THE LATER MIDDLE AGES
1272-1485

George Holmes

The Later Middle Ages is a survey of the
years from the accession of Edward I to
the death of Richard III. One of the
most turbulent and obscure periods of
English History, it covers Edward I's
wars with Scotland, the Black Death,
the Hundred Years' War, and the Wars
of the Roses, which paved the way for
the Tudor Dynasty.

The author has skilfully combined a
narrative survey with separate chapters
on government, society and the Church.

"An excellent and original survey."—
DAVID KNOWLES

"Lucid, comprehensible, and enjoyable
history."—G. R. ELTON

Volumes in the series

THE LATER MIDDLE AGES
1272-1485

A HISTORY OF ENGLAND

General Editors

CHRISTOPHER BROOKE, M.A., F.R.Hist.S.
Professor of Mediaeval History
University of Liverpool
and
DENIS MACK SMITH, M.A.
Fellow and Tutor, Peterhouse, Cambridge

TO MY MOTHER

The Later
Middle Ages
1272-1485
GEORGE HOLMES

SPHERE BOOKS LIMITED
30/32 Gray's Inn Road, London, W.C.1

First published in Great Britain in 1962 by Thomas Nelson
Second Impression, with corrections 1967
© George Holmes 1962
First Sphere Books edition 1970

Set in Linotype Plantin

Printed in Great Britain by
Hazell Watson & Viney Ltd
Aylesbury, Bucks

GENERAL EDITORS' PREFACE

Knowledge and understanding of English history change and develop so rapidly that a new series needs little apology. The present series was planned in the conviction that a fresh survey of English history was needed, and that the time was ripe for it. It will cover the whole span from Caesar's first invasion in 55 B.C. to 1955, and be completed in eight volumes. The precise scope and scale of each book will inevitably vary according to the special circumstances of its period; but each will combine a clear narrative with an analysis of many aspects of history—social, economic, religious, cultural and so forth—such as is essential in any approach to English history today.

The special aim of this series is to provide serious and yet challenging books, not buried under a mountain of detail. Each volume is intended to provide a picture and an appreciation of its age, as well as a lucid outline, written by an expert who is keen to make available and alive the findings of modern research. They are intended to be reasonably short—long enough that the reader may feel he has really been shown the ingredients of a period, not so long that he loses appetite for anything further. The series is intended to be a stimulus to wider reading rather than a substitute for it; and yet to comprise a set of volumes, each, within its limits, complete in itself. Our hope is to provide an introduction to English history which is lively and illuminating, and which makes it at once exciting and more intelligible.

C. N. L. B.
D. M. S.

MAPS AND DIAGRAMS

LIST OF ABBREVIATIONS

C.H.J.	Cambridge Historical Journal
E.H.R.	English Historical Review
Econ.H.R.	Economic History Review
H.T.	History Today
P. and P.	Past and Present
T.R.H.S.	Transactions of the Royal Historical Society

AUTHOR'S PREFACE

My aim has been to write an intelligible introduction to this period of history for those who are reading about it for the first time. I have not, therefore, tried to be original and I have drawn constantly on the works of other scholars. I hope that the authors whose writings I have plundered for this purpose, and perhaps misused, will forgive me. My debt to them is all the greater since our understanding of many aspects of the subject has been transformed by researches published in the last thirty years.

I should like to thank the following for granting permission for extracts to be quoted: Dr Helen M. Cam (*Liberties and Communities in Medieval England*); the Chancellor of the Duchy of Lancaster (Public Record Office document D.L. 5/1, f. 90 v.); Mr P. B. Chatwin and the Birmingham and Midland Archaeological Society ('Documents of "Warwick the Kingmaker"' by P. B. Chatwin, published in *Transactions of the Birmingham and Midland Archaeological Society*, 1935); the Delegates of the Clarendon Press (*A History of Antony Bek* by C. M. Fraser, and *The Thirteenth Century, 1216–1307* by F. M. Powicke); the Editors of *The Economic History Review* ('Labour Conditions in Essex in the Reign of Richard II' by N. Kenyon, published in *The Economic History Review*, 1934); the Librarian, Lambeth Palace Library (Register of Archbishop Whittlesey, f. 121); the Librarian, Louvain University Library ('Walter Burley's Commentary on the *Politics* of Aristotle' by S. Harrison Thomson, contained in *Mélanges Auguste Pelzer*); Lutterworth Press (*The Lost Villages of England* by M. W. Beresford); Manchester University Press (*The Anonimalle Chronicle, 1333–1381*, ed V. H. Galbraith); and the Syndics of the Cambridge University Press (*The Abbey and Bishopric of Ely* by E. Miller, and *Canterbury Cathedral Priory* by R. A. L. Smith).

I should also like to thank Miss Susan Flower and Dr R. L. Storey for their help in choosing illustrations; and I am grateful to the following for permission to reproduce photographs: the Air Ministry and the Cambridge University Committee for Aerial Photography (photograph by Dr J. K. St Joseph, Cambridge University Curator of Aerial Photography; Crown copyright reserved); the Bodleian Library, Oxford; the British Museum; the County Archivist, Essex Record Office (D/DGh M 14, mem. 2, from the records of Guy's Hospital); the Courtauld Institute of Art; Mr A. F. Kersting; the National Buildings Record; the Pierpont Morgan Library, New York; the Public Record Office (Crown copyright reserved); Mr Lawrence Stone; and the Wool (and Allied) Textile Employers' Council, Bradford. The drawing of the village of Boarstall, Buckinghamshire, is reproduced by permission of Major Sir H. L. Aubrey-Fletcher and the Institute of Historical Research, University of London.

I am particularly grateful to four people who have generously spent a great deal of time, and shown much patience, in helping me to improve the book: to Professor C. N. L. Brooke and Mr Denis Mack Smith, to Mr James Campbell, and to my wife.

G. A. H.

CONTENTS

PART TWO 1361–1485

CHAPTER ONE

INTRODUCTION

THIS book is about the later 'Middle Ages' in England, so I must begin by saying what I mean by this famous and elusive phrase. It was invented by the historians of the seventeenth century to describe the long stretch of time in the 'middle' between the ancient world, which ended with the fall of the Roman Empire in the fifth century, and the modern world which they thought was created by the Renaissance and Reformation in the sixteenth century. Nowadays we also use 'Middle Ages' or 'medieval' in a slightly narrower sense, which I shall adopt here, to describe the European civilisation which appeared in the eleventh century after the turmoil of the invasions by Arabs and Norsemen, and which grew and flourished until the fourteenth century, chiefly in the lands which we now call Italy, Spain, Germany, France, and England. The 'Middle Ages' did not of course have any clear beginning or end. The Renaissance and Reformation made fairly rapid changes in some branches of intellectual and religious life, but most aspects of life changed only gradually between the thirteenth and sixteenth centuries. It can be very misleading to think, as people tend to do, of a civilisation as an organic thing which blooms and decays. It is best to think of the 'Middle Ages' as an impressionistic description of a phase in the continuous process of historical change. It conjures up for us a picture of certain characteristic institutions which were prominent in the thirteenth century: a single Christian Church, crowned by the remote authority of the popes at Rome; a countryside divided into thousands of small estates or 'manors', tilled by peasants, many of whom were unfree serfs, and owned by lords, who had authority over their tenants; armies of knights fighting on horseback with armour and lance; stone castles; cathedrals and monasteries in Gothic architecture; scholastic philosophy, friars, town gilds. The ways in which kings ruled their kingdoms and bishops their dioceses, knights fought, philosophers argued, and monks prayed were remarkably similar throughout Europe from Austria to Wales, from Sicily to Scotland, and also different from the institutions of the neighbouring civilisations of Byzantium and the Arab Near East. England in 1272, when this book opens, was part of this medieval world.

In the chapters that follow I have two main purposes. The first is to describe medieval society and the way in which it was evolving into a society of a somewhat different kind by the late fifteenth century. In the first half of the book I shall attempt to describe England as it was at the end of the thirteenth and the beginning of the fourteenth centuries. I shall start with the land and the way people tilled it, the division between freemen and unfree men, the lords, the towns, and the trades. Then we shall look at the Church, the clergy, bishops, monks and friars, cathedrals and universities; finally the king's government—his courts, officials, and taxes, the parliaments in which he consulted with his subjects. There is a point, which I hope will become clear, in this method of working from the bottom upwards. Though religion and government evolve to some extent by their own momentum, independently of the material conditions, they are also largely dependent on the society which supports and respects them. The medieval Church cannot be understood unless we realise that it lived on the revenues of its estates in a largely agricultural society, nor can the monarchy be understood unless we know how kings maintained courts and armies by taxing the incomes of landowners and the exports of merchants. In the second half of the book I shall argue that medieval society was fundamentally affected by the great fall in population which started with the Black Death of 1349, and show how village society was transformed, how serfdom disappeared, the great estates became less important, industry grew, the commodities and directions of trade changed. We shall have to look at the heretical movement initiated by Whycliffe in the thirteen-seventies, and at the tendency for the Church to become less powerful as society was laicised. Finally, we shall see

2

changes in the organisation of royal government: the growth of a parliamentary system at the end of the fourteenth century, the collapse of this system in the next century, and the emergence of a new kind of kingship.

The second purpose of the book is to describe politics, the relations of the kings of England with neighbouring rulers and with their own subjects. A medieval king had to keep his authority intact in the face of powerful individuals, earls and bishops, and powerful classes of gentry and townsfolk, all jealous of their privileges. His kingdom included modern England, Wales (after the conquest by Edward I), a part of Ireland, and (until 1453) the Duchy of Aquitaine in France. The king of Scotland could be a troublesome neighbour; the king of France could be very dangerous; the land of France was a temptingly rich field of conquest. The king of England had to be constantly vigilant against attack and, if possible, a successful warrior himself. Success in battle against other kings was one of the best ways to keep the respect of his own subjects and no large army could be raised without their support, so that foreign and domestic politics, though they are separated for convenience in telling the story, are closely interdependent. This period includes the successful conquest of Wales by Edward I (1272–1307) and his unsuccessful conquest of Scotland. After the reign of Edward II (1307–27) the dominions of the king in the British Isles were roughly fixed until the sixteenth century. Because of the English king's position in Aquitaine, war with France was a recurrent feature of the whole period. There was a big invasion of France in 1297 by Edward I. The series of wars known as the Hundred Years' War (1337–1453) began with Edward III's attempts to invade in the years 1337–40, followed by the forays into France which culminated in the victories of Crécy (1346) and Poitiers (1356), and the Treaty of Brétigny (1360), which gave Edward III control over all south-west France. After a long period of French recovery the English attack was revived by Henry V (1413–22), who conquered much of north-west France. These gains were gradually lost by his son, Henry VI, who finally abandoned all English possessions across the Channel, except Calais, in 1453.

In home politics we shall have to take account of the

characters of kings and of their circumstances. We shall see how the ambitious designs of so effective a king as Edward I brought him into conflict with his subjects in 1297; and how the tragedy of Edward II's reign, ending in his murder, sprang from his failure to control his court and lead his magnates. We shall see a somewhat similar tragedy in the reign of Richard II (1377–99), leading to the revolution which brought the new dynasty of Lancaster to the throne. We shall see the complete collapse of royal authority in the long and ineffective reign of Henry VI (1422–61), leading to the Wars of the Roses, the overthrow of the Lancastrians, then of the usurping house of York, and the final victory of the first Tudor, Henry VII (1485–1509).

Many passages of medieval politics seem to the modern reader like mere feuds of bandit leaders, undignified even by the national or class interests which modern politicians commonly use to justify their plans. The repeated wars against France in this period were profitable to those who fought in them; it is doubtful whether they did much good to anyone else except a few army contractors and exporting merchants. We shall certainly notice the influence of class interests on government, and attempt to understand changes in the constitutional basis of kingship—just as we might discuss class interest and taxation in a modern state. But the motives of medieval politicians are comprehensible only if we remember that they belonged partly to a world of ideas quite different from ours, in which regal power and warlike prowess, tempered only by the 'chivalry, truth and honour, freedom (i.e. liberality) and courtesy' of Chaucer's Knight, were the proper ambitions of great men and needed no extra justification. This is one illustration of an important general truth: that the understanding of a distant society requires an effort of the imagination, exercised as far as possible without nostalgia, sentimentality, or contempt. We must be both realistic and appreciative. We must remember that a high proportion of the wealth of the country was controlled by a nobility who spent it chiefly on personal splendour, entertainment, and fighting; that war was a practically continuous scourge of border districts; that many men were unfree serfs, liable to be oppressed at the caprice of their lords; that spiritual and

4

intellectual life were controlled by a Church which played a full and ruthless part in economic exploitation and imposed its system of belief on a largely illiterate population. We must remember also that those who thought at all thought within the framework of an elaborate, subtle, and deeply rooted religion; that, though this was a poor society by our standards, it devoted a higher proportion of its wealth than we do to aesthetic and religious purposes, building cathedrals and supporting scholars and monks; that all those who survived the maladies of childhood lived in a world of much greater natural beauty than the modern city dweller. There is of course no reason whatsoever to suppose that medieval men differed in any essential human characteristics from us. They were, so far as we know, neither more nor less intelligent, grasping, or pious than people are today. But they had, and the distinction is important, some very different customs and ideas.

How do we know what happened in medieval England? The historian is like a man visiting a distant country, trying to understand a society vastly different from his own in which people speak a strange language and think and act in unfamiliar ways. His task is even more difficult than that of the traveller, for he cannot speak to the dead; he can only interpret the remains which they have left. These remains are not always what he would like to have—medieval England has left us no newspapers, few memoirs or eyewitness accounts, not many personal letters. The first book was printed in England in 1477. Before that time all books were manuscripts, written laboriously by scribes, generally on sheepskin until paper began to be common towards the end of the fourteenth century. The most obvious sources of information are the chronicles, contemporary annals written up year by year, usually by monks as part of their intellectual vocation. Chronicles, such as those compiled by Bartholomew Cotton of Norwich Priory in the reign of Edward I, Henry Knighton of St Mary's, Leicester, in the reign of Richard II, and Thomas Walsingham of St Albans in the reign of Richard II and after, provide the main account of political events. Other chronicles were compiled outside the monasteries—the most important are the chronicles of the wars between England and France compiled by a French secular clerk, Jean Froissart, who moved in high places among the laity in the later fourteenth century. In the early fifteenth century narrative accounts in English became commoner, but the great chronicle tradition of the monasteries petered out and this is the main reason why the political history of that century is difficult to write. Literary works, such as Chaucer's *Canterbury Tales* and Langland's *Piers Plowman,* give an insight of a different kind into the conditions of society. Biographies are rare: the *Life of Edward II,* written by a contemporary cleric called John Walwayn, and the *Book of Margery Kempe,* which is the autobiography of an early fifteenth-century lady of Lynn, are two of the few examples. Personal letters are also rare, though the great collection of letters preserved by the Paston family give a wonderful insight into the life of Norfolk in the time of Henry VI and the Yorkists.

Much of what we know about these centuries has to be pieced together laboriously, not from narrative accounts but from 'records', documents made by people in the normal course of their business lives and kept for reference: the title deeds of their lands, orders from the kings to their officials, receipts for money, financial accounts. Since England's history has been relatively peaceful for the last four centuries, these have survived in enormous quantities. If we want to discover how the king's government worked, the best way to do this is to examine the records of his Chancery, Exchequer, and law-courts, which are still preserved in the Public Record Office in Chancery Lane. When the clerks of Chancery and Exchequer sent out letters in the king's name they kept copies for reference on long 'rolls' of sheepskin, and the rolls still survive for nearly every year from the thirteenth century onwards. Many of the doings of the archbishops of Canterbury can be discovered from the registers of their letters which are kept at Lambeth Palace. To discover what a medieval village was like, we must read the records, which are also rolls, in which the officials of the manor kept accounts of crops sown and reaped, and the buying and selling of stock, and on which they entered the proceedings of the manorial courts. Because medieval people preserved their business records and not their private letters, and did not write autobiographies, we often know a great deal about their official lives and very little about their personalities.

Besides the written records, there are the material remains of medieval towns and villages. Everyone has seen a medieval cathedral. It is still, no less than when it was built, the most splendid material creation of the medieval world. Perhaps the easiest way to get a glimpse of the lost world is to stand in a cathedral and try to imagine the aims of its builders, or to stand at one of Edward I's castles in North Wales and try to imagine how it was defended. In recent years archeologists have begun to apply to medieval history the techniques which they have developed for prehistoric ages. They have photographed villages from the air to show the plans of buildings and fields hidden under the soil. They have shown us that the ridges in modern fields often correspond with the strips of medieval fields. It is partly thanks to aerial photography and archeology that we know that large numbers of medieval villages were abandoned at the end of the Middle Ages.

Our knowledge will always be very imperfect and fragmentary. Many of the explanations and even the facts of what happened in the Middle Ages are uncertain or disputed amongst scholars. What follows is one historian's attempt to summarise the present state of our understanding. It is for the reader to go behind it to the sources and histories on which it is based and to make up his own mind.

PART ONE

1272–1361

CHAPTER TWO

MEDIEVAL SOCIETY

(1) VILLAGE AND MANOR

IN THE thirteenth century most Englishmen lived in villages. The typical village, so far as one can speak of such a thing, was firstly a nucleus of houses with a church, a mill, and possibly a manor-house. Apart from the church, and perhaps the manor-house, there would be no buildings in stone. In some parts of the country it was usual to build cottages with walls of a mixture of mud and clay, hardened by the sun, and a thatched roof. Many peasant houses were made of timber, constructed by standing together pairs of 'crucks' (curved wooden beams reaching from the ground to the apex of the roof to form an arch), joined by a pole at the top. The outside walls would be filled in with timber or mud. By adding to the number of pairs of crucks the house could be lengthened indefinitely; but it was generally small, with one or at most two rooms, sometimes sheltering ani-

Construction of a cruck house: a pair of crucks with tie-beam

mals as well as people, and warmed by a single smoky fire. The cottages were ranged on either side of a village street or, in a more complicated plan, several streets and a green. Most of them would be set in small crofts or gardens running back from the street. Beyond the crofts were the open fields stretching to the borders of the next village.

A typical modern farm commonly contains a single group of fenced fields adjoining each other; the lands of a medieval peasant were generally arranged quite differently. The fields belonging to the whole village were split up into a large number of unfenced strips, of which each tenant, and the lord of the manor and the parson, held several, often widely dispersed in different fields (Plate 1). This arrangement was determined partly by the communal husbandry which was generally practised. So that the soil should not be exhausted, each field (containing a number of strips) was used for a 'rotation' of crops. In a typical rotation spring grain would be sown in the first year, winter grain in the second, and in the third year the field would be left fallow so that the soil could recover before the cycle was repeated. Thus all the strips in one of the fields would be laid down to a single crop or left fallow for the animals to wander over, according to the year of the rotation. Each tenant had to have a strip in more than one field in order to take part in the sowing and harvesting of a selection of crops. The division of the land into a number of scattered strips also gave a fairer distribution of good and bad soil; it was stated at Wakefield in Yorkshire in 1297, for instance, that the holding of one peasant ought to include pieces of land of each of the different qualities found in the manor.[1] The strip system was also determined partly by the methods of ploughing. A long narrow strip is easier to plough with a team of oxen. Moreover, if it uses the lie of the land, it may have advantages for drainage since channels will be formed between the strips as the earth is thrown to each side by the plough. The characteristic holding of one peasant was a collection of strips making up a 'virgate', which varied in size from district to district but was commonly about thirty acres. Besides the arable fields he might have a share in the meadows (which could be in 'common', that is open to the beasts of all the villagers, or enclosed in hedged plots), common pasture (on which each tenant had the right to graze a certain number of animals), and woodland, which was valuable for firewood and for the pasturing of pigs.

In describing this 'typical village', reservations must be made. It was not normal in the hilly country of the Pennines and the Lake District, Cornwall, and the Welsh Marches, where the population was frequently scattered in small hamlets rather than grouped in villages, though there were a number of open-field villages as well. The reasons for this are obviously

1. G. C. Homans, *English Villagers of the Thirteenth Century* (1941), p. 91. I am indebted to Professor Homans' book for much else in this section.

12

largely geographical: hill country suits the isolated farm rather than the large village. For different reasons open fields were not normal in much of East Anglia and Kent, where the peasantry often followed the rotation of crops in enclosed fields. The explanation of this eastern divergence is probably to be found far back in the different customs of the original English settlers. The bulk of England, however, was open-field country.

The arrangements of open-field agriculture naturally demanded a good deal of communal organisation in matters like the setting-up of temporary fences, the maintenance of boundaries and grazing rights. Some of these affairs were settled in the manorial court. At this court the tenants of the manor were the suitors, that is the people who were bound to attend and to take their disputes to it. They also contributed to the administration of justice by declaring the local 'customs', the ancient and remembered traditions of individual rights and communal arrangements, which were enforced in the court. Ancient custom was an important notion at all levels of this society, which had few written laws and many traditional conventions. Medieval institutions reinforced the natural bonds uniting isolated communities. In the first year of Edward II the suitors at King's Repton in Huntingdonshire, deciding who should inherit the land of one Thomas Arnold, said that 'Ralph Arnold his brother is his nearest heir of blood, but by the custom of the manor Nicholas son of John in-the-Angle is the nearest, because John in-the-Angle, who was *of the blood of the village*, married Margaret, the sister of Thomas.' In this case, however, the judgment of the lord overruled the suitors. For though the court existed partly for the villagers to manage their own affairs, it also belonged partly to a different element in rural life—the 'manor'.

Like the medieval village community, the manor was very different from any modern institution. A modern farm or estate is a piece of land which somebody owns; he may employ men to run it, but he owns only the land. A medieval manor was both a piece of land and a unit of jurisdiction over the men who lived upon it. The lord's tenant was also the lord's man and as such he performed an act of homage in the court on receiving his strips in the fields. He was bound to attend the manorial court, which was presided over by the lord or by a steward as the lord's representative. The custom of the manor was declared in the court by the suitors, but the lord also had jurisdiction in it over the buying and selling of land and over petty theft. The manor was a more universal institution than the open-field village. Most countrymen were subject to some kind of manorial jurisdiction. The variations in detail were endless and it would certainly be wrong to think of any part of England as neatly divided into villages each ruled over by a single manorial lord. In some cases one village contained several manors, each with its court; elsewhere one manor included several villages; and in the north and west it becomes difficult to draw the line between manors and large lordships, such as those of the Welsh Marches, which might cover half a modern county. There were areas where many of the peasantry had only a tenuous connection with the manor; in some cases they were not even obliged to do suit of court. At Haslingfield in Cambridgeshire in 1279 there were three manors and twenty-six freeholders outside them who held small pieces of land as tenants of other people; at Filgrave in Buckinghamshire in the same year there was a manor with only half a virgate in the lord's hands, no villeins, and some freeholders who had no connection with the manor. Nevertheless the manor can properly be regarded as the normal unit of medieval rural life. Men thought of it as such themselves and had a clear enough idea of what it typically contained, as can be seen from the contemporary treatises on husbandry and from the set of instructions used by royal officials for describing estates called the 'Extent of a manor': this typical manor had a court, tenants both free and servile holding lands and paying rents and services for them, common lands, tenant lands, and land retained in the lord's personal possession.

The land which the lord kept in his own hands, the 'demesne' to distinguish it from tenant holdings, was the core of the manor's economic function as the court was of its jurisdiction. In an open-field village the demesne, like other land, was divided into strips but it was exploited directly by and for the lord. The day-to-day organisation was commonly done by a reeve, who was elected annually from among the

14

unfree tenants and was responsible to the lord during his term of office for the profitable working of the demesne and collection of rents. In addition to money rents some of the tenants owed unpaid labour services, perhaps a certain number of days' work each week throughout the year ('week work'), or annual services at the busy times of ploughing, mowing, and reaping. Usually some wage labour was employed, often a great deal, but the manor was sometimes a compact economic unit, consisting of demesne, with tenants who supplied the labour for it as well as working their own holdings.

One basic distinction, dividing Englishmen into two very broad classes, was to be found everywhere. 'All men are either freemen or serfs,' was a legal maxim. The serf or villein was subject to the lord not only in being his man and owing suit to his court but also in being his personal property. He could be bought and sold with his descendants, his 'sequela' as they were called; he could not leave the manor or even marry without permission; and his servile status was inherited by his children. Here again the historian must acknowledge wide regional variations, stemming from geographical differences and distinctions of custom going back to the first English settlements, and perhaps beyond, when peoples with different social systems had settled in different areas. In Kent there were few villeins. In East Anglia there was a high proportion of freemen with extensive lands and little connection with manors, but also a number of large manors whose villeins owed heavy labour services. Moderately sized manors, with small demesnes and generally light services, were characteristic of the Midland counties. But the essential distinction of free and unfree and the institution of labour services are to be found in varying degrees almost everywhere.

In the manor of Borley in Essex in 1308, to take a concrete example, there were 300 acres of arable in demesne plus meadow and pasture, 7 free tenants holding varying acreages and paying money rents, 6 *molmen,* probably the descendants of men who had been freed from villeinage, owing money rents and some services, and 28 *custumarii* holding villein land. The villeins nearly all held land in multiples of 5 acres (5, 10, or 20), and they owed standard services to be performed on the lord's demesne: three days' work each week from

15

Michaelmas (29th September) to St Peter in Chains (1st August) except Christmas, Easter, and Whitsun weeks, the ploughing of 4 acres, carrying manure, weeding corn, mowing the meadow, 24 reaping 'works' between 1st August and 29th September, and so on. It is evident that in origin these men and their holdings descended from servile tenants, settled on standard plots with obligations to provide a substantial amount of the work needed for the demesne. The lord's arrangements no doubt explain the origin of villein land and villein status. At Wilburton in Cambridgeshire in the late thirteenth century, to take another example, there were three groups of tenants: freeholders who held tenements varying in size between 6 and 22½ acres, owing moderate services and very small rents; 15½ standard villein units paying a small rent and heavy labour services of 3 days' week work and 5 days in harvest time; and 10½ small cottage units paying a small rent and moderate services. By no means all manors had such symmetrical arrangements, but many had, and the land shortage of the thirteenth century made it fairly easy for the lord to maintain the system if he wished. In the Hundred Rolls, the documents which contain the results of inquiries by Edward I's officials into tenures in the home counties, East Anglia, and the eastern Midlands in 1279, about half the tenants mentioned had free or villein holdings of the standard 'virgate' (or 'yardland') or of half-virgates; about one-third had very small holdings of less than a quarter of a virgate; only about 3 per cent had more than a virgate.[1]

At the end of the thirteenth century both the geographical differences and the customary distinctions between classes in individual villages were being blurred by the effects of fairly rapid social change and economic progress. Tenements were sometimes divided between heirs who inherited jointly. Pieces of land were being bought and sold. Sometimes lords found it convenient to 'commute' the labour services of their tenants by changing them into money rents. Plots of villein land, originally held by serfs and still burdened with customary labour services, were sometimes held by free men who had to arrange for the labour to be done even though their own

1 E. A. Kosminsky, *Studies in the Agrarian History of Medieval England in the Thirteenth Century*, ed. R. H. Hitton, trans R. Kisch (1956), pp. 227ff

personal status was unchanged. Conversely it was possible for a villein, with all the personal disabilities of his class, to become a holder of free land as part of quite a large holding and to better himself by marriage and investment. Here is an example of such a man, as near as we shall ever get to the biography of a medieval villein:

'His name was Stephen Puttock, and he lived on the prior of Ely's manor of Sutton at the end of the thirteenth and the beginning of the fourteenth century. There can be no doubt about his villeinage: he was described as *nativus* in a charter; he paid a fine for the lord's licence to marry both his wives, as did his sister when she married (and leyrwite [the fine for immorality by a villein] as well). There can be no doubt that he owed labour services, for he was amerced [i.e. fined] from time to time for carrying them out with less than proper care. Yet he was an important man in the village. Almost certainly he held a full land [i.e. full peasant holding] at least. . . . He was . . . reeve 1310, a chief pledge for a quarter of a century, ale-taster more than once, a frequent member of inquest juries. Like others of his kind he was a sheep farmer. . . .

But above all he was a great buyer of land. In 1300 he bought three-quarters of an acre without licence. A charter of 1303 recording the purchase of an unspecified parcel from another villein, is still extant. In 1304, he took up Northcroft (containing 8¼ acres) from the prior. In 1305 he bought 2 acres from the prior's former bailiff and in 1307 a parcel of meadow from a free tenant. . . . In 1310 he bought 6 acres of arable for 20 silver marks. . . . Such a man was thriving into the yeomanry.'[1]

Thirteenth-century society included many people like Stephen Puttock. But, although the rigidity of social structure was mitigated in this way, the supremacy of the manorial lord and the essential distinction between free and unfree were unquestioned.

Nearly everywhere the maintenance of the lords' supremacy was made easier by one basic fact of English life in 1272 and

1. E. Miller, *The Abbey and Bishopric of Ely* (1951), pp. 150–1

17

for half a century after: the scarcity of land. In the thirteenth and early fourteenth centuries a rapidly growing population, living by simple forms of agriculture, was occupying the land of England to the limits of possibility. There are today few country villages, as the churches show, which did not exist in the Middle Ages; some have disappeared since 1300. New townships were being established by English colonists in the Welsh Marches, sometimes still recognisable from their names, such as New Radnor. The bishops of Winchester were attracting settlers to their new boroughs at Burghclere and Hindon and elsewhere in Hampshire and Wiltshire.[1] The monks of Christ Church, the cathedral priory at Canterbury, were draining Romney Marsh. Peasants were enclosing and cultivating for the first time the fenlands on the edge of the Wash in Lincolnshire and Cambridgeshire. The denes were being cut out of the ancient forest of the Weald and in many other parts of England "assarts' were being cleared in the woods to add to the village fields. It is unlikely that during the period there were revolutionary changes in technique to improve the yield of existing arable land, though landlords certainly brought seedcorn from other areas and paid attention to marling and loaming, and some villages were able to increase their turnover by the change from a two-field system (the land lying fallow every other year) to a three-field system (two crops in every three years), which gave more frequent crops from the same area. A fourteenth-century abbot of Fountains in Yorkshire, for instance, appointed a group of tenants with their consent 'to ordain the best way that they can to lay out the field in three parts so that one part shall be fallow each year'. The tendency everywhere was to use more land, more intensively, in the old ways. Prices of grain rose throughout the thirteenth century to an unprecedented height in its last years. The great floods and famines of 1315–17 and the other calamities of Edwards II's reign brought to an end a period of expansion in which the extraordinary increase of population had driven men beyond the margins of good arable land and given some areas a settlement more dense than they were to see again until the eighteenth century.

1. M. W. Beresford, 'The Six New Towns of the Bishops of Winchester, 1200–55), *Medieval Archaeology*, III (1959)

The common image of medieval society was a hierarchy of graded ranks. The notion is not peculiar to the Middle Ages and still has a tenuous survival in the nostalgic desire of some people to keep others 'in their proper stations'. In the Middle Ages it was neither nostalgia nor ideal but a living assumption which corresponded with the facts of life. When the labour problems following the Black Death of 1349 threatened the position of the landed classes they responded not with economic theory but with a statement of the social order whose maintenance was necessary to preserve a healthy economy. To curb inflation in 1363, parliament laid down the clothing which was appropriate to knights with an income of more than 400 marks a year, knights with less, esquires and gentlemen with over £100 a year, merchants (those worth £1,000 were reckoned to be level with landowners of £200 rent), artisans, down to labourers worth less than 40 shillings a year. Above these ranks were the nobility whom the Commons did not presume to regulate. There were later acts of a similar kind in 1463 and 1482, and the general social order which they describe is often to be seen in miniature in noble households with their ranks of followers from knights down through yeomen and varlets to grooms and boys.

The most important people in thirteenth-century England were the 'magnates'—*magnates regni*, 'great men of the kingdom'. On the lay side these included the earls, and the greater barons who were, roughly speaking, the wealthier nobility, below the earls in rank and power but important enough to carry weight as individuals in the politics of the kingdom. On the ecclesiastical side they included the bishops and the abbots of the greater abbeys. Below the magnates were the lesser nobility, many of whom were knights, that is to say men who had been trained in the art of warfare on horseback, who had received the ceremonial order of knighthood and could equip themselves with fine horses, weapons, and armour, much superior to those used by common soldiers. Knighthood, however, was not by any means universal among well-to-do men and the title *seigneur* or *dominus*—'sir' or 'lord' —was commonly given to all men of superior wealth or status, including parish priests and country squires, without carrying any technical meaning as it does today. Broadly speaking, the upper classes of England were the 'lords' and the greatest of them the 'magnates'.

Wealthy people nowadays generally derive their money from shares in industrial and commercial enterprises, less often from land. Though there were, as we shall see, wealthy merchants in the Middle Ages, they were a fairly small minority. Most lords and all magnates derived the bulk of their income from property in land, either in the form of rents paid by tenants, or by farming land themselves so that they had at their disposal every year a large quantity of grain, meat, or wool which they could use in their own households or sell. The great concentrations of wealth which supported the power of lay or ecclesiastical magnates were in landed property, the estates of abbeys, of bishoprics, or of earls. Further down the social scale, small estates supported the country squire or rector. Most of the estates owned by the lords were manors of the kind described in the previous section, involving lordship over both men and land. The economic tendencies of the period with which we are concerned at present—the scarcity of land and abundance of population—were very favourable to landlords, especially manorial landlords, and powerfully reinforced their superiority over the smallholders, tenants, and landless men below them. Thirteenth-century England was a country dominated by great manorial estates and by castles, cathedrals, and abbeys reared on their profits. In this section we shall see how the lords organised their estates, then look at the distinctions within seignorial society and finally see how the lords organised their servants and followers.

A small estate might consist of one manor, like that of Henry de Bray, the squire of Harleston in Northamptonshire in the reigns of Edward I and Edward II, who had about 250 acres of land which he worked himself, and 24 tenants. The largest might contain so many properties in different parts of the country that they had to be organised in geographical groups. Gilbert de Clare, Earl of Gloucester, the greatest lay magnate of his day outside the royal family, who died at Bannockburn (1314), had one huge 'bailiwick' in South Wales, another in Dorset, a third in East Anglia, centring on his castle at Clare, each including a number of manors. These groups of estates, producing rent, grain, and wool, were the units of medieval wealth and power.

In some cases they were no more than areas occupied by rent-paying tenants. The estates of Edward I's cousin, Edmund, Earl of Cornwall, scattered all over southern England from Hertfordshire to Cornwall, were nearly all held by tenants paying rents. In the prevailing economic climate, however, there were powerful incentives for the manorial lord to exploit his lands more actively, to make the most of them by direct farming. The growing usefulness of estate management in the thirteenth century made it a highly regarded profession. There were textbooks—the most famous of them was Walter of Henley's *Stewardship*—which explained how to make up accounts and how to deal with rents, labour services, and reeves. The great problem of estate management was to make sure that the official on the spot, who might be a reeve filling the office for one year, and (like Chaucer's character) an expert at cheating his masters, did his work conscientiously. Most large estates made both estimates of the yield to be expected from each kind of produce in a year and careful arrangements to make sure that the reeve did not conceal or steal crops or animals that belonged to his lord. The Priory of St Swithun's, Winchester, for instance, had a system of quotas, called *responsiones*: of grain according to the amount of seed sown, of butter and cheese so much per cow, of wool a certain average weight of fleeces. If the reeve failed to produce these quotas or to give an adequate excuse he was charged with the difference.[1]

This supervision involved an elaborate system of administration. The senior official of the estate would be the steward, a man with some legal knowledge, whose duty would be to hold the courts and to formulate the general policy of the estate. It was a responsible position which could be part of a great career: Adam de Stratton, who later became a notorious judge under Edward I, had done the work of steward for the Countess of Aumale.

Each group of estates also had its receiver to collect the

1. J. S. Drew, 'Manorial Accounts of St Swithun's Priory, Winchester', E.H.R. (1947)

money. Finally there were auditors to go round each year checking the accounts of all officials. Their corrections and notes of items 'disallowed' can still be seen on many surviving reeves' account rolls.

The agricultural work itself was done partly by unpaid labour services, partly by casual hired labour, partly by permanent farm servants, according to local manorial conditions. One Kentish manor in the reign of Edward I had a permanent staff including seventeen ploughmen and carters, but this was in an area where villeins owing labour services were scarce. Some of the manors near the lord's usual place of residence, the castle or abbey, might be home farms supplying food directly for the table. In most other cases the produce was sold locally for cash to be taken to the central treasury. 'Know, sir,' wrote the Prior of Christ Church, Canterbury, in 1323, 'that half our lands are so far from us, out of this county towards Oxford, Devonshire and elsewhere that we must sell the grain in those parts and buy grain in this country. And . . . all the grain we have apart from the seed for our lands, between Sandwich and Rochester, never suffices for the sustenance of our convent and our house beyond Pentecost, so that we have to buy 1000 quarters and more in this country.' The Prior was probably not quite telling the truth; he was trying to avoid contributing to the supplies for Dover Castle. But he described the general arrangement of his estates well enough.

The writer of that letter, Henry of Eastry, was Prior of Christ Church from 1285 to 1331 and a most astute man of business. To understand the medieval seignorial estate at its height we cannot do better than to look at some aspects of his administration.[1] The first way in which an estate could be developed was by enlarging the amount of land under cultivation by purchase or reclamation. The Canterbury monks at this period bought more land every year. They added to the reclaimed portions of their coastal lands in and around Romney Marsh and the Isle of Thanet. They could always lease out new land for one or two shillings an acre, which was higher than the rent paid by established customary tenants. Buying of land and enclosure from the waste were common features

1. Described by R. A. L. Smith, *Canterbury Cathedral Priory* (1943)

of estate policy in most places, and it could be said of many lords, as a monk of Peterborough wrote of Eastry's contemporary, Godfrey of Crowland, Abbot of Peterborough (1299–1321), 'he began a manor where there had never been a manor before but it had lain as pasture'.

A second marked characteristic of the Christ Church estates was the energetic pursuit of arable and pastoral farming. In the reign of Edward II, when the sales of grain were at their height, over 8,000 acres were sown in the Kentish estates alone. We do not know who bought the surplus. Some presumably went to feed the landless men and women of the local villages, including the very numerous labourers and domestic servants. Some was perhaps sent to the towns; the English manors of the Norman Abbey of Bec at this period sold grain from Lessingham to Norwich and from Ruislip to London. The Abbey of Crowland in Lincolnshire had farms which specialised in rearing cattle for milk and meat. This was probably unusual, but a more common and very important type of specialisation was sheep-farming. In the reign of Edward II Christ Church Priory had 13,000 sheep on its Kentish estates, whose wool was generally sold directly to Italian merchants. Crowland had a centralised sheep farm which moved about the fen pastures round the Isle of Crowland, and the Countess of Aumale had about 7,000 sheep on her estates in Holderness. The greatest of all in this sphere were the Cistercian abbeys of Fountains and Rievaulx in Yorkshire, with great stretches of wild moorland.

This evidence has come mostly from ecclesiastical estates, whose records have generally survived better than others. It may be also that the greater continuity of an ecclesiastical estate, whose owner could not die or split up his inheritance, made for elaborate and efficient management. The essential organisation of a lay nobleman's estate was, however, the same. Four hundred years later, in the early seventeenth century, John Smyth of Nibley described the estate management of Thomas Berkeley, who reigned over his family's lands from Berkeley Castle in Gloucestershire during the reigns of Edward I and Edward II, in terms which recall clearly the monastic records of the same period. In the account rolls Smyth found 'what kinds of grain he yearly sowed according to the quality

23

of the ground as wheat, barley, peas, oats, rye. . . . And also how these kinds of grain each second or third year were exchanged, or brought from one manor to another, as the vale corn into an upland soil and, contrarily the upland and Cotswold corn sown in the vale and low ground . . . how this lord for his better profit exchanged . . . part of his cattle at certain seasons of the year from one manor to another according to the diversity and condition of the soil'. He noticed that Thomas Berkeley promoted the enclosure and consolidation of holdings and the planting of trees and hedges 'in so much as from my house at Nibley . . . I do behold them as groves or thickets through the nearness of the hedges in those small enclosures. And myself having at the felling of some of the fairest oaks in these places told their ages (a thing certainly and easily to be done by the grain made in a circle in every kind of tree by the yearly ascent and consolidation of the sap) I have constantly found their risings and plantings to answer this very time'.[1] A manorial steward himself, Smyth recognised and saluted the climax of demesne farming from the closer vantage-point of the seventeenth century. Never again in English history was the great estate to dominate society quite as it did in the lifetime of Henry of Eastry and Thomas Berkeley.

A social survey of the villages of Warwickshire, based on the Hundred Rolls of 1279,[2] shows that about half of them had each a single lord of the manor. The others were divided between several lords. These lords were partly the layer of local seignorial gentry—twenty or thirty laymen who held between one and three manors each—partly the religious houses, and some were really big magnates. The biggest landowners in the county were the Benedictine Abbey of Coventry and the Earl of Warwick, followed by the Augustinian Canonry of Kenilworth and the Cistercian Abbey of Combe. These landowners and their like in other counties were the upper classes of England. If Warwickshire was untypical, it was as a county dominated less by the really big estate

1. J. Smyth, *The Lives of the Berkeleys*, ed. J. Maclean (1883–5), 1, pp. 155–6, 161
2. R. H. Hilton, 'The Social Structure of Rural Warwickshire in the Middle Ages', *Dugdale Society Occasional Papers*, 9 (1950)

and more by the gentry and small religious houses than the average.

The clergy are left for another chapter. Lay society was crowned by a group of about a dozen or fifteen earls. Some were of the royal blood, like the earls of Lancaster, descending from Edward I's brother, Edmund Crouchback; others members of ancient families descending from the Anglo-Norman aristocracy, like the de Vere earls of Oxford and the Bohuns of Hereford. Some of these families died out in the early fourteenth century and some new ones were added to them such as the Mortimers, who became earls of March through the efforts of Roger Mortimer, the rebel who overthrew Edward II in 1327, or the Montagues, who became earls of Salisbury through the efforts of William Montague who overthrew Mortimer in 1330. All of them held extensive territories in different parts of the country. Below them were other barons, twenty or thirty families, who were substantial enough to be included amongst the 'magnates of the realm'. These were usually families with somewhat smaller and more localised properties. The Berkeleys in Gloucestershire belonged to this class, as did the Mortimers in the Welsh March before they became great, the Percies in Yorkshire and Northumberland, the Cobhams of Kent, and many others. Below them again were the knights and gentry down to the lords of fractions of villages. The greatest of these families were related to the king and some of them were creations of the royal blood, younger sons of kings. The magnates were closely linked by blood, tenacious defenders of their common rights but also sometimes quarrelsomely divided into factions.

This was the world of knighthood, chivalry, and heraldry. Most landowners were not knights, though some were wealthy enough for Henry III and Edward I to attempt to compel them to take on knighthood—a device by which it was hoped to increase the resources of cavalry for the royal army. They were country gentlemen, sufficiently occupied with estate management and hunting. But there was a large number of men, probably somewhere between 500 and 1,000, who had actually been 'girded with the sword' and formed a military and social *élite*. They included of course the magnates and barons. At the end of the thirteenth century it was becoming common for the nobility and gentry to have coats of arms which would be blazoned on their seals and shields. We still have a number of rolls of arms, manuscripts giving lists of knights who were present at a particular tournament or military enterprise, with coloured paintings of the armorial bearings which they had carried into battle. Apart from the ability to fight on horseback with lance, sword, and heavy armour, knighthood also involved the code of chivalric adventure which plays so large a part in medieval literature. Most of the stories in medieval romances, stories of King Arthur's knights or of the Trojans, came originally from remote antiquity, but they were invested with the chivalrous attitudes of the knight-errant. Orpheus for instance was turned into a knightly king called 'Sir Orfeo' in an English poem of the early fourteenth century. One poem called *Sir Gawayn and the Grene Knight* (telling how one of Arthur's knights faced heroic and chivalric temptations), written down in the form we know in or near Cheshire about 1350, is generally regarded as outstanding for its literary qualities. A great many other romantic legends written in both French and English were current at the end of the thirteenth century and after, and must have been for the nobility an important constituent of their world of ideas.

The nobility as a whole had in common their dependence on landed property and, to some extent, their initiation into the warlike arts of knighthood; but there were obviously wide differences between the country knight, absorbed in the management of a small estate, hunting, and the politics of the shire, and the great earl who was a power in the court and the kingdom. Medieval society can be regarded as a hierarchy of concentric communities. At the bottom was the village world, presided over by the lord and peopled by the free and villein peasants. Above that was the community of the shire which had its central institution in the shire court, attended by the gentry and more prominent freemen, an ancient assembly, much less important in justice than it had once been but still frequently convened and now acquiring the important new power of electing knights for parliament. Embracing them all was the kingdom, in which, apart from the king and the court, only magnates and prelates had an acknowledged right to influence. It was a stable society in the sense that there was relatively little movement into the nobility from below. The bulk of an estate descended from father to eldest son and it was amongst the chief concerns of a nobleman's life to maintain and extend his inheritance. On the other hand there were always younger sons, who had to make their own way in the world and therefore depended more on their prowess in war or in counselling kings and magnates to win them wealth. Success in war was always a way to rise and it was possible for a man who was favoured in this way to rise from the squirearchy to the nobility or from the lesser to the greater nobility. The Church and the law also offered careers where individual talent could overcome low birth and make a man into a bishop or into a judge with the opportunity to found a great family.

From Beowulf to the Duke of Omnium, as long as lords were exalted above the men who served them, one hub of lay society was the hall in which the great man entertained his dependents. Every baron and gentleman in the Middle Ages had a house of which such a hall was the central feature. The manor-houses of the central Middle Ages which survive today are naturally often uncharacteristically elaborate examples, such as Stokesay Castle in Shropshire or Little Wenham Hall in Suffolk. They all show, however, the central importance of the hall, and most of those which existed in the reign of Edward I probably contained little more than a hall for the whole household, with a kitchen at one end and the private rooms of the lord at the other. Often the hall was raised above ground-level to make it more defensible, and even the sumptuous palace built by Edward's Chancellor, Bishop Burnell, at Acton Burnell in Shropshire, was constructed partly for defence. Especially in the Marches of Wales and the north, resistance to a siege could still be a major consideration; the seignorial residences of these areas were small castles rather than houses. The greater magnates all had castles of some magnificence: those of the Beauchamps at Warwick, of the earls of Arundel at Arundel in Sussex, and of the Veres at Hedingham in Essex are examples which still survive in part. Though the greatest castles built in this age were without question the work of Edward I (to be described in a later chapter), this period saw the building of two great structures which approached them in grandeur: Caerphilly Castle in Glamorgan, built for the Clares in the reign of Edward I, and Dunstanburgh in Northumberland, begun for Thomas of Lancaster in 1313. Significantly they were both in the Marches (the borderlands between England and Wales, and England and Scotland respectively) and supported by the two largest magnate inheritances.

All landed property was held ultimately of the king by feudal tenure, so called because the commonest unit of tenure was the knight's fee (*feudum* in Latin), the holder of which was obliged to do the service of fighting for his lord as a knight for forty days in each year. Knights' fees varied considerably in the areas of land which they contained, but they were fairly uniform in the duties to which they obliged their holders. 'Tenants-in-chief' held their fees directly from the king, and did homage to him for them, after which they owed him a special allegiance, and made a general promise to perform service in his feudal army, to give him financial help ('aids') when his eldest son was knighted or his eldest daughter married, and to give him counsel. If the tenant died without heirs his land 'escheated' into the king's hands. If he died leaving a son under age, the king held the land in 'wardship' until the heir came of age. Other men held knights' fees from the tenants-in-chief, with similar obligations, and these held them in turn from the king. The magnates were mostly tenants-in-chief, holding their estates directly from the king, who thus had some control over the movements of their property. Lesser men might hold either from the king or from another lord, and the greater magnates had large numbers of feudal tenants, some of them organised in 'honors' with central courts for the settlement of disputes relating to feudal tenure.

By the reign of Edward I, however, the feudal system below the rank of the tenants-in-chief had become largely a form of land tenure which did not usually involve any close personal tie between lord and man. The honorial courts were falling into decay and the whole of feudalism was becoming something of an anachronism. In practice the organisation of a lord's power and influence depended on relationships in

28

which feudalism played little part. Each great estate, as we have seen, had an administrative organisation of officials. At its centre was the household, for which it supplied the food and money. In 1287, for instance, the household of Lord Willoughby d'Eresby, a baron but not a great magnate, included a steward of the household, a 'wardrober' who managed the accounts, a chaplain, and a staff of more than twenty-five other servants, such as butlers, cooks, ushers, and porters. A great earl would have a much larger staff. Every magnate and prelate had a council of substantial people, officials, lawyers, and friends, retained to advise on matters of business. The Countess of Aumale counted among her council at the beginning of Edward I's reign, for instance, a royal judge, a prominent London merchant, and the Constable of Carisbrooke Castle.[1] Officials and councillors were commonly granted annual fees and robes which were the accepted marks of their relationship to the lord.

If a magnate wished to extend his influence and following beyond his household and estates he could do so by retaining other men to give advice or military service in time of need. The kind of arrangement by which a manor in Yorkshire in 1323 was 'charged to Sir Thomas de Bolton knight for life by the deed of Ralph baron of Greystoke in 20 marks, two robes, one with fur and the other with linen and a saddle fitting the status of a knight'[2] was common in this society. Some wealthy and ambitious magnates employed the device of retainder on a very large scale. The most notable perhaps was Earl Thomas of Lancaster in the reign of Edward II who had a large number of men, including some important knights, retained for lifelong service in peace and war in return for grants of land or annual rents: Sir William Latimer, retained to come when requested with forty men-at-arms, and Sir Robert Holand who treacherously failed his lord at the critical moment before the battle of Boroughbridge, though he had been 'preferred' to a yearly living of 2,000 marks'. This contract system has been called by historians 'bastard feudalism' because it has seemed like a debased version of the older feudalism, based on annuities instead of grants of land in

1. N. H. Denholm-Young, *Seignorial Administration in England* (1937), pp. 7, 29

2. *Calendar of Inquisitions Post Mortem*, VI, p. 304

knights' fees. In fact there was probably nothing very new about it. Since the days of Beowulf lords had attracted and retained followers by the promise of rich rewards; and the exercise of 'patronage' by which lords gave advancement and help to faithful dependents was not essentially different in the fourteenth century from what it was to be in the eighteenth, though it was less peaceful and more ostentatious.

The contract system was important in two ways. Firstly, it enabled the magnate to raise an army quickly in time of war, (as Lancaster and the Despensers did in the reign of Edward II), though he would have to add temporary mercenaries to his permanent retinue. Secondly, it gave form to the lord's wide influence in politics and in society below him, made it easier for him to build up an 'affinity' of men who owed some special allegiance to him, and expected his help and protection in return. Royal authority and justice were limited and corruptible. 'Notwithstanding the many appointments by the king of keepers of the peace,' says a complaint in 1334, 'felons and transgressors escape due punishment because they are maintained by magnates and others who retain them in their households and in their pay and livery, because gaol deliveries of such felons take place sometimes before they have been indicted, sometimes by surreptitious means or by dishonest and cowardly juries. . . .'[1] Retinues and lordly influence were not necessarily as vicious as this but, for good or ill, they were as essential as the open fields to medieval society; neither the magnate nor the commoner could imagine a world without them.

(3) COMMERCE AND TOWNS

One of the earliest handbooks of commerce, compiled by a Florentine merchant in the early fourteenth century, includes a list of over 180 English religious houses which produced wool, with estimates of the qualities and quantities which were to be expected of them, and of the costs of transport to Italy by way of Gascony and Provence. This document from distant Tuscany illustrates two important things about the

1. *Calendar of Patent Rolls, 1331–34*, p. 573

commerce of the central Middle Ages. Firstly, England was involved in regular large-scale trade over long distances; secondly, trade was conducted in basic commodities at least as much as in dispensable luxuries. Though fairs held annually and markets held weekly or monthly were an essential part of the life of the countryside and the country towns, in international trade the days of the occasional peddling merchant were long past. The international fairs, such as St Giles' Fair at Winchester, or even Stourbridge Fair near Cambridge which was by far the most important in the later Middle Ages, were less prominent than they had been in the twelfth and early thirteenth centuries compared with the regular business done by merchants settled in the commercial towns.

The biggest import trade was probably in wine from Gascony, paid for with English cloth, fish, and grain. The two economies were so complementary that a Bordeaux merchant could ask, 'How could our poor people subsist when they could not sell their wine or procure English merchandise?' The chief English exports were tin from the stannaries of Cornwall, corn, and fish, sent especially to Gascony, cloth, which was beginning in the thirteenth century to find a market in Italy, and, above all, wool. Kings, magnates, merchants, and all Englishmen whose way of life was assisted by overseas commerce could agree with the thanksgiving of a later Nottinghamshire stapler:

> I thank God and ever shall,
> It is the sheep hath paid for all.

Wool, either as raw material or, later, as cloth, was the chief basis of large-scale commerce. Most peasants had a few sheep to be sheared, and the great estates, especially those of the Cistercian abbeys, had developed huge flocks, whose fleeces they supplemented by acting as collecting agents for the wool of smaller growers. The biggest producers were the monasteries of Yorkshire and Lincolnshire, such as Fountains, Rievaulx, Kirkstead, Revesby, and Spalding, but there were sheep of different kinds everywhere, producing a variety of recognised qualities from the finer grades of the Welsh border, the Cotswolds, and Lindsey to the rough, short wool of Yorkshire. The annual export at the beginning of Edward I's reign was

31

over 32,000 sacks (or about 5,800 tons) and that level was roughly maintained until the middle of the fourteenth century. The chief exporting places were the main east-coast ports, conveniently placed for the areas of large production: Hull, where the greatest of medieval English merchants, William de la Pole, started his career, Boston, and London.

Like many countries in other centuries which have been dominated by large and prosperous estates, medieval England had some of the characteristics of a colonial economy. Industry was rudimentary compared with that of Flanders and Tuscany; more cloth was imported than exported. The high development of commerce, which had an importance out of proportion to the percentage of national production involved, was due largely to the penetration of foreign merchants with wider horizons and more capital than the natives. About two-thirds of the wool exported at the beginning of Edward I's reign was taken by aliens and most of it was carried in foreign ships. The chief groups of foreign merchants were the Hansards, the Flemings, and the Italians.

The merchants of the Hanseatic towns, particularly Cologne and Hamburg, had long been active in this country and enjoyed very wide privileges by royal charter, extending, in the reign of Edward III, even to the payment of lower customs duties on some articles than native merchants paid. They had a Gildhall and the 'Steelyard' (the name is derived from a German word meaning a courtyard in which wares were set out for sale) in London, and colonies in other east-coast towns. (In 1270 one Gottschalk of Almain called himself a burgess of Lynn.) They exported wool, cloth, and tin, and brought cloth from Flanders and timber and furs from the Baltic. Some of them did a large trade (Tidman of Limburg was one of the chief lenders of money to Edward III) and they remained an important element in English life throughout the Middle Ages and after. The Flemings, on the other hand, were already declining from their earlier importance. Their position was based on the export of wool for the textile towns of Flanders and the import of cloth, but their native industry was already starting on its long decay. It was hard hit by the wool famines, deliberately created as instruments of policy by Edward I and Edward III, when they temporarily banned export in 1297

32

and 1337; on the latter occasion a number of Flemish weavers were induced to emigrate to England.

The Italians were the most wealthy, influential, and expert of the aliens. Industry, commerce, and banking were all more highly developed in the cities of Tuscany and Lombardy than anywhere else and much of Europe was entangled in their economic imperialism. Firms like the Riccardi of Lucca and the Frescobaldi of Florence, which were the most active in England in the reign of Edward I, were far more elaborate and wealthy than any contemporaries in northern Europe. Lombard Street in London had already taken its name from the Italians living there in the fourteenth century. Their entry into England had been assisted by their work as agents for the collection of papal taxes, which gave them large balances of cash in this country and connections with the religious houses. At the end of the thirteenth century most abbeys sold their wool in bulk to visiting Italians, often years in advance. Fountains contracted in 1282 to supply an Italian firm with twenty-six sacks a year for five years. The Italians exported from Hull, Boston, London, and Southampton. Most of the wool went overland, but, in the reign of Edward I, Genoese galleys began regularly to make the direct voyage from the Mediterranean to the Channel. The Italians dominated finance as well as trade. Many abbeys were in debt to them, the king found them indispensable as lenders of money for his wars, and Archbishop Pecham paid for his installation with a loan from the Lucchese.

These aliens, like the Jews who were expelled in 1290, depended on royal protection. However essential they may have been to the economic growth of the country, they were not loved by competing English merchants. To kings they were an unrivalled source of profit in customs and loans, which amply repaid the generous and unpopular patronage given them in return. Edward I was happy to overrule the privileges of London in their favour and, throughout the Middle Ages, kings checked the desire of English merchants to impose restrictive conditions upon aliens. But the natives were growing in strength and during this period one organisation of English merchants was evolved—the Company of the Staple —which was powerful enough to compete with the foreigners for royal favour and to gain an unassailable position in European trade. A 'staple' was a place designated by royal ordinance as a special centre of commerce with privileges or monopolies. The word became particularly attached to the centre of trade in the main English export—wool. The idea of a staple of wool originated in the mutual interests of the king to have an organisation which would be easy to manipulate, and of the greater merchants to consolidate their position by monopoly. The first staples were set up at Dordrecht and Antwerp in the years 1294 to 1297, to help Edward I's plan for loans of wool and high customs duties on it to finance his invasion of France. The first compulsory staple, which all wool exporters were bound to use, was set up at St Omer in 1314. At the beginning of the Hundred Years' War, in and after 1336, the staple was again established at various times at Antwerp and Bruges for the same reason as had moved Edward I, the easing of war finance. The arrangement suited the bigger English exporters, some of whom were very substantial men, like Lawrence of Ludlow, who helped Edward I to set up the first staple and built Stokesay Castle, and William de la Pole, the financial genius of Edward III, whose son became Earl of Suffolk. A single foreign staple under their control was a disadvantage to the foreign merchant, who would rather buy wool from a grower or local dealer in England and take it directly to his market. The foreign staple also seems to have been disliked by the Commons in parliament, probably because it gave a single group of exporters an easier control over the prices paid to growers. The Commons several times pressed for staples at home and, in the years immediately after the Black Death, when the trade was very hard hit, their wishes were temporarily enforced by the Ordinance of the Staple (1353), which named staple towns in this country and gave the maximum advantage to growers and aliens by forbidding natives to export. The arrangement quickly broke down. English exporters were becoming too important and too indispensable to the king. The Florentine firms of Bardi and Peruzzi, which had been prominent under Edward II and in the early years of Edward III, had collapsed in the thirteen-forties, and the Italian empire in the wool trade and in royal finance went with them. In 1363 a group of twenty-six English merchants was established as the Company of the Staple at Calais (close to Flanders but a possession of the king of England) with complete monopoly of wool export except for the trade directly to Italy by sea.

The Company of the Staple is the supreme example of the common tendency of medieval merchants, industrialists, and craftsmen to form themselves into exclusive organisations to regulate and monopolise particular trades. This tendency was very prevalent in the towns, where the shopkeepers and craftsmen following a distinguishable 'craft' or 'mistery' commonly organised themselves into a gild—say of bakers or weavers—to promote their common interests and keep business in their own hands. The members of the gild would be the men established in the craft, who had the sole right to practise it and to train apprentices who might eventually become masters themselves, or might remain for ever wage-earners. Many towns also had a 'gild merchant' including all the traders, and this, as can be imagined might be a powerful organisation. The character of this economic organisation may be illustrated by the ordinances made for the Cordwainers (shoemakers) of London in 1271. They were distinguished from the workers in cowhide and inferior sheepskin, who were forbidden to meddle with their trade; the selling of shoes was confined to one market in Cheapside, near Cordwainer Street; a premium of forty shillings was fixed for the entry of apprentices, who could rise to be masters; each master was allowed to have eight servants, but no servant might employ an apprentice. Like the towns themselves, the crafts were exclusive organisations which did their best to preserve a monopoly and exclude outsiders. Business was carried on by relatively well-to-do men who employed wage-earners (the entrance fee of forty shillings was the wage of a skilled worker for several months). London naturally had an unusually large number of organised crafts—111 were listed in 1422. They were divided in the fourteenth century into the greater 'misteries'[1] including most of the wealthier merchants and aldermen, and the lesser gilds, which were made up more predominantly of small shop-

1. Grocers, Mercers, Fishmongers, Drapers, Goldsmiths, Woolmongers, Vintners, Saddlers, Tailors, Cordwainers, Butchers and Ironmongers were listed as the greater gilds in 1351.

keepers and craftsmen. Similar craft gilds existed, however, on a smaller scale elsewhere. There were organised Cobblers, Saddlers, and Fullers at Norwich at the end of the thirteenth century, and apparently Tanners, Weavers, and Tailors at Oxford about the same time. Apart from the municipal constitution itself, they provided the framework of town life, organising business and fighting the battles of their members against their employees and other trades. They were frequently also charitable associations which looked after members in distress, and religious fraternities attached to particular saints or churches, such as the gild of Weavers of Lincoln 'constituted in the name of the Holy Cross'. Primarily, however, the gilds were monopolies. The town was the world of communal monopoly, as the countryside was the world of lordship; all medieval traders, from the Staplers of Calais to the cobblers of a small town, aspired to the highest degree of exclusive independence which they could extract from the king or impose upon their neighbours.

By no means all the activities which we should call 'industries' were carried on in towns. Mining was already important in most of the English coalfields: coal from the estates of the Bishop of Durham was carried by sea through the port of Newcastle and there were quite elaborate pits in some places. Iron-mining and iron-making were important in the Forest of Dean and the Weald of Kent. Tin from Cornwall was an important English export. Mining was sometimes valuable as a manorial right, exercised by lords or leased out by them, but in both the Forest of Dean and in Cornwall there were 'free miners' outside the usual manorial system with special privileges enabling them to prospect and extract freely within a certain area. Cloth-making was another trade widely practised in the countryside, often as a sideline by peasants. It involved a number of different skills, already carefully distinguished. The wool had to be dyed (alum and woad were imported for this) and combed before it was spun into thread and woven into cloth. Then the cloth had to be fulled, by being beaten in water, to make it clean and thick—this was already being done in the thirteenth century with mechanical fulling-mills driven by water-power—before being stretched on 'tenters' and 'sheared' to give it an even texture.

The only industries which were developed to any magnitude in medieval England were the primary crafts of building and cloth-making. Great enterprises like the building of cathedrals or of Edward I's castles required hordes of workmen in addition to the master masons. More than 500 men were employed at a time in the rebuilding of Windsor Castle, in the middle of the fourteenth century. Some English towns were famous for their cloth, notably York, Lincoln, Stamford, Beverley, Colchester, Oxford, and Winchester, and it appears from the records of substantial Leicester burgesses, who were employing weavers, fullers, and dyers at the end of the reign of Henry III, that the industry could grow into relatively big business. But already the movements were afoot, assisted by the increasing use of fulling-mills situated on country streams, which made clothing chiefly a rural industry. The greater English towns were predominantly commercial rather than industrial centres. The most notable were seaports, London, Newcastle with its coal trade, the wool ports of Boston, Lynn, and Hull, granted its first charter by Edward I, Bristol, with its Gascon and Iberian connections, and Southampton; or the market centres of rich agricultural regions like York, Lincoln or Winchester.

A society in which agriculture and commerce flourished rather than manufacture, in which foreign merchants were as important as natives, in which the traditions of the Mediterranean cities had not taken root, and in which the kings exerted an unusually comprehensive judicial control, was a poor soil for the vigorous growth of urban independence. With the sole exception of London, there was no city in England comparable in size and independence with the bigger cities of Italy, Flanders, or the Rhineland, and no possibility of urban institutions achieving a comparable importance. Most towns were small and struggling communities, pockets of unusual customs in a world dominated by barons and bishops. There was much hostility between towns and their neighbours and overlords, shown perhaps most vividly during the political revolution of 1327, when the townsmen of Bury St Edmunds and Abingdon attacked the abbeys which ruled them and restricted their privileges. So important a place as Coventry did not achieve independence of the jurisdiction of the earls of Chester and the priors of Coventry—though it was unusual in this— until the townsmen obtained a royal charter in 1345. Most of the trading communities, which gave towns their social peculiarity, were also relatively small. Although they were sometimes enclosed in defensive walls, most towns were also closely connected with the surrounding countryside and a proportion of the inhabitants were engaged partially or entirely in rural pursuits, so that the town lands which stretched far beyond the walls were important to them as well as the streets and shops within. Oxford, for instance, had its own fields and meadows stretching up the Thames and Cherwell to about two miles north of the town.

By the end of the thirteenth century, however, there were well over 100 places, large and small, which had acquired privileges as boroughs, marking them off from the feudal and manorial world outside. The simplest characteristic of a borough was that its inhabitants held their land by 'burgage tenure', paying rents in money and exempt from the customs and services usual in a manor. This right was granted by lords to many places which were little more than villages, such as Higham Ferrers in Northamptonshire, but were sufficiently distinguished as market towns to claim and receive some urban privileges. There was a vast difference both in economic importance and in legal status between these and the bigger urban communities with larger liberties, such as York, Bristol, or Norwich. Urban independence was based on charters granted by local lords, or, in the case of most of the more important towns and many of the lesser ones, by the king, and the extent of their privileges depended on their bargaining powers. The charter granted to the city of Lincoln in 1327, confirming the privileges which it had built up in the past, gives an idea of the independence which might be enjoyed by a larger town. The mayor and citizens paid the king a 'fee farm' of £180 as an annual lump sum to cover their dues in rents and the profits of their courts. They also had the right of receiving and executing the king's writs (the judicial orders sent out from his Chancery). They were thus largely exempt from the jurisdiction of the king's sheriff of the county. Legal disputes within the city were heard by its own court, the 'burghmanmot', held by the mayor and bailiffs every Monday.

They had the right to impose a tax on merchandise sold in the city and to hold markets three times a week and an annual fair from 17th to 29th June. It would be impossible to construct a list of privileges which was absolutely typical of the greater English towns, for the variations were considerable. But privileges of this kind were characteristic of many towns which had trading communities, and therefore both needed to organise their life in freedom from the restrictions of the manor, and were wealthy enough to buy the right to control their own affairs and to maintain the monopoly of their trade in the hands of their own citizens. Lincoln itself was the centre of the Lincolnshire wool trade and a weaving town of some importance.

Walter Hervey, the mayor of London who held office when Edward I came to the throne, had been elected by a tumult of people crying, 'We are the Commune. We ought to elect the Mayor.' Again in 1312 and 1346 there were serious attempts to alter the city's constitution to make aldermen more responsible, by imposing upon them councils chosen by the gilds. For the most part these efforts failed. London was ruled by a mayor and twenty-four aldermen, who were elected by the city wards and mostly from the greater merchant class and were largely unrestricted by the mass of their fellow-citizens. The aldermen tended to hold office for long periods and thus to constitute a persistent oligarchy. A royal charter of 1319, which forbade immediate re-election after a year of office, was disregarded. The same provision was temporarily reintroduced in 1376 with little effect. The only serious attempt to democratise the constitution of London was the imposition in 1376 of a Common Council, elected by all the gilds and bound to meet every quarter as a check on the aldermen. But this experiment, which took place in a period of social unrest in the city (see below, p. 157), ended in 1384, and for much the greater part of the fourteenth and fifteenth centuries aldermanic control was unquestioned.

Urban constitutions, like urban privileges, varied considerably. In many cases the government of the town was inextricably bound up with that of the gild merchant of traders, which was sometimes identical with the body of burgesses. Some towns were ruled by councils of varying kinds, such as the twenty-four who were elected at Exeter towards the end of the thirteenth century and whose existence may suggest a democratic element. It is difficult to discern the balance of power which lay behind the formal constitutional arrangements. But the signs of popular restiveness were common enough: in 1290, for instance, complaints that the richer citizens of Lincoln had sold the city tolls and exacted money from the poor seem to have given the excuse for a temporary suspension of liberties by the king, and in 1304 the 'poor men of the commonalty of Lynn' complained of the exactions of their rulers. The burgesses, who had some say in government, were not the whole population of the town, and even the burgesses generally had only a remote control over the officials. At Oxford, for instance, the only freemen were the members of the gild merchant, but the government of the borough was carried on by the mayor and a council of twelve, including four aldermen, elected for life, and eight others probably co-opted, over whom even the freemen had little control. It is probable that most larger towns were governed in practice by oligarchies of their more prosperous citizens, 'the better people' rather than 'the whole commonalty'.

CHAPTER THREE

THE CHURCH

(1) THE CHURCH AND THE CLERGY

In thirteenth-century England about one man in fifty was a cleric of some sort and the Church owned a huge proportion of the country's landed wealth, in estates varying from the 'liberties' of abbeys and bishoprics, carrying jurisdiction over large areas,[1] to the 'glebes', land set aside in each parish to support its local church. Many of the clergy, it is true, were men in minor orders, deacons and sub-deacons, with no more knowledge than was necessary to conduct services, and a high proportion disobeyed the rule of celibacy. A visitation of nineteen parishes around Romney Marsh in the twelve-nineties discovered six rectors absent, four 'doing no good in the parish', most of the inferior clergy living with women, and several churches with ornaments and books inadequate to carry out the services. But the Church also contained examples of great piety and learning. Both the gap between the best and worst in the Church and the gap between the piety of a few and the brutality of lay life were greater than they are today. Thousands of men and women had taken vows to abandon themselves entirely to the communal religious life as monks and friars. Independent hermits, living in solitude, and anchorites, permanently enclosed in small houses for the purpose of constant devotion, were revered and supported in many places. Every village was dominated by its parish church, where the wall paintings of Doom and other religious subjects were the most vivid works of art ever seen by common folk. Sophisticated learning, the monopoly of the clergy, was crowned by a school of philosophers remarkable for the breadth and subtlety of their thought; and the cathedrals towered with equal magnificence over the houses of the cities. Religion was a greater power in the minds of men and in their material

1. For the definition of 'liberty' see below, p. 59

41

society than it has ever been before or since. At the climax of its struggle to control the world by the spirit, the Church had succeeded astonishingly in embodying in massive institutions the elusive impulses of devoutness.

The basic units of ecclesiastical life were the parishes, with an average population of three or four hundred people. In the towns they were closely packed, often covering only a few streets, so that the large number of churches in the middle of an ancient city, like York or Norwich, is today very surprising. In the countryside the parish would cover a village, or sometimes a group of hamlets, with subsidiary chapels in the outlying centres. The parish church and its clergy were supported partly by glebe land, annexed permanently to the church, partly by the tithes of parishioners, a proportion of their agricultural produce which they were legally obliged to pay annually to the rector. In theory and origin this income was intended to maintain the church in the parish itself. In practice much of it went elsewhere. A benefice in the Middle Ages was a piece of property as well as a cure of souls. The owner, having the right to appoint the rector, might be the local manorial lord, or an abbey or bishop, or the king. The rights of the patron were jealously valued and guarded, as were the rights of the incumbent. Some parishes had resident rectors in full command of their resources, but it was also possible for a rector to live elsewhere by permission, as a university scholar, or as an ecclesiastical official, supported by the income of his parish. In may cases parishes were 'appropriated' to abbeys, cathedrals, or colleges, so that their proceeds went to the support of a distant religious institution. These arrangements were part of normal ecclesiastical organisation. They might lead to scandalous absenteeism and pluralism, like the famous case of Bogo de Clare in the reign of Edward I, who drew income from a number of neglected parishes whilst he lived the life of a wealthy courtier, but in most cases they were probably necessary for the maintenance of the normal hierarchy. Many parishes were therefore in the care of a vicar, who performed the necessary duties for a stipend from the rector. The Church had its own social divisions, and the masses of salaried and often unlettered priests (who, according to the philosopher and intellectual

Medieval dioceses, with some abbeys and towns

snob, Roger Bacon, 'recite the words of others without knowing in the least what they mean, like parrots and magpies')
lived in a very different way from the cultivated and wealthy
monks and prelates.

The parishes were grouped in archdeaconries, about the
size of counties, and then in dioceses, each with its bishop and
cathedral, of which three—York, Carlisle, and Durham—were
in the Province of York and the others in the Province of
Canterbury (see map). In their own dioceses it was the
bishops' business to ordain clergy and to maintain ecclesiastical
discipline. They did this partly by occasional visitations, in

43

which they perambulated the diocese, inquiring into the state of each parish. The visitations carried out by Archbishop Pecham (1279—92) were extremely searching and revealing and so, no doubt, were those of many other bishops who have left less record. The bishop had a court, usually presided over by his archdeacon, for ecclesiastical cases. He held regular synods of the diocesan clergy, in which constitutions were issued to be obeyed by them, and the two archbishops held councils of their provinces for the same purpose.

Some of the dioceses, Winchester for instance, were very richly endowed with episcopal lands, and Durham was notable for its palatinate (see below, p. 60), which made the bishop almost an independent ruler. The road to a bishopric was not by success as a parish priest but by distinction in the more aristocratic world of the monasteries, the universities, and the bureaucracies of bishops, popes, and kings. The Church certainly did offer a way of advancement to the man of humble origins, who could not conceivably rise to a comparable position in lay society. Robert of Holy Island, Bishop of Durham (1274-83), was a poor man's son who had been a monk in Durham Priory; and John Pecham, the only Franciscan Archbishop of Canterbury (1278-92), was the son of a Sussex farmer, who had distinguished himself at Paris and Rome as a theologian. But Antony Bek, the gentleman and king's clerk who succeeded Robert of Holy Island as Bishop of Durham, was more typical in his social origins. Royal influence in episcopal appointments was considerable and bishoprics were often rewards for service to the king: Robert Burnell, Edward I's Chancellor and Bishop of Wells (1275-92), and William Airmyn, Keeper of Edward II's Privy Seal and Bishop of Norwich (1325-36), are examples. But kings might fail to get their nominees appointed. Edward I failed to secure a further promotion for Burnell to the archbishopric of Canterbury. Edward III failed to get York for his former Keeper of the Privy Seal, William Kilsby. Probably most bishops rose to the position through some sort of ecclesiastical distinction and some of them were considerable scholars. Pecham and Robert Winchelsey, Archbishop of Canterbury (1294-1313), were striking examples of ecclesiastical careers ending in episcopates of great distinction.

Parish priests and vicars were the secular clergy. Standing apart from them were the regulars, who might also become priests or bishops but whose vocation was to live the religious life for its own sake rather than to minister to the needs of laymen. The most prominent were the Black Monks who followed the Rule of St Benedict. Most of the abbeys were by this time ancient houses and they included some very great foundations like St Albans, Bury St Edmunds, Glastonbury, and St Mary's, York, not to speak of the cathedral priories. A later wave of foundations in the first half of the twelfth century had established the Cistercian Order. Their houses were also mostly old-established by 1272 and included such great abbeys as Fountains and Jervaulx in Yorkshire. On entering the abbey a monk abandoned his freedom of movement and his right to private property, to become part of a communal life with a prescribed routine of liturgy, work, and diet. Monks were no longer in the forefront of religious, intellectual, or artistic life, as they had been at some earlier periods, but they were still important in national life apart from the weight carried by their prestige and wealth. We should, for instance, know very much less about the history of this period if they had not written chronicles. Since the early thirteenth century the Benedictine houses had been subjected to regular inspections or 'visitations' by their own Order as well as by the bishops. They also held regular assemblies called 'chapters', attended by representatives of many houses, which had powers of government over the whole Order. They received new constitutions in 1277 which attempted to reduce the hours devoted to liturgy in favour of more study which the intellectual movements of the previous century had made fashionable. Though the eating of meat was forbidden by the Rule, it had become common in practice and the constitutions attempted only to restrict it within reasonable limits. This monastic legislation suggests that the difficulty at this period was less to curb excessive zeal than to retain the spirit of the Rule in institutions whose wealth and immemorial security could encourage their members to live like prosperous laymen, at worst devoting themselves to hunting and hawking, like the Prior of Leominster in 1286, at best more interested in their estates than in the religious life. It is of course impossible,

45

however many stories of piety and scandal survive, to measure how far the monks lived up to the main purpose of their life. All that can be said is that at this period they seem to have been a stable and traditional element in society rather than a leaven.

In contrast to the monks, the Mendicant Orders of friars, Franciscan and Dominican, had been in this country for only half a century when Edward I came to the throne and were still obviously fired by the ideals of their founders. The fame of St Francis (1181–1226) and St Dominic (1170–1221), the originality of their aims, and the position which their followers soon acquired as leaders of intellectual life gave the friars an enormous attraction for the spiritually minded of the thirteenth century and a great influence. They were joined by many of the greatest thinkers and eagerly patronised by the laity. St Francis had intended his followers to live an exemplary life of apostolic poverty and simplicity; St Dominic aimed to found an Order of men also living in poverty, but devoted particularly to preaching and instruction against heresy. Hence the distinction between the titles of Friars Minor and Friars Preachers. In practice they had come to live an increasingly similar life, owning no personal and relatively little communal property and concerned particularly with the evangelical work which the parochial clergy were ill-fitted to perform. Their own ardour and the admiration of their contemporaries quickly made them outstanding bodies within the Church. They were exempted by papal bulls from the ordinary jurisdiction of bishops. One evidence of their rapid penetration into everyday ecclesiastical life is a bull of 1281, allowing them to carry out all the functions of priests without permission of either bishops or rectors, which met with much opposition and was later modified. They were much suspected by many of the secular clergy but eagerly sought by many of the laity to preach, confess, and bury. They were ruled by their own chapters and their own provincial 'ministers' and 'priors', linked into a European organisation. In the reign of Edward I they had about a hundred houses, chiefly in the bigger towns. In both the universities, where they quickly penetrated and took the lead, and the ordinary urban parishes, they were easily the most vital force in the thirteenth-century Church.

For two centuries before the time when this history begins priests in England and abroad had been pressing their claim to be a separate order of men, set apart from the laity by their sacramental powers, independent of the temporal jurisdiction of kings and magnates, and owing a spiritual allegiance to the popes at Rome, successors of the apostle Peter. The heroic age of this movement was long past and the largely accepted division between the two swords of Church and State had introduced a fundamental cleavage, unparalleled in the homogeneous societies of antiquity and modern times, which is the most remarkable peculiarity of the medieval world. No king, however powerful, could be entirely master in his own house when a numerous, wealthy, and indispensable body of his subjects belonged to a European organisation, which allowed him only a limited authority; while the Church acquired an independence and a power for good or ill impossible in a society where it is regarded merely as a department of the State or a spiritual adjunct to everyday life. In important respects the clergy not only claimed to be but actually were independent of the authority of laymen.

In the thirteenth and early fourteenth centuries the papacy was at the height of its power, combining, as never before or since, the temporal independence of the Papal States in central Italy with a world-wide spiritual jurisdiction over the whole of western Europe. The transference of the popes to Avignon, which took place in 1308 because of political difficulties in Italy and lasted until 1377, reduced their political independence—later popes played a less ambitious part on the diplomatic chess-board than Innocent III (1198–1216), Innocent IV (1243–54), or Boniface VIII (1294–1303)—but it did not diminish their position as the heads of the ecclesiastical hierarchy. Natural administrative growth and the mounting financial needs of the papal Chamber prolonged the movement of centralisation until the difficulties and divisions of the late fourteenth century undermined it. Direct political intervention by the pope was often of some importance even to a monarch as remote as the king of England. Cases of this are Boniface VIII's mediation between Edward and Philip the Fair in 1298, his support of Scots independence in the next few years, and Benedict XII's efforts to prevent the early developments of the Hundred Years' War. In this sphere, however, the papal court could generally act as little more than a benevolent United Nations, encouraging the warring parties to come to terms by respecting each other's rights. More tangible results flowed from the pope's exercise of his direct headship over the clergy in England. This was manifested in three important ways. Firstly there was the papal right of 'provision'—nomination to benefices. The number of circumstances in which the pope might exercise the right to nominate the next incumbent of a parish or a canonry, when the last holder had died or been promoted, was much increased by the popes of the thirteenth and early fourteenth centuries. The power was used frequently in the case of bishoprics. Pecham and Winchelsey, for instance, were papal nominees, and a large number of bishops were appointed by the pope, sometimes in opposition to the wishes of both cathedral chapters and kings. Cathedral chapters themselves included a proportion of canons appointed by the pope, and to a lesser extent he interfered also in the selection of the ordinary parochial clergy. The right of provision had become recognised in the thirteenth century and was extended by Pope John XXII (1316–34). It was criticised on several occasions by the English laity, notably in the making of the Statute of Provisors in 1351, but throughout this period and after it was a normal and, in practice, accepted method both of supporting papal administration by giving sinecures to its officials, and of improving the personnel of the higher clergy. Secondly there was papal judicial authority, exercised in the acceptance of appeals in spiritual matters to the courts at Rome or Avignon. This again was criticised and slightly limited by the Statute of Praemunire in 1353, but generally accepted. Thirdly there was the papal right to tax the incomes of the clergy. Tenths were levied between 1274 and 1291 for a Crusade which never took place. From 1291 to 1329 frequent tenths were levied on the basis of the new assessment of ecclesiastical income made by Pope Nicholas IV; thereafter they were rarer.

The English clergy themselves were poised between the papal supremacy, which was acknowledged though often irksome, and the royal power, which consorted uneasily with a body of men claiming exemption from lay interference. In the last resort a king might use brute force to coerce churchmen, in a way which was difficult for a spiritual organisation to resist. Edward I imprisoned the Archbishop of York in 1292 for excommunicating his favourite, Bishop Antony Bek of Durham. This sort of occurence was rarer, however, than in previous centuries. The conflicts arose mostly because of the uncertain boundaries between the lay and temporal worlds, without calling into question their separateness. Like the pope, the king was interested in the appointment of churchmen, in jurisdiction and in taxation. Taxation of such a wealthy part of the community was irresistibly attractive. It produced one complete breach between Church and State in 1297, but in general it was reluctantly accepted by the clergy and formed an important part of royal financial resources. The greater part of the money levied by the pope in the reigns of Edward I and Edward II went in fact to the king to reconcile him to the export of the remainder. Nomination to bishoprics and benefices was an important part of royal patronage, essential for the rewarding of clerical administrators, and caused constant friction between king, pope, and chapters.

The conflict between lay and ecclesiastical jurisdiction flared up into a serious controversy in the episcopate of John Pecham. Pecham was determined to assert the rights of the Church. In a provincial council at Reading in 1279 he pronounced a general excommunication against those who impeded the jurisdiction of ecclesiastical courts by procuring the withdrawal of cases into lay courts and against royal officials who refused to execute ecclesiastical punishments. Ecclesiastical law claimed to deal both with crimes committed by clergymen and with moral offences of laymen. It was set out in the great corpus of canon law, evolved in the previous century and quite distinct from the common law of England, and it could be enforced by excommunication, cutting off the victim from the sacraments, which was a serious, if not always an effective deterrent. The boundary between lay and spiritual law was difficult to define, not only because the cleric might claim immunity from lay courts in ordinary, temporal crimes but also because questions of marriage, contract, and the ownership of benefices, which vitally affected lay society, also came partly under ecclesiastical jurisdiction. Edward I was not prepared to yield to Pecham's claims. He retorted with the Statute of Mortmain, which limited the power of the Church to acquire property from laymen, and by requiring Pecham to withdraw his general excommunication. Further quarrels led to the issue of the royal writ, *Circumspecte Agatis*, which defined some of the legal cases about moral offences, such as disputes over tithes and offences against the clergy, which even the king acknowledged to be the proper business of Church courts. Thereafter the lay and spiritual powers lived in an uneasy harmony which was often disturbed by recrimination from one side or the other but never broke down into a wholesale conflict.

(2) CATHEDRALS AND UNIVERSITIES

The centre of each diocese was a cathedral, which was also the church of a community of secular canons or monks. Several of the English cathedrals, like Canterbury and Durham, were the churches of great Benedictine abbeys. This meant that the monks formed the cathedral chapter, their abbey buildings were adjacent to the cathedral, and, in theory though generally not in practice, they elected the bishop. Elsewhere the chapter was made up of secular canons who lived in the close. The administration of the cathedral was maintained by the dean, the precentor, the chancellor who was sometimes also the master of the cathedral school, the treasurer, the resident canons, and the vicars choral who performed the duties of non-resident canons. Secular cathedrals whose canonries carried prebends (i.e. incomes without parochial duties) were the special field of pluralism and non-residence. A large and growing proportion of canonries was held by clerics who were really in the royal service, or papal nominees who never visited England. The main work of the chapter, monastic or secular, was to maintain a complicated programme of liturgy which went on throughout the day every day in the cathedral. It was the great wealth of these landowning corporations and also their prestige, which enabled them to attract special gifts from the people of the diocese, that made possible the erection of such huge buildings.

Though the cathedral was, in the thirteenth century even more obviously than today, the chief expression of the majesty of the Church, it is not easy for us to imagine just what it meant to a medieval man. It was certainly not a large parish church, for the streets around were generally well supplied with their own churches. The nave of a medieval cathedral, encumbered with a large number of small altars and chapels, would be less suited to receive a large congregation than it is today, but it was often a normal meeting-place of laymen, even a centre for the transaction of business; it would be attended by crowds at certain festivals and it was an object of pride to the inhabitants of the diocese. Many cathedrals contain masterpieces of architecture but, though the medieval masons worked by strict and elaborate rules of geometrical proportion, they rarely had the opportunity to construct a whole building to a single plan—Exeter and Salisbury are the only cases approaching this amongst the English cathedrals. Many have substantial portions in widely different styles from each of the medieval centuries; they seem to have grown like a landscape rather than to have been built. Their great size, their rich painting and glass, and the height of their vaults made them incomparably the most splendid buildings that the medieval man ever entered.

When Henry III died most of the English cathedrals were ancient and some of them (Durham, Salisbury, and Lincoln, for instance) already contained the chief architectural features which make them outstanding today. The late thirteenth and early fourteenth centuries, however, witnessed a remarkably lively development of architecture, in which the cathedrals shared with the greater monastic churches. In the major rebuilding of Westminster Abbey Henry III himself had carried out the enterprise which was perhaps nearest to his heart and which introduced new and influential motifs into England from the cathedrals of France. The period from 1250 to 1350 is the time when building in this country reached the heights of elaborateness and sophistication, developing from earlier medieval styles in something like the way that the baroque of the seventeenth century grew out of the simpler

Renaissance classicism before it. The cathedral of the early thirteenth century was by comparison a severe and simple building, sharply divided into nave, aisles, transepts, and presbytery, with fairly narrow windows between the massive pointed arches necessary to hold up the roof. The characteristic features of the building of the period covered by this book are firstly a greater richness of sculptured decoration, and secondly a freer and subtler conception of the spatial relationship between the parts of the church. It would be difficult

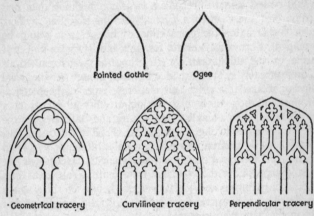

Pointed Gothic   Ogee

·Geometrical tracery   Curvilinear tracery   Perpendicular tracery

Types of arch and window

to distinguish the influences of wealth, technical advance, and aesthetic sensibility in producing this change. They combined to make possible the outstanding artistic achievements of medieval England.

Perhaps the most striking of the decorative inventions was the ogival arch, with its double curve inwards and upwards to a point, for purely decorative effect. It was used in the Eleanor crosses, which Edward I set up about 1300 in memory of his queen (one still stands at Geddington in Northamptonshire), and more elaborately in the tracery above the tomb of Edward II in Gloucester Cathedral. The stone canopies above the sedilia of the Lady Chapel at Ely (about 1340), in which the arches bend in a complicated manner outwards as well as vertically, exhibit this decoration at its richest. The spaces between the lines of the arches are filled with small effigies and luxuriant sculptured foilage, which are also characteristic of this period. The most remarkable foilage sculpture is to be seen in the leaves of identifiable trees carved in the late thirteenth century around the capitals of the pillars of Southwell Minster. Less naturalistic leaves and other decorative additions to arches and pinnacles are common. Windows were also growing both in size and in elaborateness. The simpler 'geometrical' tracery of the thirteenth century, in which windows were broken up by stone shafts into arches, circles, and trefoils, evolved into 'curvilinear' or 'flamboyant' tracery with more complicated and flowing lines. The great east window at Lincoln, with its narrow shafts to allow wide expanses of glass, capped by a rose, was built about 1275–80. The east window at Carlisle was made about 1320 and the development in this period reached its climax in the windows of the choir of Gloucester Cathedral (then the church of St Peter's Abbey), built in the mid-fourteenth century, where the stone shafts are reduced to thin divisions in a wide expanse of glass. The ribs of stone in the roof cease to be merely structural devices to hold it up, and flower into complicated patterns running over the ceiling for decorative effect. These can be seen in the choirs of Tewkesbury Abbey and Gloucester, built early in the reign of Edward III.

The way in which advanced engineering skill could contribute to architectural effect is seen about 1338 in the cross arches set, like massive Gothic girders, between the piers at the centre of Wells Cathedral to support the tower above. Most remarkable perhaps is the octagonal lantern built at the end of the reign of Edward II to replace the fallen tower at Ely Cathedral. It is supported by a framework of wooden beams behind the walls and creates an open, windowed space, of impressive height between the transepts. The main architectural advance, however, was the breaking of the sharp divisions between the parts of the church. At Ely the eye of the spectator is carried upwards by mounting arches from the choir to the octagon. The east end of Wells Cathedral was rebuilt about 1300 with the addition of a Lady-chapel, whose space appears to flow out of the choir to the west of it. In the new work in the choir of St Augustine's, Bristol, in the reigns of Edward I and Edward II, the arches dividing the choir from the aisles were raised to the roof to give the effect of a single space, lit by the windows of the aisle walls instead of by the clerestory windows above the aisles, as in earlier churches. (See Plates 6 and 7.)

The early part of the reign of Edward III saw the invention of the perpendicular style which was to dominate the rest of the Middle Ages. It is uncertain how much this owed to the examples of west-country building at Bristol and elsewhere, how much to the London school of architecture, patronised by the court, whose work was to be seen in two important buildings destroyed by fire in modern times, old St Paul's and St Stephen's Chapel, Westminster. The new style reached an early consummation in the rebuilding of the choir at Gloucester. Here the effect of a single broad space was achieved by cutting off the side aisles more completely from the choir. Broad windows were placed in the upper part of the walls with panels of stone and open arches below them, carrying the flat plane down to the floor, and thin piers up the walls topped with ribs opening into an elaborate tracery on the roof. The arches are flattened by comparison with thirteenth-century work and the whole effect is of a great hall, not narrowly pointed and dimly lit, as in buildings of the early Gothic, but wide and open. This style, evolved before the middle of the fourteenth century, set the fashion for the architecture of the rest of the Middle Ages. Gloucester clearly belongs to the same manner of building as much later examples like King's College Chapel, Cambridge, or St George's Chapel, Windsor, and it closes the period of daring architectural invention on either side of 1300 (Plates 8 and 9).

Sculpture and painting were, in the Middle Ages, also largely subservient to religious purposes. The most developed forms of sculpture were those employed in effigies on the tombs of prominent people and in the details of church architecture; most of the paintings which survive are miniature illustrations to religious books, stained-glass windows, or paintings on the walls of churches. These arts also were progressive and inventive in the early fourteenth century. Sculpture in stone was inseparable from architecture: we have already mentioned some of the most remarkable examples—the leaves of

Southwell, the Eleanor crosses, the sedilia at Ely, and the tomb of Edward II (Plate 10). The richness of this decoration and the profusion of sculptured foliage and small figure-scupture which is found in so much building of this period shows, however, that sculpture was increasingly being developed for its own sake. The effigy of Queen Eleanor at Westminster was the first known attempt in this country to accomplish the technically difficult feat of casting a life-size figure in bronze. The effigy of Edward II, placed beneath the elaborate canopy of his tomb at Gloucester, is a magnificent work in alabaster, which was quarried in the northern Midlands and became an increasingly characteristic material of English sculpture. There is also some similarity in feeling between the sculpture of this period and the miniature illumination of the East Anglian school—so-called because many of the finest examples were produced in monasteries of that region such as Ramsey and Bury St Edmunds, though the best-known work is perhaps the Luttrell Psalter, written for a Lincolnshire gentleman about 1340. The pages of these books are illustrated with a rich profusion of human figures, birds, animals, and battle scenes (Plate 5). Most medieval art is anonymous. We know a little about some of the patrons, for instance the royal court and the monasteries, and we know some of the names of the masons who designed buildings and of the 'imagers' who carved effigies; but their biographies are almost completely lost. Their works, however, suggest that they were just as ambitious and subtle as the artists of later ages whose personalities have become famous.

The artistry of the cathedrals was paralleled by the equally remarkable if less attractive development of the intellectual side of religion. By the end of the thirteenth century the universities at Oxford and Cambridge had been in existence for some time and, though Cambridge remained a smaller and more local university, at least until the fifteenth century, Oxford was already one of the leading centres of European thought and learning, estimated to contain 1,500 masters and students in the early fourteenth century, and the home of several thinkers of the first rank. Most of the students were aspirants to the ecclesiastical preferment which degrees would help them to obtain, living in lodging-houses in the town or with their masters. A few colleges had been founded in the thirteenth century to provide homes for poor advanced scholars (University, Balliol and Merton at Oxford, Peterhouse at Cambridge) and there were convents of student friars and a house for Benedictine monks at Oxford. The basic subject of study was the curriculum for the degree of Master of Arts, the seven liberal arts of Grammar, Rhetoric, Logic, Arithmetic, Music, Geometry, and Astronomy, studied in the books of ancient authors, such as Boethius and Aristotle. Beyond these the persistent student could proceed to Theology, Medicine, or Law. The full courses were lengthy: six years for the mastership in Arts, another eight for Theology. Most of the intellectual discipline consisted in reading prescribed texts and lecturing and disputing on them. Every aspirant to the mastership in Theology had to lecture on the theological and philosophical texts assembled in Peter Lombard's twelfth-century complication, the 'Sentences'. Thus philosophical and theological writings even of the leading philosophers tended to be in the unpalatable form of question and answer, which removed most of the literary graces from the masterpieces of medieval thought. Oxford trained the intelligentsia of medieval England, but it was, of course, essentially an ecclesiastical institution, its scholars mostly clerics, its privileges subject to the visitation of the archbishop.

Thirteenth-century thought had been to a large extent dominated by the problem of incorporating the newly discovered and intellectually compelling works of Aristotle into a Christian philosophy. When Edward I came to the throne the Dominican St Thomas Aquinas (1225–74) was composing in Paris his *Summa Theologica*. This carried the reception of Aristotle to the furthest tolerable point, but provoked an episcopal condemnation, in 1277, which was repeated at Oxford by the Archbishop of Canterbury, Robert Kilwardby (1272–8), also a Dominican and a distinguished philosopher. Thomism, however, had its supporters at Oxford and elsewhere and it was reinstated in the next year when Kilwardby was recalled from England to become a cardinal. The new Archbishop, the Franciscan John Pecham, was also a distinguished theologian, who had been in conflict with Kilwardby at Paris over the question of apostolic poverty as practised by the two Mendicant Orders. He visited Oxford in 1284 to condemn Thomist propositions which were being taught, and to assert the superiority of the intellectual tradition contained in the writings of earlier Franciscans, notably St Bonaventure.

These quarrels illustrate two important general points. Firstly, the philosophical ferment of the thirteenth and fourteenth centuries, though clothed in abstruse academic terms, had as much importance for the Church as a whole as the eucharistic and Biblical controversies of the sixteenth century for the Reformers, or the niceties of Marxist dogma for the modern Communist hierarchies. Aristotelianism tended to exalt the power of the individual intellect to acquire understanding of the universe by reason independent of revelation. It bound the soul more closely to the body than had been customary in Christian thinking—this was in fact one of the particular points which Kilwardby condemned in 1277—and could, if carried too far, restrict the sphere of operation of God and faith. The thiteenth-century thinkers debated at great length and with complicated subtlety the abstract problems of the nature of Being, Essence, and Ideas, which are perennial problems of philosophy, but with particular reference to the nature of God and His connection with the world, and in the hope of constructing a metaphysic which would be true both to the logic of the human mind and to Christian beliefs. The questions at issue therefore affected the whole dogmatic basis of the Church.

Secondly, scholastic philosophy in the thirteenth and early fourteenth centuries was largely dominated by a series of remarkable thinkers in the Mendicant Orders, whose ideals tended to attract the best speculative minds. The second point is particularly true of Oxford. Ever since Bishop Grosseteste, himself one of the originators of Oxford's tradition of speculation, had sponsored the foundation of the Franciscans at Oxford early in the reign of Henry III they had attracted and nurtured its leading philosophers. Roger Bacon, who died at Oxford in 1292, was a Franciscan and one of the boldest and most learned thinkers of his age, remembered particularly for his advocacy of the study of Greek, for the better understanding of ancient philosophers, and of mathematics. The most notable Oxford thinker of our period was another Franciscan, John Duns Scotus (died 1308), who constructed a theory of Being and Form which sharply reduced from its Thomist level the power of the human intellect to understand God and religion rationally, and tended to restrict the operation of sense and reason more to the comprehension of the natural world.

CHAPTER FOUR

GOVERNMENT

(1) THE KING'S LAW

MEDIEVAL men were divided into the free and the unfree. The bondman was his lord's property, to some extent at the lord's mercy and subject to his manorial court in matters of tenure and petty theft. It is impossible to know just what proportion of Englishmen had this status in 1272, but it was certainly a very large number, possibly a quarter of the population. Villeinage, however, was not slavery. Though the villein's rights against his lord were restricted, in his relations, civil and criminal, with all other men, he was in exactly the same position as a freeman. All men were therefore potentially subject to the king's law. But this law was not valid in the same way in all places or over all men. While the serf, at the bottom of the social scale, was distinguished by his subjection to a lord, other men in the higher ranks of society had judicial powers much greater than those of the ordinary freeman. 'Liberty' in the Middle Ages does not mean the equal right of all subjects to manage their own affairs without interference from above. A 'liberty' was a special right held by one man or group of men and not by others. Thus when kings acknowledged the 'liberties' of the Church they were admitting that churchmen had special judicial privileges. If a lord had special judicial powers over the men in his lordship, these powers, or the area in which they were exercised, would be described as a 'liberty' or 'franchise' or an 'immunity' from royal jurisdiction.

Apart from the king's justice the main kinds of jurisdiction were these:

(i) The Church claimed the authority of the bishops' courts, not only over the behaviour of priests in their ecclesiastical duties, but also over crimes committed by them and over some spiritual affairs of laymen, particularly marriages and wills.

(ii) Jurisdiction over petty offences by tenants and also over disputes about their holding of land were settled in the courts of lords of the manor all over England.

(iii) There were several wide 'franchises', notably the lordships of the Welsh March (including parts of the modern counties of Monmouthshire, Herefordshire, and Shropshire), the county of Chester, the palatinate of the Bishop of Durham, the liberty of Ely, and the liberty of the Abbot of Bury St Edmunds. The Bishop of Durham's steward claimed in 1302 that 'there are two kings in England, namely, the lord King of England wearing a crown as symbol of his regality, and the lord Bishop of Durham wearing a mitre in place of a crown as symbol of his regality in the diocese of Durham'.[1] The Bishop of Durham, with his own justices, sheriffs, and chancery, claimed and exercised all the rights of justice pertaining to the king in other places. This was the extreme case. Even the lords of the franchises in East Anglia, however, received the fines and confiscations from criminals, which went elsewhere to the king, and had the powers of distraining and presenting criminals which were exercised by the king's sheriff elsewhere, though the actual judgments were given by the king's justices.

(iv) Many lords of manors also had the right of court leet, that is to say the right of exercising privately the sheriff's power of summoning the community regularly to the 'tourn' to see if there were any criminals to be presented for trial and of fining for small offences. Many also exercised these rights over the wide area of a 'hundred' (usually including many villages), which was the basic ancient unit of criminal jurisdiction, now falling into disuse.

(v) By the time of Edward I there was a large number of boroughs holding charters of liberties from the king. A few of them had the franchise of 'return of writs' like the lords of Ely or Peterborough—that is the right of executing the king's judicial orders, which would in other places be exercised by the sheriff. All had the right to hold courts for civil pleas and petty crimes.

These were all in a sense acknowledged limitations to the

1. C. M. Fraser, *A History of Antony Bek* (1957), p. 98

power of the crown. Bishops, monasteries, lay lords, and towns therefore had judicial rights, 'liberties' embodied in customs and charters, which even the king would hesitate to infringe. They might have to defend themselves but their independence was likely to continue from generation to generation. There is a famous story that, when the Earl of Surrey was challenged by Edward I's judges to say by what warrant he held his lands, 'he produced an old and rusty sword and said, "Here, my lords, is my warrant. My ancestors, who came with William the Bastard, conquered their lands with the sword and I will defend them with the sword against whoever tries to occupy them."' Although this is probably a legend and rather anachronistic in tone, it expresses a real attitude. For more than a century kings with growing resources and growing pretensions had been extending the authority of the judges whom they appointed, and of the 'common law' which those judges created, making more effective the king's claim to be the supreme fount of justice for the whole of England. By Edward I's day this process had been carried a long way. Most of the rights in temporal justice exercised by the holders of immunities, except in the far north and west, were either concerned with fairly trivial matters or had become subsidiary parts of a judicial system controlled from Westminster. The bailiffs of franchises, for instance, often executed judgments which were made by royal justices. But it was still true that many Englishmen, not only those in the remote Marcher lordships, were as much affected by the jurisdiction of their local lords as by that exercised directly by the king's officials. A man who lived in the area covered by the 'liberty' of the Church of Ely might be subject in some judicial matters to his manorial lord, a tenant of Ely, in others to the bishop or prior, as holders of the liberty, in others to the king. Royal justice was dominant and had to a large extent made the franchises its servants, but it was not all-pervading.

The supreme tribunal of the justice which emanated from the Crown was the king and his council (including his chief ministers and clerks), which might meet alone or in the solemn publicity of a parliament. Important or doubtful cases might be referred by the judges to the council and some notable trials were held in parliament, with the magnates participating as judges. An example is the famous case of Nicholas de Segrave, who was condemned to death in parliament in 1305 for committing treason while fighting on the Scots border, and then pardoned by the king. Much judicial business was done as a result of petitions to the king and council, in or out of parliament, by subjects who had failed to get justice elsewhere. The main legal business, however, was concentrated by this time in three royal courts at Westminster: Exchequer, which dealt with matters affecting the king's finances; Common Pleas (the 'Bench', as contemporaries called it); and King's Bench, which was then called *Coram rege* ('In the king's presence'), because of its close relationship to the king and its special concern with matters affecting him. The judges of King's Bench and Common Pleas were sometimes clerics with an academic training, and often expert professional lawyers. During the fourteenth century the Chancery, whose main business was to write royal letters, also developed into an important court, exercising equitable jurisdiction in cases which could not be decided by the ordinary rules of common law.

Much royal justice was also done outside the courts at Westminster, for the king had power to issue commissions to hold trials anywhere in the kingdom, within the limitations imposed by private franchises. Commissions were frequently issued for judges to hear the 'assizes' concerning property disputes in particular counties and also commissions of *nisi prius*, to hear on the spot cases begun in the local court; of 'gaol delivery', to try prisoners in gaols; and of *oyer* and *terminer*, to 'hear' and 'determine' whatever cases might be named. The judges empowered by these commissions were by no means always professionals, but they were the forerunners of the assize judges on circuit of later times. Sometimes a comprehensive commission was issued to a group of judges and local notables to hear all pleas in a county. This was the general 'eyre', the most impressive demonstration of royal justice. The men of Cornwall had been known to flee to the woods on the coming of the eyre and in 1301 it was said that Edward I 'amassed great treasure' by it, which reminds us that justice in these days was also a way of imposing power on unruly subjects and of making a profit out of them. The eyre was so hated that it became traditional never to hold it in a county more than once in seven years and, though eyres were characteristic of the reigns of Edward I and Edward II, they were practically abandoned after 1330.

The executive side of royal justice was mainly the business of the king's sheriff in each county. Besides being responsible for the Crown lands, it was his duty to execute the writs from Westminster, to produce criminals for the royal courts, and to distrain their property if necessary, to empanel the juries, and to hold his tourn (see above, p. 60) regularly in the hundreds. The sheriff might or might not be a local gentleman; in any case he was, as far as his office went, essentially the king's servant. Another important custom of this period was the entrusting of royal justice to the local gentry, to act temporarily for the king in the way that Justices of the Peace do in modern times. For many years kings had appointed coroners in the shires to inquire particularly into cases of sudden death and felony. It was also common at this time to find local gentry appointed as Keepers of the Peace in their counties, with the duty of keeping order, apprehending criminals and presenting them to the royal justices. In the reign of Edward III their powers were considerably increased, partly, perhaps, as an alternative to sending out justices in eyre from Westminster and probably partly because the Commons in parliament pressed for judicial responsibility to be given to the local gentry of the shires rather than to the king's servants. A statute of 1368 gave them full power to hear and try felonies.

Medieval justice was always a compromise between the king's will to rule with his bureaucracy centred on Westminster, and the jealous resistance of those who were important in their own localities and resented intrusion. The king's acceptance of local franchises was part of this compromise. The existence of Keepers of the Peace, who acted in virtue of the king's commission but were chosen for their local prominence, was another part of the balance of power between the king and his more important subjects. The balance was maintained for centuries. In medieval times royal judicial power never extended much beyond the limits reached by Edward I, and there were times of weakness in the fifteenth century when it appears to have receded considerably.

By 1272 the conception of all-embracing royal justice had already received its classic expression in the book *The Laws and Customs of England* by the greatest medieval English jurist, Henry Bracton (died 1268). Bracton was both an experienced royal judge and a scholar learned in Roman and canon law. His treatise is a systematic statement of royal justice as it actually happened, illuminated by general principles which would occur to someone influenced by the theories of law descending from antiquity; the combination of the two marks impressively the emergence of a developed, civilised system of royal law in England. The common law had grown mainly out of the precedents established by innumerable disputes about property and criminal offences decided by the king's judges. Most of the book is a guide to the elaborate growth of precedents which had taken place by this time. It also presents a point of view. Bracton sees the king as the fount of justice, who should rule according to the accepted law of the land, not as a capricious despot. Further, he thinks that all jurisdiction in the land emanates in principle from the king and that no man has a right to hold a court, with the kind of superior jurisdiction which the king normally exercises, unless he can show royal authority for it. 'Those things which are matters of jurisdiction and peace . . . pertain to no-one except the crown and the royal dignity. Nor can they be separated from the crown, since they make the crown. . . . Jurisdictions of this kind cannot be transferred to persons or tenements or possessed by a private person . . . unless it was granted to him from above as delegated jurisdiction.'

Bracton had several literary imitators under Edward I, when the views of the king's judges were in the main those which he had propounded. His principle of royal judicial supremacy was in conflict with the facts of English history, for many of the judicial immunities owed little to royal consent; they had been won by the sword or descended by ancient prescription from times long before there were kings of England with even the pretension to jurisdiction over the whole country. Nevertheless the Crown had grown so strong by the thirteenth century that kings could make a serious effort to wrest the whole complex of jurisdictions into a system conformable with Bracton's theory that all court-holders acted by leave of the king. The principle which came to be accepted was that an immunity could be allowed only if it had either been granted by a royal charter or had been used before the reign of Richard I (1189–99). The process of enforcing this had been carried far by the writs of *quo warranto* ('by what warrant?') issued to start inquiries into titles to liberties in the reign of Henry III. It was completed by the investigations and statutes of Edward I. The general inquiry into local rights, ordered in 1274, produced a mass of evidence about liberties, which is entered on the Hundred Rolls, and led to insistence on the proper execution of royal writs in those liberties which had 'return of writs' in the Statute of Westminster I (1275). Then the principles of the *quo warranto* writ, hitherto applied to particular cases, were generalised into the Statute of Gloucester (1278), which said that no liberty was to be exercised until its holder had justified it before the king's judges. After years of litigation, following from this bold statement, the Statute of *Quo Warranto* (1290) maintained that a franchise, which was claimed simply on the basis of long use, must be confirmed by a royal charter. In fact, of course, most of the franchises remained—Edward had tried not to destroy them but to limit them as far as was possible without offending against established custom—but the assertion of judicial supremacy had been carried as far as it could be in medieval society.

The statutes of Gloucester and *Quo Warranto* were part of a series of acts, which made Edward I's reign a very notable period in the history of English law. Most of medieval law was not statute but custom or precedent, and, before Edward's time, there had been very little of what we should call legislation. Kings and judges frequently changed the law in detail in the course of administering it, and medieval men did not distinguish clearly between legislation and the growth of precedent. It is clear enough to us, however, that Edward made some serious attempts to define not only royal jurisdiction but also the important part of the law relating to feudal property.

As we have seen earlier, most of the land of the gentry and nobility was held by feudal tenure, and it is from the custom governing this that modern English property law descends.

Feudal tenure had originated in the grants of land made two centuries earlier after the Norman Conquest and, like any property arrangements, it had become extremely complicated by the passage of more than six generations, during which lands had been repeatedly divided between heirs and granted out by temporary agreements which became permanent. This would not matter in a modern régime of freehold property. It mattered in the thirteenth century because feudal property was never freehold but always held of a lord with reciprocal rights and duties between lord and tenant. Ultimately all land was held of the king, but there might be a long chain of intermediate lords between the king and the man who actually lived on a piece of land. 'In Edward I's day Roger of St German holds land at Paxton in Huntingdonshire of Robert of Bedford, who holds of Richard of Ilchester, who holds of Alan of Chartres, who holds of William le Boteler, who holds of Gilbert Neville, who holds of Devorguil Balliol, who holds of the King of Scotland, who holds of the King of England.'[1] All these tenants and lords had rights and duties to each other. The tenant owed military service, or alternatively the money payment called scutage, and, if his heir inherited while still under age, the holding reverted to the lord in wardship until he grew up. The difficulties of enforcing these rights and duties were important both to the king and to many of his subjects. In the Statute of Westminster II (1285) Edward tried to settle the legal rights of both sides in a case where the lord distrained on the property of a tenant for failing to perform his services. In the same statute he tried to settle the rights of people who granted away their land conditionally, for instance to a younger son with the proviso that it should revert to the main line of the family if he had no children. In the Statute of Mortmain (1279) he forbade property to be granted to the Church (because such a grant meant that it forever escaped the lord's hands, since abbeys and churches never died), unless the lord licensed it. Finally, in the Statute of Quia Emptores (1290), he altogether forbade his subjects to create new feudal tenures. In future, if a tenant B held of A, he could grant his land to C only if he dropped out of the

1. F. Pollock and F. W. Maitland, *History of English Law before the Time of Edward I*, I, 2nd ed. (1898), p. 233

Quia

chain himself, so that C held of A. All land was still held of the king by feudal tenure down to the seventeenth century, but after *Quia Emptores* it was impossible for anyone except the king to reward a follower by making him a feudal tenant. Thus in practice, though the king's feudal relations with tenants-in-chief were still important, further down the scale the ties of feudal tenure became less significant and land was commonly conveyed by outright grants or leases. These are some of the prominent points in a complicated series of statutes. They did not settle the law of property, which went on evolving and proliferating throughout the Middle Ages, and we can see from the records of the courts that it was often a long and difficult business to establish ownership, but they provided important points of reference.

(2) THE KING'S MINISTERS

The modern State, with its supreme powers and huge staffs of officials, has grown very gradually out of medieval government. The continuity is more obvious in England than in most countries because we still have institutions like Parliament and Chancery which retain medieval names and some vestiges of medieval organisation. It is important, however, not to be misled by this continuity into thinking that medieval government, or indeed the government of the sixteenth and seventeenth centuries, was just a smaller version of the modern State. The medieval State, like ours, existed to keep order, to raise taxes, and to defend national interests; but in some essential respects it had a different character and purpose which were only gradually abandoned between the sixteenth and the nineteenth centuries. Firstly, the powers of the king were not so sharply different from those of other great men as the powers of a modern government are from all organisations within the State. The king was one lord among many. Though he was far above the others and had attributes of regality, which he shared with none, his government was in many ways similar to the organisations maintained by the greater lords. The Duke of Lancaster and the Bishop of Durham had chanceries and substantial judicial powers, and every earl and bishop kept high state in his household as far as he could afford it, had a council to advise him, and a treasury to manage his money. Secondly, government was less concerned with national welfare than it is today and more with the glorification of the king. Medieval men, as we shall see later, did not think a king was without duties to his subjects—they had a conception of political co-operation and no doubt many of them benefited by the more impartial justice administered by the king's judges—but neither did they think of government as being primarily utilitarian. Royal magnificence, exhibited in a splendid court, in the wearing of jewels, the maintenance of a large retinue, the building of lavish castles such as Edward III's at Windsor, and the waging of expensive wars in support of the claim to France, might sometimes be resented by those who were squeezed to pay for it, but it was generally accepted as a proper object of policy. We shall understand royal administration better if we think of it in terms of the *ministri regis*, the king's ministers, rather than as the State.

Outside Westminster most of the men who were responsible for the king's business were part-time officials. We should add to the coroners and Keepers of the Peace on the judicial side the assessors and collectors of taxes on property, who were usually local men appointed temporarily, and the merchants, who collected the king's customs in the ports as a sideline to their main business. The escheators, who administered lands which fell into the king's hands as feudal 'escheats', were sometimes more professional. The sheriff had been, from time immemorial, the king's chief representative in the shire, collecting the dues from his lands and the profits of justice and executing the judicial writs. He was still important, but his isolation had gone with the appointment of hundreds of other men to do pieces of royal business as collectors and justices. Though there was no full-time bureaucracy outside Westminster, except for the few clerks employed by sheriffs and collectors, a great many men of the middle ranks had some occasional responsibility for enforcing the king's rights up and down the country.

A considerable staff of clerks, working permanently for the king, was partly established at Westminster and partly followed the court on its travels. Some of these, like William Airmyn, Keeper of the Privy Seal to Edward II and then

Bishop of Norwich, or the great William of Wykeham, rose through the king's service to become prelates; most of them were obscure functionaries for life, lucky if they could collect a benefice to add to their income, literate but connected with the church only by Minor Orders, if at all. These were the forerunners of the civil service. The central government can be divided into four main parts: council, household, Chancery, and Exchequer. The Chancery is the easiest of these to describe. It was the royal writing office, with a staff of clerks, who wrote the letters and charters issued by the king and kept copies of them for reference on long, narrow rolls of sheepskin. It was presided over by the Chancellor (usually a prelate, sometimes the Archbishop of Canterbury), who was given authority by his custody of the Great Seal, which was appended to royal charters. Like the Chancery, the Exchequer was an ancient and revered institution, usually presided over by a great prelate, the Treasurer. The chief business of the barons of the Exchequer and the lesser clerks was to account for the king's money as it came in from all over the country. The Exchequer had originated out of the ancient custom by which sheriffs came to Westminster twice a year with the money due to the king from their shires. After handing it in at the Lower Exchequer and receiving tallies (pieces of wood with notches to show the exact sums they had paid) as receipts, they proceeded to the Upper Exchequer, where their accounts were solemnly investigated and entered on the Pipe Roll for the year. By this time the Exchequer's business had grown more continuous and complicated, for it received money from many other collectors, besides the sheriffs, and there was much clerical work involved in reckoning not only the sums received but also the payments made locally or to other officials by royal warrant, and setting them against the totals due from the accountants. In 1323 the Treasurer, Bishop Stapleton of Exeter, found that the confusion made it necessary to separate all accounts except the sheriffs' from the main Pipe Roll (the Cowick Ordinance). But the methods of the Exchequer remained essentially the same in spite of the elaboration of government and taxation with which it had to deal.

The apex of the royal administration, as of that of other great lords, was the council, the body of superior officials, king's friends, courtiers, and clerks, which stayed about the monarch and advised him on his actions. Because of the way medieval archives have survived (generally the official files of Chancery and Exchequer, not the important letters and memoranda containing policy), we know much less, unfortunately, about the council than about the minute details of tax collection, but, from the little that we know, we can infer that it was the most important of royal institutions. Rebellious subjects several times tried to control the government by controlling the membership of the council. The most striking case was in 1318, when the baronial factions meeting at the Treaty of Leek nominated eight bishops, four earls, four barons, and a banneret of the Earl of Lancaster, the most powerful magnate, 'to stay by the king and counsel him'; but neither these imposed councils nor the regency council appointed for the minority of Edward III were characteristic of the body as it normally existed. Its function was not to be representative but simply to include those men whose advice and loyalty the king most valued. Probably its most constant members were the king's leading clerks and judges, ministers like the Chancellor and the Keeper of the Privy Seal, and occasional magnates in the king's confidence. In 1304, for instance, it was said to consist of Bishop Langton of Lichfield (the Treasurer), Henry de Lacy, Earl of Lincoln (a close associate of Edward I), Roger de Brabazon, and other judges. Some of the members at least took an elaborate oath of loyalty to the Crown and much important business was entrusted to them.

Like other great lords, the king lived in a large household. Edward I's Household Ordinance of 1279 lists over fifty established domestic officials, including important people like the stewards and marshals who organised the court, and less important like the cooks, the ushers of the Chamber and clergy of the chapel, all of whom were entitled to receive robes from the King. It laid down rules about matters like weighing the candles every day to see that they were not wasted and making sure that courtier knights did not bring too many followers to eat freely at the king's table. The household had its own administrative offices, the Chamber and the Wardrobe, which also had considerable importance beyond purely domestic matters. Unlike Chancery and Exchequer, the clerks of the Chamber and Wardrobe travelled about with the court and they were concerned less with the general supervision of the royal finances than with the spending of the money. It was therefore natural that, when Edward I fought in France in 1297–8 and Edward III in 1338–40, the Wardrobe should control most of the payment of troops and other war expenses. This was a matter of convenience, but it was not confined to war time, and it also meant that large quantities of money raised by taxation were never seen, sometimes not even accounted for, by the Exchequer. The Exchequer was a more public, accessible institution than the household offices, and the tendency for it to lose its grip on the whole royal financial system sometimes seemed sinister to opponents of the court. One of the points on which the ordainers tried to insist when they were restricting Edward II's power in 1311 (see below, p. 111) was that all money used by the Wardrobe should be properly accounted for at the Exchequer. They regarded financial control by the Wardrobe as part of a dangerous conspiracy by the king's *domestici* at court to run the government without consulting the magnates. The king also had in the household a Privy Seal (distinguished from the Chancellor's Great Seal) to authenticate letters sent out directly from the court instead of going through the office of Chancery to receive the Great Seal, and the Keeper of the Privy Seal became an important official. In 1338, when Edward III temporarily reorganised his administration, before taking his household abroad at the beginning of the Hundred Years' War, the Keeper, William Kilsby, became in effect the King's chief clerical officer, and, in the political crisis which followed in 1340–1, he was the bitterest opponent of Archbishop Stratford, who had been Chancellor. In general, however, the distinction between the household and the great offices 'out of court' was not a matter of political importance. Nobody denied the king's right to organise his officials as he wished, unless there were strong motives of personal jealousy for attacking him or them.

71

It is now time to turn from the ways in which the king exercised his authority to the ways in which he negotiated with his subjects. Unless the king was a tyrant there was a constant process of intercourse and compromise between him and lesser men. This is the parliamentary side of medieval government. Before proceeding to parliament itself we must understand taxation, which was the chief practical reason for parliament's existence in the form it took, and taxation is comprehensible only in the light of war. In a previous chapter we have seen something of the wealth of England, which was partly mobilised in taxation; the other side of the picture is the fighting for which it was used. There were few years in the Middle Ages when the king or his soldiers were not fighting on one front or other. War was not, as it is today, a plague which civilised society aspires to eradicate. Its visitations could be terrible enough for the plundered and mutilated defenceless; there is evidence for instance that Northumberland, Westmorland, and Cumberland were seriously wasted by the Scots invasions of the reign of Edward II, and the ravages of the English companies in France in the reign of Edward III became a byword for horror. For the nobility and the knightly classes, however, war was a normal and almost essential part of life. 'Prowess,' as Froissart, their chronicler, said in the later fourteenth century, 'is so noble a virtue and of so great recommendation that one must never pass over it too briefly, for it is the mother stuff and the light of noble men and, as the log cannot spring to life without fire, so the noble man cannot come to perfect honour or to the glory of the world without prowess.' Prowess was in fact by no means the sole temptation to war, for many made large profits out of ransoms and plunder, but Froissart's words reflect the truth that war was essential to the noble society of his contemporaries.

War was in one sense a more serious version of the tournament, which was fought for entertainment and practice, and tournaments were held a number of times in the reigns of all three Edwards. Retainers were sometimes obliged to do service for their lords in both war and tournaments. Edward I held a Round Table, which was a kind of tournament, at

Nefyn in 1284 to celebrate his victory in Wales. Later on he prohibited tournaments, because they so easily became connected with serious fighting, but they were allowed early in Edward II's reign, when they seem to have been one of Gaveston's delights, and again in the early chivalrous days of Edward III. During this period the tournament was changed from the murderous *mêlée* of two bodies of armed knights, which it had been in the early Middle Ages, into the courtly ceremonial of the Round Table, within the 'lists' before spectators, which kings could regard as less of a danger to public order. But it was still a dangerous sport and its existence shows the blend of serious intent to kill and ransom with the pursuit of sporting adventure, which made up medieval war. At any rate, many noblemen, like the Black Prince, were 'never weary nor full satisfied of war'.

The royal army in the field at this time normally consisted of a mixture of cavalry, armed with sword and lance, mounted archers, and foot-archers. Edward I's army in Flanders in 1297 consisted of 7,810 infantry, three-quarters of them Welsh, and 895 cavalry, of whom 140 were knights. Edward III's armies contained a higher proportion of mounted men (the Black Prince in the Poitiers campaign probably had about 1,000 horse-archers in a force of about 2,600) but the core of knights remained small. The mixture was essential to contemporary tactics, for the infantry and archers were needed to break the attack of the enemy's cavalry and cavalry was needed for pursuit. The disaster of Bannockburn was caused by the cavalry's muddled attempt to go it alone without proper support, and the victories of Maes Moydog (1295), Falkirk (1298), Halidon Hill (1333), Crécy (1346), and Poitiers 1356) were all won by a judicious mixture of the two arms. The graded ranks of the army were a microcosm of English rural society. The bulk of the numbers were archers and foot-soldiers, and the half-naked Welshmen whom a Flemish observer described with surprise in 1297. The core of the army was a relatively small group of noblemen and gentlemen, who had received the order of knighthood, were skilled in knightly fighting, and could afford the mail armour and fine horses essential to the knight. The knight carried shield, lance, and sword. His basic armour was a suit of chain mail, reinforced with steel plates at crucial places such as knees and shoulders (Plates 4 and 5). During the fourteenth century the proportions of plating to mail were being increased until eventually the plate armour of the fifteenth century, covering nearly the whole body and replacing the shield, was developed. This heavy equipment tended to make rapid movement and fighting on foot difficult. One of the main developments in warfare at this period was the greater use of archers on horseback, necessary for mobility in border warfare with the Scots. Yet more decisive was the introduction of the longbow in the reign of Edward I, giving greater range and firing power to the infantry which showed to such good effect against the French knights at Crécy.

The king had the right to call on the military service of his subjects in two acknowledged ways. The first was the feudal host. The unit of feudal land tenure was the knight's fee (*feudum*), whose holder was theoretically obliged to perform military service as a knight for forty days in the year and to do the service by deputies if he held more than one fee. The magnates between them held thousands of knights' fees of the king and, though the numbers were largely fictious when it came to actual service (since there were only a few hundred knights in the whole of England), the king could still call out a large body of cavalry in this way, and the feudal army was used a number of times, chiefly for fighting against the Welsh and Scots, by Edward I and Edward II. Thereafter it fell into disuse. The second traditional source of fighting men was the ancient right of the king to summon his able-bodied subjects to service on foot. This right was restated in the Statute of Winchester (1285) and exercised many times in the succeeding century by commissions of Array which were issued to local gentry (like Shakespeare's Justice Shallow) so that they might levy soldiers in their shires. These rights, however, were not, in themselves, nearly enough to provide an army. The feudal host generally had to be paid at least for that part of its service which extended beyond the forty days' limit; and, as Edward I had discovered to his cost in 1297, though feudal tenants were useful for war in Scotland it was very difficult to persuade them to fight overseas. Edward I tried to expand his resources of cavalry by making all prosperous landowners, owning land worth more than twenty pounds a year, liable for service on horseback, but this too was stoutly resisted and was one of the factors in the crisis of 1297. Edward II met with resistance in his efforts to make local communities pay for their own contingents to the levy. In practice they too had to be supported by the king's food and money.

The three Edwards therefore increasingly developed a purely mercenary army of contingents, engaged by contracts to fight for the king during a stipulated period with fixed wages. This system was used for the army in France in 1297 and perfected in the French wars of Edward III, when the army, although it still contained levies, consisted entirely of paid troops. To call this a mercenary army is not to imply it was regarded as less honourable and chivalrous than the feudal host. Edward III's army, though it included contingents of famous captains well below baronial rank, like Sir Walter Manny and Sir John Chandos, who were in a sense professional soldiers, also included leading magnates of the realm, fighting for pleasure and honour as well as profit. The mercenary army was, however, enormously expensive. All its members were paid wages, graded from 2d a day to 2s for a knight and 8s for an earl, and the total cost of a big expedition, including transport overseas, replacement of horses, and extra rewards, might be of the order of £50,000. This was a very large sum in the Middle Ages, over half the king's annual revenue, and a permanent expansion of taxation was needed to support the grandiose military ambitions of the Edwardian period.

The king's financial resources could be divided into two kinds: accepted rights of his prerogative, which required no consent, and taxation, which had to be granted by those who paid it. In the first of these categories the first source of money, to which the king had an undoubted right, was the income from his estates, collected by sheriffs and escheators. The king was the greatest landowner in England and his estate could be swelled considerably by the lands of tenants-in-chief forfeited in time of civil war, or those which were held in wardship while their heirs were under age, or fell to the king through the extinction of the families which held them. But, except possibly in the later, rapacious years of Edward I, there does not seem to have been any serious attempt to accumulate a larger estate by these means; most of the lands which fell to the Crown were quickly granted away to other magnates. Next there were the profits of justice, which again were capable of expansion, but not without causing discontent, as when the magnates in 1300 objected to Edward I's exercise of his rights of holding courts to punish trespassers in the royal forests. The king's right of buying up supplies for his household at cheap rates, purveyance, was extensively used in time of war, but it also was liable to abuse, which caused bitterness, notably in the financial crises of Edward I's later years and the early French campaigns of Edward III. Finally there was the right, which the king shared with other lords, of imposing levies of 'tallages' on his estates and royal boroughs. This right was resisted during the reigns of Edward I and Edward II and transformed into taxation for which he had to obtain the consent of representatives of the boroughs.

The principle of 'no taxation without consent' was accepted before 1272, but it was left to Edward I and Edward III to develop an efficient system of taxation by consent to exploit the surpluses of their more prosperous subjects. Three main kinds of taxation were developed concurrently: taxation of the clergy, property taxes on laymen, duties on imports and exports.

Regular taxation of the clergy went far back into the thirteenth century, to the decades after King John had become a vassal of the Pope. Most of the money which Edward I got from the Church in the earlier part of his reign had been intended for a Crusade and was directed by the Pope to the King. After this most clerical taxes were directly granted by the clergy to the king, usually in the form of a tenth of their property. That is to say that all cathedrals, abbeys, and rectors paid a tenth of the assessed value of their annual incomes, the assessment used for most of the period covered by this book being the 'Taxation of Pope Nicholas', made in 1290. Like all medieval assessments it was a gross underestimate; the king was not really getting anything like a tenth. Still it was a large sum. Well before 1272 the clergy had developed a right to consent to their taxation in representative assemblies, and they were also protected by the papal rule that kings were not to tax their clergy without papal consent, which was an important element in the political crisis of 1297 (see below, p. 108), when it was made temporarily stricter by Boniface VIII's *Clericis Laicos*. The attitude of Rome became less important with declining papal prestige in the fourteenth century, when the question of clerical taxation was largely a duel between the king and the Church of England. All the Edwards raised a great deal of money from the Church; more, in the early part of the Hundred Years' War, than they raised by the property taxes on the laity.

The form taken by general taxation of the laity was similar: a fraction of their movable property and income. Throughout the thirteenth century the Crown intermittently taxed the shire communities in this way. At the same time kings levied tallages on the royal demesne and boroughs. During the reign of Edward I, arbitrary tallages gave way to property taxes granted by representatives of the boroughs, and from 1294 these were amalgamated with joint grants from the shires. The fractions varied from time to time, but from the early years of Edward III they were normally a fifteenth of movable property in the shires and a tenth in the towns. This remained the standard 'lay subsidy' for the rest of the Middle Ages. The bulk came from the shires, where it was levied according to assessments of property made by local men in each village. Great feudatories were to some extent exempt and poor men with little property entirely exempt. Most of the money was paid by the middling landowners: gentry and peasants. From 1334 the assessments for boroughs and villages were standardised so that a lay subsidy could be reckoned to yield always about the same amount, £36,000. This was not a regular annual tax—each subsidy had to be separately voted by a parliament, and the king could never rely on getting it.

It was the particular good fortune of the kings of England that their kingdom was an island with a foreign trade, which could be easily controlled and taxed at the ports. From Edward I's time they made full use of this asset, and for the rest of the Middle Ages duties on imports and exports were easily their largest single source of income. In 1275 parliament granted Edward a tax on exported wool, which remained basic and unquestioned thereafter and came to be called the Ancient Custom. It was 6s 8d on a sack. Wool could bear far heavier taxation than this. In the twelve-nineties Edward I made agreements with the exporting merchants for £2 a sack. This imposition was abolished as a result of the outcry in 1297, but in 1303 Edward made a comprehensive agreement with foreign merchants to permit the New Custom, not only on wool but on almost every other commodity going in and out of the country. The New Custom was abolished by the Ordinances of 1311 but revived in 1322, and thereafter, though often resisted, it remained. Under Edward III the customs system was extended to cover native as well as alien merchants and brought under parliamentary control. By about 1350 all goods imported and exported were taxed, but by far the most important and profitable was the tax on wool: a bulky, standardised commodity, exported in huge quantities and so much in demand abroad that it could stand a tax of 25 per cent—'Albion's chief richesse' from the king's point of view as well as the merchants'.

In spite of these powers the king's income remained precarious and uncertain. Each grant of taxation had to be separately squeezed out of the consenting body and there were often long delays in collecting it. The royal treasury was sometimes nearly empty. To keep up a regular supply of money, and, even more, to raise large sums quickly for emergencies, the king's ability to borrow in advance on the proceeds of future taxation was extremely important. The usual way of raising loans was to promise the lender repayment out of future taxes (the customs were the most useful for this, since they were the most stable form of taxation and one in which the merchants themselves had a large interest), either by assigning the proceeds to them or by allowing them to 'farm' the whole tax and collect it themselves. In the late thirteenth century the chief lenders were merchants, especially Italian merchants. This was one of the main reasons why alien merchants were protected by the Crown. Up to 1294 Edward depended largely on the Riccardi, a firm of merchants from Lucca, who controlled the customs entirely for most of this period and at one time and another loaned him nearly

£400,000. The Riccardi withdrew at the time of crisis when Edward most needed their help. They were replaced in 1299 by the Frescobaldi of Florence, who were expelled by the Ordinances of 1311 because of their close ties with the court. When Edward II recovered control in 1322 he used the Bardi and Peruzzi firms, also of Florence, who lasted until they were bankrupted, partly by Edward III's failure to repay them, amongst other calamities, in the thirteen-forties. Thus for most of the central Middle Ages the king was vitally dependent on Italian financiers, who had a large share of the wool trade and put their enormous resources at his disposal, partly for profit and partly to secure privileges, rather like English oil companies in the Middle Eastern kingdoms in the twentieth century. Edward III's need for unprecedented sums at the opening of the Hundred Years' War, plus the collapse of the Italians, led him to make more use of English wool exporters. The Dordrecht Scheme of 1337 (see below, p. 119) was to be run by Englishmen and in 1339 William de la Pole raised about £100,000 for the king. Between 1343 and the Black Death of 1349 the wool customs were regularly farmed to syndicates of English merchants. Thereafter the manipulation of royal finance was generally in the hands of Englishmen, particularly those connected with the Company of the Staple, but, as we shall see, the great days of the medieval wool trade and of royal finance based on it were passing; later kings never raised money in this way on the same scale as Edward I and Edward III.

(4) PARLIAMENT

In the Middle Ages disputes in lay politics were rarely caused by the kind of ideological differences to which we are accustomed. It is nearly always a mistake, for instance, to interpret medieval political disputes as conflicts between those who believed in parliamentary government and those who did not. At different levels of explicitness, however, medieval men held important principles of government, which we must attempt to grasp. Well before 1300 the ideas and inspiration provided by ancient writers, particularly Aristotle, had led to the formation of sophisticated political theories, of which the most famous was probably that contained in the *Government of Princes*, written, partly by St Thomas Aquinas, about 1270. Ideas of this kind were familiar to many English scholars and churchmen. William of Ockham wrote several political treatises in the thirteen-thirties and thirteen-forties, and Walter Burley wrote a commentary on Aristotle's *Politics* about the same time. The scholastics believed that political society was a natural good; not just a convenience or an unfortunate necessity, to be endured by Christians looking to the other world, but something divinely ordained and essential for the proper development of man's powers. They believed that kings ought to rule for their subjects' as well as their own benefit. 'When government is unjustly exercised by one man who seeks personal profit from his position instead of the good of the community subject to him, such a ruler is called a tyrant,' said Aquinas, and he went so far as to think that subjects were right to depose tyrannical kings. The theorists believed that kings ought to rule according to law and in co-operation with the other great men of the land. 'Even in a kingdom,' writes the Oxford philosopher, Walter Burley, about 1340, 'a plurality of men, including the king and the great and wise men of the kingdom, take some part in the government. They do as much as or even more than the king alone and therefore the king summons a parliament to deal with difficult affairs.'

Ideas of this kind were echoed at a different level by the lawyers. Bracton had said in a famous passage, 'The king himself should be under no man, but under God and under the law, wherefore the law makes the king. . . . There is no king where will dominates and not law.' And in another place, 'The king as a superior, namely God; secondly the law by which he is made king; thirdly his court, that is the earls and barons, for the earls are said to be the king's companions and whoever has a companion has a master.' Probably these were common sentiments of educated opinion. Both the philosophers and the lawyers were writing to some extent under the influence of classical authors and it was not very easy to fit the ideas of political commonwealth, evolved more than a millenium before on the shores of the Mediterranean, with the existing facts of lordship. The quotation of

Aristotle has a certain strangeness in the world of Edward III. Nevertheless there was a conception of a political society. The idea of a community organised for the common good, which stemmed from antiquity, obtained some support from the deep-rooted northern ideas of a king's duty to guard his followers and to act justly to them. It finds expression, for instance, in the coronation oath of Edward II: 'Sire, will you act in all your judgments with justice and discretion, in mercy and truth, according to your power? . . . Sire, do you grant to hold and keep the laws and the right customs which the community of your realm shall have chosen and to defend and enforce them to the honour of God, according to your power?' 'I grant and promise.'

We often associate political ideas today with revolutions, the conflict of ideologies, the will to change society. Medieval Englishmen had no theory of revolution, except the deposition of an out-and-out tyrant and the defence of their ancient rights. Their disputes were about conflicts of interest and personalities, for in general they subscribed to one theory of government: harmony and the preservation of existing rights. The ideal which governed political thinking, as it appears in political life, was the harmonius co-operation of king and people. This was often difficult to realise. If it was accepted that the king was a supreme lord, answerable only to God and the law, of which he was also the exponent, and yet ought to rule for his subjects' good, who was to decide between him and his people when they disagreed? The Commons could say to the king in 1341, 'as to the Chancellor and Treasurer, the king can make his ministers as it shall please him and as his ancestors have done in all time past. But may it please him to make such ministers as are good and sufficient for him and his people.' They could not say explicitly that they would force him to make good ministers, because that did not agree with their theory. But in practice subjects sometimes imposed their will on the king, even by outright rebellion. It was this difficulty that inspired some magnates in the troublous times of Edward II to take refuge in the idea that the person of the king was separate from the abstract Crown, so that the former could be coerced to preserve the interests of the latter; but it was not a theory which found general acceptance. Though they attacked and deposed kings in practice, medieval politicians generally stuck to the view that government should be a harmonious concord of parts in which no one part should overrule the others. To express this they frequently used the metaphor of the 'body politic'. In 1337 the Bishop of Exeter wrote to the king in a letter defending his rights: 'The substance of the nature of the Crown is principally in the king, as head, and in the peers of the land as members, who hold of him by certain homage, and in particular the prelates; and this is so attached to the Crown that it cannot be severed without division of the realm. . . .' Most commonly the idea was expressed in political documents as the co-operation of the king and the community of the realm, notably, for instance, in the Statute of York which revoked the Ordinances in 1322: 'The things which are to be established for the estate of our lord the king, and his heirs, and for the estate of the realm and the people, are to be treated in parliaments, by our lord the king, and by the assent of the prelates, earls, and barons and the community of the realm.' It is instructive that this statement of the importance of parliamentary co-operation came from the king in a moment of strength, asserting that his right to be a party to political decisions had been trampled on while he was weak, and not from his opponents; for it suggests that what he was saying was common doctrine and not the policy of a faction. We cannot define precisely what the 'community of the realm' included, nor indeed several other words in that famous passage, but its essential meaning is clear enough. Good government was a concord of king and magnates, not the domination of one by the other; in particular it involved the meeting of king and people in parliament.

The history of parliament goes back before 1272 and is connected in its origins with the Great Councils, where earlier kings consulted and judged together with their magnates and prelates. After the magnates had insisted on it in the Provisions of Oxford (1258), parliament met fairly regularly, generally about twice a year in the earlier part of Edward I's reign. Its composition varied but it generally included the king and his council and great individuals, such as earls and bishops, and its functions were political discussion and the giving of judgment. Parliament was partly what we should call a political assembly. Edward I wrote to the Pope in 1275 that he would take counsel with his magnates in parliament and that he could not do anything affecting the rights of the realm without such counsel. Edward's chief statutes were promulgated in parliaments. Parliament was also a supreme court of justice, an assembly where grievances were aired and wrongs righted. In 1285 the Bishop of Winchester wrote to another bishop, asking him to suspend action in a dispute relating to the ownership of the goods of a suicide priest 'until the next parliament where we may be more fully informed of the law or custom'. The famous quarrel between the Earls of Hereford and Gloucester was settled in a parliament in 1292, and innumerable petitions were heard about lesser cases. Sometimes the assembly was enlarged by the presence of knights of the shire and burgesses. Knights attended to grant the Ancient Custom in 1275 and to hear the judgment on David ap Gruffydd in 1282.

Scholars have argued over the problem whether parliament was essentially a court or a political assembly to discuss action and grant taxes. It is to some extent an unreal question, for medieval men did not distinguish clearly between judicial and political affairs, but the truth is probably that it became in course of time rather less a court and rather more a taxing and debating assembly than it had been in 1272. The legal book called *Fleta*, written about 1300, says, 'The king has his court in his council in his parliaments', and most of the documents which have survived from Edwardian parliaments, written on the 'parliament rolls' by the clerks of the parliaments as a record of the business transacted, are petitions. There was a regular procedure as early as 1278 by which the less important petitions were handed to receivers, who sorted them into categories to be dealt with by the Chancellor, Treasurer, and justices. A parliament was also clearly an occasion for debate. The writs from Chancery, which summoned magnates, knights, and burgesses, regularly stated that they were to treat with the king and Council of the business of the king and his realm. Finally, it became the occasion for the granting of taxes and, while a great many people continued to use parliament as a supreme court, there is no doubt that the king's need to summon it for taxation was the chief historical cause for the form and importance which it assumed from the last decade of the thirteenth century. The power of holding the purse-strings was as effective then as now. This factor caused the change in the character of parliament during the most important phase of its development at the end of the reign of Edward I.

To explain this, we must again refer to the crisis in Edward's affairs caused by his military expeditions and huge expenditure in the years around 1297, when he was forced to demand money from his subjects with unusual frequency. In 1294 the merchants granted him the *maltote* on wool in addition to the Ancient Custom, an assembly of clergy very reluctantly granted him a half of clerical revenues for a year, assemblies of knights and towns granted a tenth and a sixth. In a parliament in 1295 the knights, towns, and clergy granted, respectively, an eleventh, a seventh, and a tenth. In a parliament in 1296 the laity granted a twelfth and an eighth, while the clergy, taking their stand on *Clericis Laicos*, and already well mulcted, refused money. In 1297 the King took a forced loan from the merchants and persuaded a thinly attended lay assembly to grant him an eighth and a fifth, which the insurgent barons tried to prevent the Exchequer from collecting. This tax was replaced in a parliament in the autumn of that year by a ninth, amid discussions which led to the Confirmation of the Charters. We shall see in the political history that there was bitter division in the realm. The constitutional results were far-reaching. Firstly, the Confirmation of the Charters accepted for the first time that all taxation should be granted by the whole community of the realm, not just the merchants or shires which paid particular taxes. There is no mention of parliament in it and the decision was in any case quickly ignored by the King, but it was the principle which later grew into parliamentary control of finance. Secondly, parliaments ceased from this period to be summoned with the regularity of the earlier years. They met at haphazard intervals, generally whenever the king needed them for money. Thirdly, the Commons first emerged as normal members of parliament. There were two kinds of Commons. All cities and some boroughs were each ordered to send two burgesses. In each shire the sheriff was ordered to arrange the election of two knights in the county court to represent the whole community of the shire. The county court was one of the ancient communal courts of the early Middle Ages. It had now lost many of its judicial powers and was not very important in the judicial structure, but it still met occasionally, attended by many of the leading gentry and freemen. It was the growing connection of the gentry and the city burgesses with the powerful political assembly of parliament which produced the change from the aristocratic meeting envisaged in the Provisons of Oxford (the constitution which had been imposed on Henry III by the magnates in 1258) to the fourteenth-century parliaments, in which knights and merchants dared to stand up and criticise the king's ministers. The 'Model' parliament of 1295 included all those whom Edward ever summoned to his parliaments: councillors, magnates, bishops, proctors elected to represent the lesser clergy, knights, and burgesses. To the parliament of 1305 were summoned 95 bishops and abbots, 145 representatives of the lesser clergy, 9 earls, 95 barons, 74 knights, 200 burgesses, and 33 councillors. This parliament granted no taxation but dealt with Scots affairs and some more important judicial matters, and all but the council were allowed to go home before it ended. The composition of a parliament was not yet fixed and its main business was not always taxation, but it came increasingly to include both lords and commons.

The parliaments of Edward II's reign still had varying membership and functions. Though it was not a period of extravagant royal demands for money and there was therefore no marked growth in the importance of the Commons, two striking expressions of the wider constitutional importance of parliaments come from this reign. The first is the unique document called the *Modus Tenendi Parliamentum* ('the way of holding a parliament'), which was probably written in the middle years of the reign. The *Modus* is not a description of parliament but the theory of a well-informed person about how it ought to be organised. It says that parliaments should include prelates, magnates, knights, and burgesses, that knights should have a greater voice than earls in the granting of taxes, and that parliaments ought to be used for settling difficult matters of war and peace, both outside the realm and within. The second is the activity of the parliament which deposed Edward II in 1327. Though it was not summoned by the King, it included magnates, prelates, and Commons. The deposition was announced to the King by a deputation of two earls, three bishops, four barons, four friars, four knights, and perhaps representatives of the towns. In one sense this was merely a revolutionary assembly, but it regarded itself as representing the 'community of the realm' and called itself a parliament.

In the reign of Edward III parliament finally assumed a form which was to endure into the Tudor age, and powers which were to make it of outstanding political importance at the end of the fourteenth and the beginning of the fifteenth century, before they receded in the changing conditions of the Lancastrian period. First of all it became, unlike some of the Continental parliaments, definitely a lay body. Although Edward I had successfully initiated the summoning of the clergy and later kings followed suit, the clergy had from the first intermittently questioned the King's right to summon them to a predominantly lay assembly. Archbishop Winchelsey insisted in 1311 that they were not bound to obey the King's summons unless it was reinforced by the Archbishop's order. In the reign of Edward II they sometimes joined parliaments and sometimes met separately in their convocations. There was also the difficulty that they resisted attendance at assemblies outside their provinces and, since there were two provinces in England, it was impossible for all to meet at the same place. From about 1337 the King gave way to clerical resistance. From that time onwards bishops and abbots attended parliament as barons of the king, but the lesser clergy were allowed to meet separately in their convocations. This did not much affect the granting of subsidies, and convocation often met at the same time as parliament for the same purpose, but it meant that parliament now represented largely the interests of laymen.

While it lost control of clerical taxes, parliament gained control of the customs. This had been foreshadowed by the Confirmation of the Charters in 1297 but was not enforced for half a century after. All three Edwards found that it was easier to make bargains with the more important of the merchants, who actually exported wool, than to seek consent in a large and critical parliament. Edward II held at least two assemblies of merchants, one of which consented to the reimposition of the New Custom in 1322. Edward III held several merchant assemblies to arrange his financial schemes at the beginning of the Hundred Years' War. In the years 1336–41, as in 1294–7, heavy financial burdens stimulated opposition and parliamentary growth. Three lay subsidies were granted in 1336. A parliament in 1338 allowed Edward to purvey half the wool of England for his schemes. When parliament was asked to give another lay subsidy, the Commons eventually responded with the 'ninth sheaf, fleece and lamb', on condition that the extra customs allowed by the merchants should cease after a year and be renewed only with parliamentary consent. This was the first definite application of the Confirmation of the Charters to parliament and, like the Confirmation, it was accepted by the King and then ignored. In the next decade the Commons returned several times to the attack. In 1351 they petitioned that 'as the tax of 40s. on the sack of wool which the merchants have granted the king falls in no wise on the merchants but on the people, that it may please the king for the relief of his people that the said 40s. be not henceforth demanded or levied, and that commission be not made for such special grants except in full parliament and that if any such grant be made outside parliament it may be held of no effect.' Though it is doubtful whether the Commons were as hard hit as they said, the King eventually acquiesced. From this time customs were granted in Parliament and there were no more assemblies of merchants.

After 1327 the Commons' right to be present in every parliament was recognised. In return for grants of money they expected their grievances to be listened to and they presented them in the form of the Commons Petition. The early parliaments had received a mass of petitions from individual persons and communities. 'Singular petitions' of this kind were still accepted and dealt with by receivers and triers, but there was a falling off in their number and importance, partly because of the growing jurisdiction of Chancery in cases which could not be dealt with by the courts of King's Bench and Common Pleas. Parliament was no longer the high court for all and sundry that it had been in the days of Edward I. A typical Commons petition (1373) began with a formal request for the maintenance of Magna Carta, then proceeded to some requests of general interest, such as that regulations should be made about the size of cloths sold and that bad Scots money should not be allowed to depreciate the value of English currency; then included some desires of less general interest, such as that the fishing on the river Brent should not be spoilt for the men of Middlesex. The Commons petition included those things which the Commons desired for the general good and some more particular requests which they were prepared to sponsor. The successful petitions became statutes and this is the origin of parliamentary legislation by Bill of the Commons, converted into Act.

A parliament still resembled a tribal council in some respects, rather than a modern House of Commons. Thomas of Lancaster in the reign of Edward II had retainers, whose duty it was to support him with armed men when he attended, and several parliaments in the fourteenth century were over-awed or interrupted by armed force. But the characteristic procedure was now in being. It began with a solemn address, often from the Chancellor, explaining the king's needs. Then the whole body split up into two houses. One house consisted of the lords who had been individually summoned because of their personal importance—the earls, the barons, bishops, and the abbots of greater abbeys. The Commons deliberated separately and negotiated with king and lords until agreement was reached over the grant of money to be made. It was generally over in a few weeks and the knights went back to their shires, many of them never to attend a parliament again.

CHAPTER FIVE

ENGLAND AND THE CELTIC LANDS

(1) THE CONQUEST OF WALES

THE nearest neighbours of England are the Celtic lands of Wales, Scotland, and Ireland. In the thirteenth century each of these had a population, a language, and native institutions entirely its own and separate from England, but each of them had been in different ways affected since the Norman Conquest by the expansion of the Norman aristocracy beyond England. Much of eastern Wales had been conquered by English lords who now ruled great Marcher lordships and had imported English colonists. Much of Ireland had been conquered and colonised in the same way. Southern Scotland, though independent, was ruled by a Norman aristocracy, many of whom, like Bruce and Balliol, had ties and lands south of the border. The English penetration into Wales at least was connected with the prevalent expansion of population and land hunger of the thirteenth century. And, like the colonisation of the land at home, this expansion into the remoter parts of the British Isles was carried to its furthest limits at the end of that century. Edward I conquered Wales, made a bold attempt to subdue Scotland and wielded more power in Ireland than his predecessors and successors.

At the beginning of his reign in 1272, Edward's most dangerous rival (and an old enemy) was Llywelyn ap Gruffydd, Prince of Wales, who had profited from the disorders of the Barons' Wars of Henry III's reign to build up a great principality, recognised by the Treaty of Montgomery in 1267. The east and south of what is now Wales were held by English Marcher lords like the Clare earls of Gloucester, who held the lordship of Glamorgan; the Bohun earls of Hereford, who held Brecon; and Roger Mortimer, who had a lordship around Wigmore Castle in Herefordshire and lands farther west in Radnorshire. The modern counties of Caernarvon,

Merioneth, Flint, and much of Denbigh, Montgomery, and Radnor, however, formed a united bloc, held of the king of England by feudal homage but virtually independent. It might have continued so if Llywelyn had not been ambitious and offensively undiplomatic. His new enmity with Edward flowed from several sources of discord. Firstly he would not do homage to the new King, because he suspected or affected to suspect that Edward was supporting his brother David who was plotting against him whilst in exile in England. Summonses from Edward and conditions from Llywelyn were exchanged throughout the years 1273–6, the Prince of Wales becoming more and more clearly in Edward's eyes a rebellious vassal. Then in 1275 Edward's ships intercepted Eleanor de Montfort, the daughter of another old enemy, on her way from France to marry Llywelyn. The result was war in 1277.

In this, his first major aggressive campaign, Edward revealed immediately the quality of efficient determination which made him a great soldier. One historian has thought that his army was 'the best controlled, as it was the best led, that had been gathered in Britain since the Norman Conquest'.[1] Certainly it put all the many previous assaults on Wales into the shade. The enemy was restricted and softened in advance by a three-pronged attack directed partly by Marcher lords: by Roger Mortimer and the Earl of Lincoln into the upper Severn valley, by the Earl of Hereford into Brecon, and the Earl of Lancaster into Cardinganshire. By the time Edward's main army moved west from the Dee in the summer, prepared to overthrow Llywelyn and replace him by his brothers, David and Owen, the Marches had been cleared of the Welsh. The army of about 5,000 foot, partly feudal and partly paid, advanced into Gwynedd along the north coast, accompanied by labourers to cut roads and with a fleet of ships from the Cinque Ports, standing off the coast. Llywelyn was overawed rather than defeated and, in November 1277, made the Treaty of Conway, by which he gave up his acquisitions in the Marches and the four 'cantrefs' (ancient Welsh divisions) of Perfeddwlad, to the east of Snowdonia, and was restricted more narrowly to the north-west of Wales. He bound himself to Edward by a large fine and did the homage which he had

1. F. M. Powicke, *The Thirteenth Century, 1216–1307* (1953), p. 411

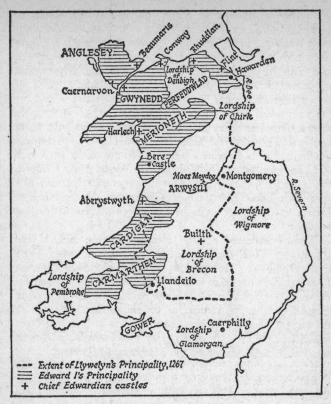

The Edwardian conquest of Wales

previously refused. In return he was allowed to keep the title of Prince of Wales as a feudatory of the King and to marry Eleanor de Montfort. The Treaty held for over four years.

Welsh independence was in any case doomed in the long run by Edward's insistence on his rights as overlord, backed by an England more united, wealthy, and powerful than ever before. One clause in the Treaty, however, was the source of bitter discord, which led to a rapid and decisive climax. The many property disputes in the lands between the principality and the Marches were to be decided by English judges according to Marcher or Welsh law, as was appropriate in each particular area. There were many cases and the difficulty was often to decide which law was appropriate, for these were lands where English and Welsh lordship had flowed back and forth during more than a century. One case in particular concerned Llywelyn's own claim to the large district of Arwystli on the upper Severn. He accused Edward and the judges of bad faith and the judicial question increasingly poisoned the air. The final outbreak was started once again by David. Edward had given him land in the four cantrefs but he had a discontented and troublesome spirit. In March 1282 he captured the Justiciar of north Wales, Roger Clifford, in Hawarden Castle. His brother Llywelyn and all free Wales rose with him. The Earl of Gloucester was defeated at Llandeilo but the last act in the loss of Welsh independence had begun.

Edward collected a large mercenary army and, in the summer of 1282, began again the invasion of north Wales' from Rhuddlan. He quickly occupied the four cantrefs. Llywelyn does not seem to have been conscious of the danger. He refused the offer, made through Archbishop Pecham, of an English earldom in return for his submission and had an encouraging success in November against an English force which tried to cross from Anglesey into Snowdonia. But he was killed in December by the Marchers, while invading the lordship of Builth. North Wales was then occupied fairly quickly. The last stronghold, at Bere Castle, in the wilds near Cader Idris, was taken in April 1283. David was captured in June and executed at the Shrewsbury Parliament in October, and the new order of a Wales without an independent principality was proclaimed in the Statute of Rhuddlan in 1284. This was not quite the end of Edward's troubles in Wales. There were two more substantial revolts before the end of his reign. While he was abroad in 1287, the last of the descendants of the great twelfth-century lords of south Wales, Rhys ap Maredudd, the holder of a big lordship in modern Carmarthenshire, rebelled because of judicial grievances and had to be put down with a large army. It was quickly done. At the end of 1294, when Edward's attention was again turned towards France, and Wales was denuded of troops for the biggest overseas effort of the reign, there was another revolt. This time it was more general and serious and demanded a temporary abandonment of Edward's Continental plans. After a serious invasion the chief rebel, Madog ap Llywelyn, was defeated at Maes Moydog in March 1295. The essential conquest of Wales had been achieved, however, in the years 1277–84; and it is notable that this aim, which had eluded so many English kings, was reached so quickly.

In a sense it was Edward's most solid and lasting achievement. The settlement of 1284 laid down the shape of Wales as it was to be until Henry VIII's Act of Union of 1536. Wales remained a land of big lordships, unlike the manors of England. The north and west were held directly by the King and administered for him by the Justices of north Wales (Caernarvonshire, Merionethshire, and Anglesey) and south Wales (Cardiganshire and Carmarthenshire). English criminal law was introduced into the new shires and hundreds, but the Welsh tenants continued to hold their land in the old Welsh fashion. The rest of Wales was divided as before between Marcher lordships, each generally consisting of a large area of country held by Welsh tenants and centring on a nucleus of a castle with an English manor or borough. Many of them were very extensive territories and their holders great magnates. The Principality was surrounded with a line of fortresses, which gave the Crown an enduring grip on the Country. In the castles which Edward built at Flint, Rhuddlan, Builth, Aberystwyth, Conway, Harlech, Caernarvon, and Beaumaris, during and after his campaigns of conquest, medieval military architecture reached its summit. The great mason who designed them, Master James of St George, summed up all the long experience of past development and, since they were built towards the end of the age of siege warfare, they were never surpassed. The Edwardian castle was at the furthest remove from the old, simple plan of a single, impregnable keep. A large central space was surrounded with a very thick stone curtain wall. Built into the wall at intervals there were massive towers, from which the approaching enemy could be swept with fire. The main rooms were generally incorporated into a particularly huge gatehouse tower, defended against entry by a complicated series of drawbridges, gates, and arrow-slits. The system can still be seen, in almost its original magnificence, at Conway and Harlech, rising sheer from steep cliffs; at Rhuddlan and Beaumaris (Plate 3), which are on lower ground, with outer moats and walls; and at Caernarvon, with its splendid gatehouse. At most of these places Edward also established new boroughs, sheltering under the castle walls and themselves defended by walls. In this way he further consolidated his hold on the conquered country.

(2) THE SCOTS WAR OF INDEPENDENCE

Most of Edward's wars were fought ostensibly about the principles of feudal overlordship. This is not to say that he was fighting only to assert principles, but that the disputes of his age took this form, as today they might take the form of quarrels about national boundaries. In the thirteenth century kings, with growing powers, were everywhere in Europe turning their vague rights of suzerainty into clearly defined kingdoms. The political boundaries of modern Europe emerged out of this process. In Wales Edward fought to assert his own overlordship; in France as a feudatory against the overlord. In Scotland he also fought on these terms, in one of the classic cases of feudal principle, and here he stretched both his rights and his material resources further than they would go.

Scotland began to be important to Edward in 1289. In that year an agreement was made for the marriage of the King's son, Prince Edward, to Margaret, 'the Maid of Norway', heiress to the throne of Scotland, vacant since the death of Alexander III in 1286. Such a marriage would have brought the two kingdoms close together; Edward II would have ruled, like James I, in both countries. But the Scots nobles, naturally jealous of their independence, were anxious to insist on the maintenance of a complete separateness and this was embodied in the Treaty of Brigham (1290), which settled the marriage with the proviso that no Scots parliamentary or judicial business was to be done in England. The situation was unexpectedly altered in the same year by the death of the Maid of Norway, the only descendant of Alexander III. All the claims to the throne depended on relationships going far back into the past. Two claimants, both Anglo-Scots noblemen, stood out from the others: John Balliol and Robert Bruce. The problem was to decide between them and it was this that first made Edward's overlordship in Scotland important. That overlordship had always been vague, depending on an undefined homage which had been made customarily by the kings of Scotland to the kings of England,

The Scots War of Independence

as by Alexander III to Edward I. Now it had to be defined and this provided the occasion for bitter war.

The Scots nobility in general turned to Edward as arbitrator and he met them in May 1291 at Norham on the English side of the border, where he was clearly accepted as 'Supreme Lord', who should both settle the succession dispute and take charge of the country during the interval before a new king was chosen. Edward took the kingdom into his own hands, progressed through part of it to accept the more important castles and announced that his writ would run in Scotland as in England. He also set up a court of arbitration to deal with the 'Great Cause' between Bruce and Balliol. Eventually, in November 1292, the verdict was given in Balliol's favour, after recourse to English law to settle the principles of succession, and the kingdom was surrendered to him. But now the lasting effects of the interregnum were seen. Not all Scotsmen loved Balliol; it was difficult for some of them to give up the advantage of looking to Edward as king, and tempting for Edward to keep some of the direct power which he had temporarily exercised. Most of the Scots nobility wished to keep to the principle of separateness enunciated in the Treaty of Brigham, but not all. People went on carrying their judicial claims to Westminster, and it happened in October 1293 that Balliol found himself, the King of Scotland, summoned to parliament at Westminster to answer a plea by one of his own subjects, Macduff of Fife. Edward insisted on the acceptance of his own superior jurisdiction as overlord.

The case was never settled, for Edward's great war with France, starting in 1294, gave Balliol and the Scots the opportunity to treat him as an enemy and to ally with the French. They did this in October 1295. Just as he had to sacrifice the French plans of 1295 to the necessity of subduing Wales, Edward had to give up the year 1296 to the conquest of Scotland. Like the earlier conquest of Wales, this operation was carried out with great speed and efficiency. The English army assembled at Newcastle in March 1296 and marched up the east coast, through Berwick, supported by a fleet standing off-shore. In April the Scots were decisively defeated at Dunbar and the way was open. Edward marched through the Lowlands, received Balliol's abdication, and rapidly journeyed round the Highlands before bringing back to England as a trophy the stone of Scone on which the kings of Scotland were traditionally crowned. In August he held a parliament at Berwick, at which he received the homage of the Scots and named the Earl of Surrey as guardian of the kingdom in his absence.

For the first time one man was direct ruler of all Britain; but the Scottish settlement, unlike the conquest of Wales, was not to endure. Scotland was much too big and distant to be subdued by such a rapid and superficial invasion, and the rest of the reign was in fact to be occupied with repeated and unsuccessful attempts to subject the Scots.

The first revolt came out of the blue in the autumn of 1297, while Edward was preoccupied with the crisis in England and preparations for the invasion of France, and while Surrey and some of the chief noble supporters of the English régime were out of Scotland. It was led by a gentleman, not one of the great magnates, called William Wallace, with a good deal of miscellaneous support, including the adherence of Robert Bruce, grandson of the Bruce who had claimed the throne in the Great Cause, and the inheritor of his claim. A small English expedition in the summer persuaded Bruce and his friends to abandon the rebellion and seemed to have restored order, but Wallace's leadership was seriously underestimated. In September Surrey himself was defeated at Stirling Bridge and by the end of the year Wallace was harrying the north of England.

From 1297 to 1304 the situation in Scotland remained confused. Some English garrisons and administrators remained and some Scots leaders were loyal to Edward, but the English hold on the country was in reality very slight and the fortunes of war fluctuated. In the year after Wallace's rising, 1298, Edward himself led a serious invasion, defeated the Scots at Falkirk and destroyed Wallace's leadership of the country, but captured neither Wallace nor Bruce. Substantial English invasions were necessary again in 1300, 1301, and 1303. At the beginning of 1304 Edward was able to come to terms with the bulk of the Scots nobility, including the powerful John Comyn the Red of Badenoch, and to hold a parliament at St Andrews, in which he received their homage and took up the reins of government again. The capture of Wallace in 1305 ended this period of Scots resistance. In that year a new administration was set up, to be headed by John of Brittany, Earl of Richmond, Edward's nephew, and a Scots council. Edward seemed to have restored the situation of 1296: direct rule of Scotland with a largely separate administration but not complete independence of the English parliament and council.

However, the work was destroyed again equally suddenly and unexpectedly. In February 1306 took place the sudden quarrel of Comyn and Bruce at Dumfries and Comyn's murder.

Bruce, who had hesitated for years to take an extreme position, appeared at the head of a powerful movement of independence and was crowned King of Scotland in March. His decision was ultimately to be decisive. He was defeated by Prince Edward and William de Valence at Methven in the first year of his reign, but escaped to rise again and turn the tables on Valence in 1307. King Edward was about to cross the border in yet another attempt to restore his power when he died in July 1307. Scotland was his greatest blunder. Its vast areas of wild country made it impossible to quell all the centres of resistance and the hopeless enterprise prevented Edward from concentrating his energies, like his most illustrious descendants, on the richer opportunities of glory in France.

(3) ENGLAND AND HER NEIGHBOURS AFTER EDWARD I

It was probably to the ultimate advantage of both England and Scotland that Edward II was not man enough to continue wholeheartedly with the struggle begun by his father. If he had been it might well have resulted in a partial conquest, like Henry II's invasion of Ireland, which would have bred centuries of strife. As it was, the strength of Bruce, opposed to the weakness of Edward II, produced a decisive defeat for England. During the years 1307–14 the English remained in partial control of southern Scotland, holding important castles, like Perth, Stirling, Edinburgh, and Berwick, which gave them a commanding position even in a hostile countryside, and several expeditions were sent to keep the Scots in order. But Bruce's strength gradually grew. He was able to defeat some of the invaders and, when their back were turned, to advance to the border and harry Northumberland and Durham. The English strongholds fell one by one from 1312 to 1314—Perth, Linlithgow, Roxburgh, Edinburgh. In 1313 Bruce captured the Isle of Man. The last major English effort was made in the summer of 1314. Advancing through the Lowlands towards Stirling, the English army met the Scots at Bannockburn and there the English nobility, blundering bravely but foolishly up the hill against the Scots, met one of their worst defeats. Amongst the many knights that were killed was the greatest English earl, Gilbert de Clare, Earl of Gloucester.

The restoration of English power in Scotland was not a serious possibility after this. Fighting continued, however, intermittently until 1323, with the Scots on the whole on the offensive. In 1318 they captured the castle of Berwick, which controlled the border, and were able to raid easily far down into Yorkshire. The border squabbles of these years were indecisive in the growth of relations between England and Scotland. But it is vital to remember that Edward II's reign at home was accompanied by a constant background of humiliation in the north. Edward was not even able to keep his own nobles united against the Scots menace. The Earl of Lancaster, his chief critic amongst the magnates and now the most powerful earl, was several times in alliance with the Scots and did much to frustrate Edward's attempts to deal with them. Lancaster's last rising in 1322, which ended in his defeat at Boroughbridge, was backed by the Scots. Finally in 1323 Edward was able to make the Truce of Newcastle, which put an end to the fighting in his reign. During the minority of Edward III a last unsuccessful attempt was made to invade Scotland before the Treaty of Northampton in 1328, in which Bruce was finally recognised as independent King of Scotland.

King Robert's son, David II (1329–71), was faced by a more formidable opponent in Edward III and his long rein was clouded by the contest. Edward's victory at Halidon Hill in 1333 resulted in the exile of David, his replacement for a few years by Edward Balliol, and the recovery by the English of some territory north of the border. In 1346 David was defeated and captured by an army of northern English magnates at Neville's Cross and kept in captivity until 1357. But after Halidon Hill Edward turned his attention almost completely from Scotland to France. There was a general diversion from the Celtic lands, which had accounted for the greater part of the serious fighting by kings and nobles in the years 1272–1334, to the attractions of war on the Continent.

This did not end the enmity between the two kingdoms. The constant friction on the border sometimes flared into conflicts of national importance. Richard II took an abortive expedition as far as Edinburgh in 1385. An invading Scots army defeated the English forces led by the Percies at the battle of Otterburn in 1388 and the Percies got their revenge at Homildon Hill in 1402. For much of the fourteenth and fifteenth centuries substantial forces, paid for by the royal Exchequer, were maintained on the Scots border under the command of Wardens of the Marches, usually leading nobles of that area like the Percies or the Nevilles. But the issue of Scots independence had been decisively settled under Edward II and the settlement was accepted in practice by Edward III and his successors. No later medieval king took up the struggle in earnest. There was scarcely a year without border fighting and many English expeditions were sent into the Lowlands, but much of the fighting after 1334 belongs essentially to the annals of border warfare in the spirit of the ballad:

> England and us have been lang at feud;
> Ablins we'll light on some bootie.[1]

Wales was entirely conquered and remained so, with the exception of the revolt of Glyndwr at the beginning of the fifteenth century. Ireland, like Scotland, saw a decline of English power in the fourteenth century, but there a more confused situation was created by the mixture of stubbornness on the part of the settlers and half-heartedness on the part of the English kings. In Edward I's reign Ireland, like Wales, was a country half subdued by English invaders. The eastern half of the country was partially conquered and ruled by English lords, some of them great men, such as Richard de Burgh, the 'Red Earl' of Ulster. These men owed allegiance to the king of England, who was represented by a Justiciar with a Chancery and Exchequer at Dublin. The western half was still in the hands of Irish chieftains and the boundary between English and Irish was uncertain and fluctuating. Edward initiated the system of holding Irish parliaments on the English model with representatives of the shires and made some attempt to expand the area in which English law was recognised, as in Wales, but he never set foot in the country. His reign was the high-water mark of English expansion and of control by the king's representatives, and was followed by decline. In 1315, the year after Bannockburn, Edward Bruce, brother of the King of Scotland, took an army to Ireland and roused many of the Irish and some of the English lords to an

[1] See E. Miller, *War in the North* (1960)

insurrection which at one time threatened Dublin itself. After the death of Edward Bruce in 1318, English power was partially restored under the leadership of Roger Mortimer (a great landowner in Ireland as well as in the Welsh Marches) as Lieutenant of Edward II, but never to its old extent. Irish pressure on English colonists continued in the reign of Edward III. A more serious attempt to strengthen English power was made by Lionel, Duke of Clarence (Edward III's son and also Earl of Ulster by inheritance from the extinct de Burghs) as Lieutenant in the years 1361–7. He issued the Statutes of Kilkenny, which attempted to confirm English customs and exclude the Irish from the counties of the east and thus to stabilise the boundaries of a reduced colony.

The only king in the later Middle Ages to take a serious personal interest in Ireland was Richard II. During an expedition which he led himself in the years 1394–5 he persuaded the independent Irish chiefs to do homage to him, and seems to have contemplated a new order in which English and Irish would acknowledge the peaceful division of the land and would all accept his overlordship. But Richard's second expedition in 1399 was cut short by the rebellion at home which cost him his throne and his plan had no substantial result. It was the last attempt until Tudor times to restore English power. The Irish chieftains continued to hold a great part of the country. Lieutenants representing the English king were regularly appointed but little effective power was exercised from Westminster, and the Anglo-Irish nobility, headed by the great families of Fitzgerald, earls of Kildare, and Butler, earls of Ormond, increasingly managed their own affairs.

CHAPTER SIX

THE POLITICS OF ENGLAND UNDER
THE THREE EDWARDS

(1) EDWARD I AND ENGLAND TO 1294

WE HAVE seen something of Edward I's struggles with
Wales and Scotland. It is now time to turn to the internal
politics of the kingdom of England and to the wars with
France, which imposed a much greater strain on royal resources than fighting in Britain and had therefore a more
critical effect on the relations of the monarchy with its subjects
at home. When Henry III died in November 1272 his son,
Edward I, was in Sicily on his way back from Syria. The last
English king to go on Crusade was thirty-three years old and
already a famous man in the European world. His early manhood had been passed in a time of adventurous politics which
had given him the opportunity to establish a reputation as a
successful soldier. He had saved his father's kingdom from the
rebellion of Simon de Montfort, Earl of Leicester, in 1265.
Then he had taken the Cross and led an army to Acre.
Crusading projects remained alive and, after his conquest of
Wales, Edward intended to lead an army again to the Holy
Land. But enterprises nearer home claimed his attention.
He never went to the East again but spent his long reign in
Britain and France. Edward I did not repeat his more
romantic father's mistake of allowing distant possibilities in
the Mediterranean to divert his attention from the problems
and opportunities of his own dominions. The persistent effort
at expansion and defence on his own borders—in Wales, in
Scotland, and in Gascony—is the first thing for which his
reign is important.

Its second great importance lies in the remarkable development of institutions, and this, too, undoubtedly owed much to
Edward's character. Medieval writings do not give us much
insight in depth into the characters of kings, for they were

represented as far as possible as embodiments of traditional virtues. In Edward I's case this may have been less misleading than usual. He was, outwardly at least, a magnificently successful conventional man. He was a great and active fighter from youth to death, 'erect as a palm, he maintained the lightness of youth in mounting a horse or running.' In politics he lived as expected of a king of his time, but much more effectively than most, for the utmost exaction of his rights. The man who expelled the Jews from England and Gascony to pay for the ransom of his ally, Charles of Salerno, by the forfeiture of their property,[1] was neither merciful nor particularly scrupulous in exacting his pound of flesh when he thought he had legal right on his side—as he did in his Welsh and Scots policies. 'By God's blood Syon shall not silence me nor shall Jerusalem keep me from defending my right as long as I have strength of body and the breath of life,' he is reported to have said to Archbishop Winchelsey, who had brought him the Pope's unwelcome reproaches for his aggressions in Scotland; and this on the whole seems to have been his attitude throughout. At home, in the institutions of England, this led to two things. Firstly, a process of legal definition. Edward's *quo warranto* proceedings (inquiries to discover 'by what warrant' people other than the king held judicial powers) completed the long struggle in which the Crown claimed judicial supremacy. Because of this, among other reasons, no medieval king before or after him was more powerful in his kingdom. His statutes are the most remarkable body of legislation between Magna Carta and the time of Henry VIII. Secondly, as we have seen, Edward's reign was a decisive period in the development of taxation and parliament, settling some important features of the political constitution for a century.

Edward's reign before 1294 is divided sharply in character from the later years. In foreign affairs the first period saw successful war and diplomacy in Wales, France, and Scotland, when the king achieved his objects without overstraining his resources and therefore without arousing any violent opposition from his subjects. This part of his reign was also one of tranquil relations with the great magnates. Like his grandson,

1. H. G. Richardson, *The English Jewry under Angevin Kings* (1960), pp. 213ff.

Edward III, eighty years later, Edward I had about him a group of young nobles who respected and shared his qualities. Besides those of the royal blood, his brother Edmund, Earl of Lancaster, and his cousin Edmund, Earl of Cornwall, were other young noblemen such as Henry de Lacy, Earl of Lincoln, who took part enthusiastically in the King's wars. At home he was able to proceed without serious check in the consolidation of royal power, with the aid of his great Chancellor, Robert Burnell, Bishop of Wells.

Soon after Edward returned to England in 1274, commissions were issued for a widespread inquiry into the lands and judicial rights of the Crown all over England. This led to the Statute of Gloucester (1278) and other acts which laid down the procedures for claiming franchises, to other inquests, to many cases of *quo warranto*, and finally to the Statute of *Quo Warranto* in 1290. The most striking exercise of judicial supremacy, perhaps, occurred in 1291, when the judges condemned the Earls of Gloucester and Hereford for fighting about a castle at Abergavenny and asserted that the King's prerogative could overrule even the custom of the March. At the same time Edward was asserting his rights in the dispute with Archbishop Pecham, which revived in a milder form the great quarrel with Becket over a century before. Apart from this firm and persistent emphasis on the royal authority, however, the first two decades of Edward's reign were quiet at home. The fighting was abroad.

(2) EDWARD I AND FRANCE

Apart from Wales and Scotland, Edward's main field of conflict was in France. For centuries people have spoken of the Hundred Years' War between England and France, meaning the series of wars which lasted, with long intervals, from 1337 to 1453, in which the kings of England claimed, also intermittently, that they were the rightful kings of France. We shall see later that these wars really had little unity apart from the repeated claim to the throne. Nor were they a very new phenomenon. The Hundred Years' War was a phase in the long struggle between the kings of France and England which lasted for most of the Middle Ages from the time when the Duke of Normandy, a vassal of the King of France, became King of England in 1066. From that time until 1453 the kings of England always had a substantial foothold in France, which was a potential source of friction. An important stage in this struggle was passed in the Treaty of Paris in 1259: Henry III renounced his claims to the Duchy of Normandy and in return was confirmed, as Duke of Aquitaine, in his extensive possessions in the south-west of France, around the towns of Bordeaux, Bayonne, Limoges, and Cahors, but as a vassal of the King of France. The legacy of this status and relationship, descending to Edward I, caused his bitter quarrels with France.

In the first half of his reign Edward spent two periods in Gascony. The first was in 1273 and 1274, when he lingered there on his way home to be crowned, established himself, and dealt with some unruly vassals. The second was from 1286 to 1289, when he crossed the Channel to do homage to Philip the Fair of France (Philip IV, 1285–1314) and stayed three years, mostly in Gascony, dealing with his own rights there, with the quarrel between France and Aragon, and with the plans for a new Crusade which he always kept alive until the problem of Scotland absorbed all his energies.

Until 1293 Edward's relations with Philip the Fair were good. Up to this time the story of his reign had been one of solid success; consolidation of his place in England and Gascony, conquest of Wales, acceptance of the overlordship of Scotland. The next few years saw a widening of his ambitions beyond his powers and a consequent nemesis. France played a most important part in this change. The immediate cause of the trouble that flared up in 1293 was a dispute between English and Gascon pirates; behind it was the determination of Philip the Fair to make good his overlordship in Gascony, ironically parallel to Edward's claims over Scotland. Edward refused to answer a summons to appear in court at Paris and Philip used this as an excuse to take over Gascony at the beginning of 1294. A war with France was, of course, a very different matter from a war in Wales or Scotland. It involved an enemy equal or greater in wealth, expensive invasions overseas, and, as Edward's plans developed, European alliance not unlike a smaller version of England's efforts in later

105

centuries against Louis XIV and Napoleon. For some years after 1294 this effort absorbed the greater part of Edward's resources, but was always fatally hindered by frustrations nearer home. The large expeditions which were quickly planned in 1294 came mostly to nothing because the Welsh rising of the next year demanded instant action. In 1296 it was the rising in Scotland that stopped Edward crossing the Channel. In 1297 he was greatly hindered, as we shall see, by opposition in England itself, and it was not until August of that year that he actually left the country.

Although there were modest and unsuccessful expeditions to Gascony in 1294 and 1296, the main attack was put off repeatedly for three years. In the meantime great efforts had been made to build up a big English army and a ring of allies. Wool exports were heavily taxed and wool sometimes seized between 1294 and 1297. The clergy and the laity were taxed directly. Alliances were made with Philip's enemies on the continent, the Count of Flanders, the Duke of Brabant, and Adolf of Nassau, King of Germany. Edward planned a great assault on France through Gascony, through Flanders, and through the Rhineland at the same time. Without the long delays in Wales and Scotland something might have come of the great design, but, as it turned out, the whole plan miscarried. By 1297 Adolf of Nassau had come to terms with Philip the Fair and Philip was successfully invading Flanders as well as Gascony. The English nobility refused to go to Gascony, the country was resisting taxation more and more strongly, and the money which had been collected was largely frittered away before its main purpose was reached. Edward eventually took an army to Flanders in August 1297 but its career ended ingloriously in a truce with Philip in October. At the beginning of the next year, 1298, Edward was compelled by the dangers of opposition in England and Scotland to return home. There followed five years of negotiation, partly through the Pope, which ended in peace in 1303, with a return to the *status quo* in Gascony, a marriage between Edward and Philip's sister Margaret, and another between the Prince of Wales and Philip's daughter, Isabella, which was to provide a new reason for war in the reign of Edward III.

The immense efforts and frustrations of Edward's campaigns in Scotland and France are the essential background to the troubled politics of his last years at home. Several times during the Middle Ages the strain of a great war in France produced a crisis in politics at home. As King John's duel with Philip Augustus had been in part the explanation of the events leading to Magna Carta in 1215, so Edward's duel with Philip the Fair went far towards humbling him before his subjects in 1297. The war and diplomacy carried on simultaneously in Scotland and on the Continent were on a scale greater than anything attempted by his predecessors. The pressure of war acted like a hothouse in developing the new kinds of taxation and the institution of parliament very quickly in a few years. It also became clear that the King was attempting too much for his resources, and his demands provoked an opposition which endeavoured to set some limits to his power. The later part of the reign is therefore a dramatic and important period in the domestic history of England.

During the years 1294–7 Edward used every method available to him to raise money, and used them all more extensively than ever before. Merchants were subjected to the *maltote*, a heavy duty on the export of wool, which seems to have been resented more by other people than by the merchants themselves, because it reduced the prices paid for wool to the owners of sheep. The knights and burgesses granted taxes in parliament in 1294, 1295, and 1296. The great parliament of 1295 included also the clergy, who eventually granted a tenth, though already in 1294 they had been forced to pay a tax of unprecedented heaviness, a half of spiritual revenues, in addition to the sums collected for Crusade in previous years, which had mostly passed into the King's hands. At the beginning of 1297 the opposition stiffened on two fronts: the Church, with papal support, took a more definite stand, and the goodwill of the magnates, broken by the King's assertive demands, turned for the first time in the reign to positive rebellion. The new Archbishop of Canterbury, Robert Winchelsey, who arrived in England from Italy in 1295, was an unyielding upholder of the independence of the Church. When Pope

Boniface VIII issued, in 1296, the bull *Clericis Laicos*, forbidding kings to tax the clergy without papal consent, Winchelsey refused to yield to Edward by sanctioning taxation until the Pope modified his prohibition in the middle of 1297. The assembly of the army to invade France at the beginning of 1297 provoked resistance, partly because the King was trying to extend the duty of military service to all men with more than £20 annual income from land, partly because of objections by two leading magnates, Roger Bigod, Earl of Norfolk, and Humphrey de Bohun, Earl of Hereford, who led an opposition which refused to go to Gascony if the King himself was going to Flanders. In the summer Edward tried to raise another tax from the laity without proper consent from a full assembly of knights and burgesses. The earls forbade its collection. When Edward did at last sail in August, it was with the country half in revolt behind him. Then to crown it all came Wallace's dangerous rising in Scotland.

The King's opponents had a traditional weapon to hand in the two Charters—Magna Carta and the Charter of the Forest—originally extracted from King John and Henry III in 1215 and 1217 and acknowledged thereafter as expressing the fundamental limitations on royal power. In the political crisis these documents came to the fore again and for several years became the centre of political debate. In the King's absence the Regent was driven in October 1297 to grant the 'Confirmation of the Charters' (*Confirmatio Cartarum*), which added an important statement of principle to the original documents: no taxation should be levied by the king without the consent of the whole 'community of the realm'. This appeased the opposition but the crisis of 1297 did not end in real agreement. The political atmosphere of the remaining ten years of the reign is one of suspicion on the part of the magnates and repeated attempts to curb the royal prerogative, which had seemed more oppressive since 1294. On the King's side there was an equally stubborn insistence on his prerogative as he interpreted it. The criticism of taxation was extended to the administration of royal forests (areas originally of hunting country, subject to special forest courts, which could be oppressive to the local inhabitants). After a further ceremonial confirmation of Magna Carta and the Charter of the Forest in 1299, the parliament of 1300 extracted from Edward twenty new 'Articles on the Charters' (*Articuli super Cartas*). These laid down restrictions on the rights of purveyance by royal officials, insisted that actions at common law should be initiated by letters under the great seal and not the king's privy seal, and ordered an investigation into forest rights. Though the magnates loyally upheld Edward's claims in Scotland, against papal intervention, at the Parliament of Lincoln in 1301, they once again insisted anxiously on the Charters, the basis of their liberties, and unsuccessfully demanded the removal of his extortionate Treasurer, Walter Langton, Bishop of Lichfield.

Their fears were justified for, as Edward recovered his hold on affairs in his last years, he became more grasping. In 1302 the Earl of Norfolk surrendered his lands to the King to receive them back only for life, and the Earl of Hereford's heir was married to one of Edward's daughters with the stipulation that his lands too should revert to the King if he had no children. In 1303 Edward made the *Carta Mercatoria*, a new agreement on heavy wool taxation with the foreign merchants, which was a clear violation of the Confirmation of the Charters. In 1306 he revenged himself on his most inflexible opponent, Archbishop Winchelsey, who had resisted him over the taxation of 1297, over the claims to Scotland, and over the Confirmation of the Charters in 1301. Winchelsey was a man of the firmest principle and a man of the European Church, one who refused to compromise with his conscience in matters of the Church's independence and the pope's authority, the last in the tradition of Becket, Langton, and Pecham, and very different from some of the accommodating primates from the royal household in later years. The ground was cut from under his feet when a Gascon bishop willing to be pliable to Edward was elected as Pope Clement V in 1305, and in the next year was persuaded to release the King from his confirmation of the Charters and to suspend the Archbishop. His exile, however, did not last long. Edward died little more than a year later. In some ways he was the greatest of medieval English kings, a commanding character at the time when the medieval monarchy reached the height of its power in Britain both in territorial conquest and in the comprehensiveness of its government. But though his grim abilities coincided with an auspicious age in the history of monarchy, Edward's ambitions in Scotland and France, surpassing even his capacities, made him ultimately an overreacher.

(4) EDWARD II AND THE MINORITY OF EDWARD III, 1307–30

With the death of the old king the political atmosphere changed. The years from 1307 to 1330 stand apart in the history of medieval England as a period of civil strife, culminating in intermittent civil war as vicious and violent as the Wars of the Roses (1455–85) and longer than the Barons' Wars (1258–65). To read Christopher Marlowe's *Edward II*, which is based on the English chronicle tradition and preserves the sense of bitter personal hatreds often missed by modern historians, is still perhaps the easiest way to recover the atmosphere of this age. The key to the period is the bitterness of individual rivalries in the absence of effective kingly rule. The cause of this and of the passions which it unleashed was the strange character of Edward II, who was like his father in being a powerful, athletic man, but unlike him in almost everything else: weak in political intelligence, ambition, and self-respect. He was very likely a homosexual and he was fatally liable to fall under the influence of ingratiating and unscrupulous young men. In the eyes of the nobilty his character opened the door to the worst of political ills, the rule of 'evil counsellors' and of those who 'accroached' the royal power to themselves.

Many kings made enemies of the magnates during their reigns, but Edward II was suspected and thwarted from the first. This has often been seen as evidence that the magnates were guarding against a continuation of the harshness of his father, but it is as likely that they knew enough of Edward as Prince of Wales to expect him to be weak and unreliable as king. The oath, which he took at his coronation, contained a new clause pledging him to accept in future the laws which should be chosen by the 'community of the realm'. One of Edward's first actions as king had been to recall from exile a Gascon knight, Peter de Gaveston, who had been exiled for his influence on the Prince in 1306, to raise him immediately

110

to the high and valuable title of Earl of Cornwall and to give him the place of honour at the coronation. Gaveston was disliked by most of the magnates and nearly all united in the attempt to check the King's independence. One of the greatest, the Earl of Gloucester, remained friendly, but he was killed at Bannockburn (1314) and had no son. The Earls of Lincoln, Surrey, Hereford, Warwick, and Arundel, and Archbishop Winchelsey were all critical. So, after a short time, was Thomas, Earl of Lancaster, who became, after inheriting the earldom of Lincoln in 1311, and after the death of Gloucester, easily the wealthiest of the magnates and the regular ringleader of their opposition.

This opposition grew against the background of continual, dismally unsuccessful war with Scotland, which made the King dependent on magnates and parliament for money, without making any more popular the court which he gathered about him or the policy which he followed. A magnate league, ostensibly to protect the Crown against its enemies, forced Edward to banish Gaveston as early as May 1308, but the favourite came back in the next year. There were petitions for changes in the methods of government at the Stamford parliament in July 1309. In March 1310 the King was forced to agree to the appointment of a committee of bishops, earls, and barons, which would take the administration into its own hands until Michaelmas 1311 and draw up Ordinances for the future government of the realm. These Ordinances form a long, comprehensive, and important document, embodying and expanding the various grievances voiced in the first four years of the reign. Amongst the main provisions are the following: (i) Gaveston and Amerigo dei Frescobaldi, the King's Florentine banker, were to be banished. (ii) The chief officials of the kingdom and of the royal household, such as the Chancellor, the Treasurer, the Controller of the Wardrobe (the chief department of the household), and the Keeper of the Privy Seal (which was used to authenticate letters and orders sent out in the King's name), were to be appointed with the consent of the magnates in parliaments, which were to meet twice a year. (iii) The same consent was to be required for the King to go to war. (iv) The 'New Custom', the extra duty on imports and exports by foreigners, was to

111

be abolished (see p. 78). (v) The Wardrobe officials were to receive money only through the Exchequer, which was controlled by the Treasurer, and not directly from the collectors of taxes. In this way the magnates hoped to end Gaveston's supremacy, depending as it did on control of the court and illegal taxes, and also to limit the King's independence for the rest of his reign. They produced a document which was a bone of political contention for a decade and which, like Magna Carta (1215) and the Provisions of Oxford (1258), was remembered long after as a classical statement of baronial grievances.

But the Ordinances were only an expression of a point of view. They settled nothing and, in the years that followed, one baronial faction after another climbed to power, while the country was humiliated by the inability to deal with the Scots and torn by repeated private wars (the most notable was the war in 1317 between the Earl of Lancaster and the Earl of Surrey, who carried off Lancaster's heiress wife, Alice de Lacy). Edward, unrepentant, had Gaveston back with him in time for Christmas 1311. By the spring of 1312 the magnates were openly in arms. The King's troops in the north were threatened by the Earls of Lancaster, Pembroke, and Surrey; Gaveston was handed over for trial in parliament, then seized from his jailers by one of his most bitter enemies, Guy, Earl of Warwick, and executed under the authority of the Ordinances at Blacklow Hill, near Lancaster's castle at Kenilworth. This semi-judicial murder won Edward some supporters, especially Pembroke and Surrey, who did not love Thomas of Lancaster, and for a time in 1312, when both sides were collecting armies, it looked as though there would be full civil war. They came to terms, however, and in 1313 the King was reconciled again with his nobles without submitting to the Ordinances.

Thomas, with his five earldoms of Lancaster, Leicester, Derby, Lincoln, and Salisbury, his vast estates in Yorkshire, Lancashire, and the Midlands, and his private army—perhaps the largest permanent retinue ever seen in medieval England— can be compared only with the greatest of baronial politicians, with John of Gaunt, Richard of York, and Warwick the Kingmaker. He had the same sort of independent power based on enormous landed wealth. His period of greatest influence in politics began after Edward had been further humbled by the defeat at Bannockburn (June 1314). Lancaster had taken no part in this battle and his relative power was much increased by it. In the parliaments of September 1314 and January 1315 he was able to insist once again on the enforcement of the Ordinances and the limitation of the King's power. In the Lincoln parliament of 1316 he reached the summit of his power, gaining the position of chief councillor with a right, jointly with the King, to remove any other councillor. For a time he had indeed virtually a veto on the King's actions and, in the later part of 1317, was able to overawe the royal army in the north by the superiority of his own power, based on his castle at Pontefract, and frustrate Edward's wish to make a truce with the Scots through the mediation of two cardinals sent by the Pope.

Lancaster's influence, all the same, had one decisive weakness, compared with the other men who dominated the kingdom before and after him: it was exercised from outside the court. Lancaster never had the King's friendship, which was the easiest, and indeed the essential, way to power over government. He is sometimes criticised by historians for being a capricious and unconstructive opponent. It is true that he made little attempt to play a regular part in court or council, but Edward was also at fault in making no serious effort at compromise and readily giving his ear only to Lancaster's enemies. He was supplanted in 1318 by a group of men who had acquired the King's confidence since 1314, the Earls of Pembroke and Hereford and the knights, Bartholomew de Badlesmere, Roger d'Amory, Hugh d'Audley, and Hugh Despenser the younger. These men have been called the 'Middle Party', and the phrase is just in so far as it emphasises that they aimed neither at the rule of a single, all-powerful courtier, like Gaveston, nor at destroying the King's independence from outside, like Lancaster. Lancaster's power was weakened both by the rise of this confederacy and also by his private war with Surrey. By 1318 he was much more isolated in his insistence on the Ordinances and parliamentary control of the King, and a new distribution of power was eventually recognised by the Treaty of Leek (August 1318) and the Parliament of York (October–December 1318). The Treaty of Leek was a private agreement between Thomas of Lancaster and a number of other magnates. Lancaster agreed to the setting-up of a permanent council to control the King, consisting of seventeen bishops, earls, and barons, as long as the Ordinances were enforced. This would give him some influence in government but not his old power of veto. The parliament at York confirmed the power of the knights of the Middle Party in the royal household.

The next period of the reign saw the astonishing rise of one of these knights to supreme power. The younger Despenser was the son of a trusted courtier of Edward I and was himself essentially a creature of the court. The York parliament gave him his great opportunity, or at least helped him on his way, by making him Chamberlain, that is, administrator of the King's Chamber and therefore an official in constant and intimate contact with the King. Gradually and ruthlessly during the years 1318–21 he climbed into a position of absolute ascendancy at the court. The chroniclers tell us that he eventually refused to let the King give audience to anyone unless he was present; and we know from some of his own letters that he was able to order judges to give verdicts in his favour. But his use of these powers raised up a powerful opposition to him from two quarters. The first was in the Welsh Marches. The inheritance of the last Earl of Gloucester, including a great part of modern Glamorganshire and Monmouthshire, was divided between his three sisters, who were married, with royal approval, to Audley, Amory, and Despenser. Despenser was not content with his own share and attacked the lands of the others. When he added to this offence by trying to acquire the nearby lordship of Gower with royal influence, he aroused the violent opposition of the other Marcher lords, including the Earl of Hereford and the Mortimers. The King stood by Despenser and finally, in the summer of 1321, the Marcher lords advanced on London. Meanwhile, in the north, Thomas of Lancaster was roused to opposition by his concern about the danger of such a power over the King. He and his many followers in the north held a meeting at Pontefract in May, and in June sealed the so-called 'Sherburn Indentures', pledging to support the Marchers and oust the evil counsellors. In July 1321 Despenser was condemned in a parliament at London, dominated by the armed force of his enemies, and he and his father were banished.

The story of Gaveston, however, was repeated and this time with a more lasting success. By the end of the year the Despensers were back again and Edward had raised a large army, with the help of some of the earls, to confront the rebels. He advanced towards Wales, forcing the Marcher lords to submit in January 1322. Lancaster was defeated in his own county at Boroughbridge, in Yorkshire, by royal supporters in March. Boroughbridge was one of the great civil battles of English history; immediately after it Lancaster and Badlesmere were executed. Hereford and Amory died. Many other lords perished or, like Mortimer, were imprisoned. The estates of many 'contrariants' were taken into the King's hands and a parliament at York soon after the battle finally revoked the Ordinances. Edward was vindicated as never before.

The supremacy acquired in those days lasted for four years. It ended in terrible disaster, partly because the fighting itself engendered bitter hatreds (Thomas of Lancaster, in spite of his treacherous and turbulent political career, became a popular saint and Roger Mortimer was made into a very dangerous enemy of the Crown), partly because the King's supremacy was carelessly and cruelly used. The real victor had been not Edward but Despenser, who now continued with more assurance and freedom on the course he had started before his exile. His ambitions were greater and more offensive than Gaveston's. By a mixture of force and legal trickery he soon obtained his empire in south Wales and a large number of estates elsewhere. Perhaps no man in medieval England ever had so many personal enemies as he had by 1326. His only decided supporter among the great magnates was the Earl of Arundel. Two positive achievements can be reckoned to the credit of the Despenser régime: the peace with Scotland in 1323 and the careful reorganisation of Crown finances carried out by the Treasurer, Walter Stapledon, Bishop of Exeter. But the first was humiliating to the English Crown, and the increased efficiency of the King's administration, which resulted from the second, gave no joy to his plundered subjects.

Edward and Despenser seem, moreover, to have been extra-ordinarily short-sighted in allowing effective opposition to build up against them. The first main actor in the conspiracy was Roger Mortimer, who escaped from the Tower to France in 1323. The second was Queen Isabella. She was ousted from favour by the King's friendship with Despenser to the point of confiscation of her estates, and then sent in 1325 to France to negotiate with her brother, King Charles, after the English had been defeated in a war in Gascony in 1323–4. Finally the twelve-year-old heir to the throne, Edward, was sent across the Channel to do homage for Gascony in place of his father. The Queen did not return when she was expected. In Paris she became the lover of Mortimer and they landed in Suffolk in September 1326 with the Prince and an army from the Low Countries. They were quickly joined by other magnates and bishops, including the King's half-brothers, the Earls of Kent and Norfolk, and Thomas of Lancaster's brother and heir, Henry. The royalists were driven into the Welsh Marches, the King captured and imprisoned, and Despenser and Arundel quickly executed in November.

The parliament which met in January 1327 carried through the first deposition of a king since the Conquest. It was completed by a deputation representing the various estates of the realm, which went from parliament to the King's prison at Kenilworth to extort an abdication from him. The brutal murder of the King at Berkeley Castle in September (Thomas Berkeley was a relation of Mortimer by marriage) was the last revenge of his queen and his enemies, the clearest demonstration of the passions which his rule had aroused and a dramatically fitting end to the tragedy which had started in the palmy days with Galveston.

The political effect of the revolution was only to replace one tyranny by another not much better. Edward III was a minor and had therefore to be represented by a regency council, which was naturally dominated by the partisans of Mortimer and Lancaster. By the end of 1328, however, this alliance had split. Lancaster was excluded from influence at court, while Mortimer, created Earl of March, had acquired grants of lands from the confiscations of the rebellion which made him into a leading magnate. At the beginning of 1329 the two sides were in arms against each other, but Lancaster submitted. The Earl of Kent was executed for an alleged conspiracy in the same year. The horrors of Despenser's day were being repeated. They were ended dramatically by the young King himself. Unsuspected by Mortimer or his mother, he had hatched a plot with a young courtier, William Montague, and even corresponded secretly about it with the Pope. On the night of 19th October 1330 at Nottingham Castle, Montague and his friends seized Mortimer in the room next the King's. He was condemned to death by a parliament and Edward III began to reign in fact as well as in name. This palace revolution immediately changed the face of English politics, much more fundamentally than the deposition of Edward II, by giving England once again a real king.

(5) EDWARD III AND THE HUNDRED YEARS' WAR TO 1361

In Edward III the Plantagenet line found its happiest king. Not perhaps the greatest and certainly not the most interesting personality, but the one whose designs coincided best with the temper and opportunities of his time. Edward III did not make great constitutional innovations, like Edward I, and in home affairs he was rather a passive inheritor of the legacy of his grandfather. But, unlike grandfather and father, he was essentially a successful warrior, who loved fighting and was good at it, achieved more than he could reasonably have expected, and surrounded himself with a comradely galaxy of warrior magnates and warrior sons.

Edward's first campaigns were in Scotland. The claims of the 'disinherited' nobles, who had lost their lands through loyalty to England, had not been satisfied after the Treaty of Northampton (1328), and a renewal of the quarrel between the Bruce and Balliol families allowed Edward to intervene. His first victory was the defeat of the Scots at Halidon Hill in 1333. He campaigned in Scotland again in the summers of 1335 and 1336, but there is no reason to suppose that he was engaged with the Scots very earnestly. French support for Scotland against England became more and more open, so that the campaigns on the border led easily into the great

117

business of Edward's life, the war across the Channel. It is
probably futile to look for a simple diplomatic or political
'cause' of this great struggle. Certainly causes and reasons
enough were alleged by chroniclers and by Edward. He was
thought to have been encouraged by an atractive noble
refugee from the French court, Robert of Artois. The French
took Bruce's side in Scotland. Philip VI of France (1328–50)
had refused to consider Edward's claim to the Agenais, which
adjoined his Duchy of Gascony, and practically declared war
by announcing the confiscation of Gascony in May 1337.
Finally Edward, by right of his mother, Isabella, the daughter

of Philip the Fair, claimed the throne of France itself. But these reasons are not convincing in the historical situation. It looks much more as though Edward and his young friends were attracted by the glorious prospects of an invasion of France and took any excuse that came to hand.

The preparation for the first invasion, planned most carefully on a magnificent scale and on a pattern which improved on Edward I's design of 1294 to 1297, took shape in 1336. There were three important elements in the scheme: firstly, direct invasion by Edward through the Low Countries; secondly, massive support from a line of allies in the Low Countries (where his betrothal to Philippa before the invasion of 1326 had given him a father-in-law in the Count of Hainault); thirdly, the use of the wool export trade to finance the army and the allies and also to force Count Louis of Flanders over to the English side. In 1336 parliament and the merchants agreed to wool taxes and to heavy loans, the staple was moved from Bruges in Flanders to Antwerp in Brabant, and export of wool was forbidden. This had the double object of creating a wool famine in the textile towns of Flanders which depended on English supplies and would thus be made more pliable to English policy, and of creating an artificial shortage of wool abroad which would allow a large profit to be made out of the renewed sales when export was resumed. Meanwhile arrangements were made with English merchants for them to use the king's powers of pre-emption and prohibition of export to create a huge corner in wool, which would be profitable both to them and to him.[1] By the spring of 1338 this 'Dordrecht Scheme'—as it has generally been called, because the wool was to be collected and sold at Dordrecht in Holland—had broken down through resistance from the sheep-farmers in England and difficulties about sale on the Continent, but the King made a large profit by confiscating what had been collected. At the same time, however, Edward's ambassadors had very expensively built up a great alliance in the Rhineland, involving the German king, Lewis the Bavarian; and the economic pressure on Flanders

1. The financial schemes of these years are described by E. B. Fryde in 'Edward III's Wool Monopoly of 1337', *History* (1952), and 'The English Farmers of the Customs 1343–51', *T.R.H.S.* (1958).

had produced a revolt in the textile towns which forced the Count to renounce alliance with France.

By the summer of 1338 Edward himself was able to cross over with an army and make impressive progresses between his allies in Brabant and western Germany, where, as a French chronicler said, 'it rained money'. But even the wealth of the wool trade was not really equal to this largesse. Already in 1338, before he had made any direct attack on France, Edward was borrowing very heavily from the Italian banking houses of Bardi and Peruzzi and from William de la Pole. The winter of 1338 to 1339 was spent in Antwerp. In 1339 Edward was ready to move, but his expensive allies were not anxious to help and he got no further than a small campaign on the French border in the area of Cambrai. After returning to England in February 1340 to bargain with parliament for more money, he went back to take advantage of the strongly pro-English feeling in Flanders, where power had been seized by the clothing towns, led by James van Artevelde of Ghent. On the way back he won his only great victory in this period of the war, the shattering defeat of the French fleet, which had sought to prevent his return, in the battle of Sluys off the coast of Flanders. Once he was back on the Continent he could still get no further than trivial operations on the French border. He returned to England finally in November after concluding the Truce of Espléchin that autumn.

The immediate reason for the King's return was lack of money. After the original Dordrecht scheme Edward had persuaded parliament to agree to other plans for making a great profit out of wool. In 1338 he was to buy half the wool in the kingdom, in 1340 to take 'the ninth sheaf, fleece and lamb'. But these monopolies did not work out as was hoped and meanwhile the King's debts (estimated in 1339 at £300,000, several times his annual income) grew worse and worse. In 1340 several earls had to be left behind as hostages for debts contracted in the Low Countries. Edward came back frustrated and angry and we shall see later how he worked off his anger in England. The cause of this failure had been a too grandiose strategy. The attempt to build up a grand alliance of unwilling allies was expensive and inefficient—the money ran out before anything was done. The Truce of Espléchin marks the end of this strategy and the successes of later years were the result of turning to plans of quite a different kind.

The new pattern of direct raiding into France from the coast, which was typical of the rest of Edward's reign, began in Brittany. The opportunity was given by a dispute about the succession to the Duchy, one claimant being supported by the overlord, the King of France, and the other, John de Montfort, turning for help to Edward III. In 1341 Edward was quick to give theoretical support to Montfort; in the summer of 1342 he sent a force under the command of Sir Walter Manny and in the autumn crossed over himself, defeated the French at Morlaix, overran much of Brittany, and concluded a truce early in the next year. Thereafter Brittany was an important English foothold in France for about forty years. In 1345 more elaborate plans were laid. Montfort again went over with an English army to Brittany and was successful. The Earl of Derby went to Bordeaux to start several years of harrying the French on the borders of Gascony. The King himself crossed to Flanders but arrived at the very time when the pro-English party was finally collapsing, and, recognising again the impossibility of success in that direction, he returned quickly to England.

Then came the great year. In July 1346 Edward crossed over to Normandy with a large army of about 7,000 archers, 1,000 lances, and 1,700 horse, while the main French forces were occupied in dealing with the Earl of Derby in Gascony. In July and August he sacked the city of Caen, marched through Normandy, crossed the Seine at Poissy, and then went north to the Somme, where the French king, who had been watching warily from a distance while the English plundered through the countryside, at last came to grips with him. After the crossing of the Somme, not far from the Channel, the two armies met at Crécy on 26th August, and the uncertain and divided French nobility were defeated by the English fighting on foot in one of the classic medieval victories of infantry over cavalry and the greatest of Edward's battles. Two months later the Scots, invading England in the King's absence, were decisively defeated by the northern lords and bishops at Neville's Cross, where King David II of Scotland was captured. The next year held yet more victories. In June the French were defeated in Brittany and the English position there consolidated. In August, after a year-long siege, the town of Calais fell to Edward, to remain for over two centuries a vital English foothold on the Continent.

The successes against France in the thirteen-forties and after were chiefly made by raids, *chevauchées* as they were called, by English armies into the French countryside. The armies were mobile, they plundered as they went and they had no need of allies. The proceeds of wool customs and of lay subsidies were adequate for this kind of war as they had not been for the grand strategy of the thirteen-thirties. On the eve of the Black Death of 1349 Edward's prestige and power stood high. The truce, which followed the decisive French defeat, and the economic effects of the Black Death, which temporarily reduced the yield of royal taxation, brought about a long lull in the war. The next burst of activity started in 1355 against a less formidable adversary, the new French king, the chivalrous but ineffective John the Good (1350–64). Two major expeditions set out for France in the autumn of 1355. One, commanded by the King, crossed to Calais, but, after foraging about in the surrounding countryside for a short time, returned early to England because of new Scots raids. More important was the first expedition of the King's eldest son, Edward the Black Prince, a young man of twenty-five who had fought at Crécy and was quickly to make himself a reputation as one of the greatest captains of his time. His army went first to Bordeaux. From there he took it in the autumn right across Gascony and Toulouse to Narbonne on the Mediterranean and back again to winter at Bordeaux. In 1356 France was again harried in the north and south. The Duke of Lancaster took an army to Normandy and Brittany. In the late summer the Black Prince's force again sallied forth from Bordeaux, this time northwards into the district of Berry, in the loop of the Loire, and westward to Tours. On the way back the English were pursued by a huge French army under King John himself. They met at Poitiers on 16th September and the smaller English force, against expectation, completely routed the French army, capturing many of its leaders, including King John, who was brought in triumph to England in 1357.

122

Edward now had two kings in captivity and the kingdom of France at his feet. The disorder and desolation there in the years following 1356 were extreme. In addition to the troubles resulting from the Black Death there was the political disunity caused by the absence of the King, the peasant revolt of the Jacquerie in 1358, and the bands of English soldiers, the 'free companies', who plundered and fought for themselves or for some faction of the French nobility. In 1359 the Black Prince was able to take an army from Calais in a great circle round Paris and into Burgundy without much opposition. Finally in May 1360 a treaty was made as a result of negotiations between the Duke of Lancaster and the French regent at Brétigny, near Chartres. It made the King of England's influence in France greater than it had been since the days of the Angevin Empire, a century and a half before. His possessions were extended beyond Gascony almost up to the Loire in the north, by the addition of Poitou and the Limousin, and at the other extremity to the east and south of Toulouse. King John was to be ransomed for the enormous sum of 3,000,000 crowns (about £500,000, or the equivalent of the English king's income for over five years). In return Edward undertook to renounce his claim to the throne of France. The French fulfilled their promises. The new territories were ceded and the Black Prince, who had the greatest share in their winning, went to Bordeaux in 1362 as Duke of Aquitaine, to reign in a substantial Duchy. A large part of the ransom was actually paid over in the next few years. But Edward in fact never made a full renunciation of his claims and the way was kept open for future kings to revive them.

(6) EDWARD III AND ENGLAND TO 1361

The most striking feature of politics at home during the reign of Edward III was the King's good relations with the nobility. Until he lost his grip on affairs in his later years, they were perhaps better than in any other medieval reign. This was clearly the result of his building up around him a circle of devoted magnates and keeping them engaged in generally successful foreign wars. One of the symbolic acts at the beginning of the war with France in 1337 was the creation of six new earls, including some young noblemen with whom the King was already very friendly and who were to be among his leading commanders: William Montague, Earl of Salisbury, his accomplice in 1330; Henry of Grosmont, Earl of Derby, later Duke of Lancaster; and William de Bohun, Earl of Northampton. The unhappy memories of civil war were as far as possible effaced by the restoration of Mortimer's grandson to the earldom of March in 1354 and the reversal of the judgment against the Earl of Arundel, who had been executed as Despenser's supporter. The Statute of Treasons of 1352 attempted to restrict the meaning of the word which had been used so freely to condemn political enemies in the previous reign. Later, as Edward's sons grew to manhood, and they too included several active soldiers, they were given great estates which supported the royal dignity, though they were to be the source of discord in the future: the Black Prince was Duke of Cornwall and Prince of Wales; Lionel of Antwerp, Duke of Clarence, inherited the Clare estates; and John of Gaunt inherited the estates of Lancaster, when that family died out with Henry of Grosmont. In his earlier years Edward was a great lover of tournaments; and another symbol of his devotion to the ideals of the nobility was his foundation, probably in 1348, of the Order of the Garter, an exclusive chivalric fraternity, including the King himself and his greatest warriors, both earls and knights. The extravagant praise of Edward III by the contemporary philosopher Walter Burley is not without foundation, at least as far as his relations with the magnates and barons are concerned: 'A profound love of subjects and king makes for a deep concord between the citizens and a very strong kingdom; as appears today in the case of the King of the English, on account of whose excellent virtue there is the greatest harmony in the English people because each one is content with his rank under the king.'[1]

Thus a true sphere of concord with the nobility made the reign as a whole remarkably free of serious political crises such as had occurred intermittently from 1297 to 1330. There was, however, one major upheaval following on Edward's

1. S. Harrison Thomson, 'Walter Burley's Commentary on the *Politics* of Aristotle', *Mélanges Auguste Pelzer* (1947), pp. 577–8.

return from Flanders after the Treaty of Espléchin in November 1340. During the King's absence on the Continent the administration had been divided by the Walton Ordinances (1337) between the chief ministers and departments, remaining in Westminster, and the household, which was to go with the King. The object was to speed collection of money and to keep ultimate control in the household, but there had been much criticism of the arrangements and the bishops at home had been both slower and more dubious about the rightfulness of the war than the King wished. He came home, burning with shame and anger, convinced that he had been betrayed by those who had remained in charge of the government at home, and his first actions were to dismiss the Chancellor and Treasurer, the Bishops of Chichester and Lichfield, and give those offices to laymen—the first time there was ever a lay Chancellor. He then attacked Archbishop Stratford of Canterbury, who had previously been Chancellor and had taken the largest share in the home government, for maladministration, issued a pamphlet denouncing him as the cause of all the misfortunes abroad, and ordered him to Flanders as hostage for a debt. Stratford took this as a general attack on the liberties of the Church and the rights of peers of the realm, and began to defend both. In the spring of 1341 the affair developed into a serious constitutional quarrel. As the Archbishop won support from both magnates and commons by his rational and fearless defence and his dramatic appearance at the parliament from which he was to be excluded, Edward was compelled to allow him to clear himself of the charges and to return to favour. For many years after this the Crown remained on good terms with the prelates, notably with Stratford himself and with William Edington, Bishop of Winchester, Chancellor from 1356 to 1363.

The most constant political opposition to Edward in England came neither from the nobility nor from the Church but from the gentry and burgesses in parliament. This reign was the period when the Commons' right to consent to all lay taxation became complete and the division into Lords and Commons emerged. This process was connected with the constant war taxation, which gave the Commons unusual importance and carried further the evolution of parliament which is discernible in the later years of Edward I's reign. Resistant to repeated demands for money and often unenthusiastic about the war, the Commons acted as a constant brake and exerted special political influence at two periods when circumstances gave them more power than usual. The first was the initial phase of the French War with its unsuccessful campaigns and huge expenses. When, at the end of 1339, the King asked for yet more money and confessed his debts to amount to £300,000, the magnates readily offered new taxes, but the Commons would grant nothing further without consulting their constituents; they demanded and got another parliament at the beginning of 1340. The large grants of that year were made in return for substantial concessions, including agreement that no lay taxation should be levied without the consent of parliament.

Edward was still more at the mercy of the Commons in the early thirteen-fifties. Apart from its long-term effects on society, the Black Death of 1349 had important immediate political consequences. In the first place it weakened the King by spoiling the wool export trade for a time and so destroying, temporarily, the system of finance, based on loans, from merchants to whom the king farmed the duties on imports and exports, which had sustained him for much of the previous decade. Secondly, the labour shortage, which made new difficulties for propertied people, seems to have added to the truculence of the gentry and burgesses. One result was that Edward was forced in 1353 to agree to the Ordinance of the Staple, temporarily abolishing the foreign staple and satisfying the interests of the wool-growing landowners (see p. 34). In 1351 they secured the Statute of Labourers, which imposed severe penalties on workers taking high wages. The Statute of Provisors, made in the same parliament, was, in its intention, an extreme attempt to limit the pope's right to provide clergymen to churches in England and so to strengthen the position of the local patrons. None of these measures was very effective in the long run but, taken together, they expressed a mood of aggression on the part of the Commons. There is no doubt that the power and importance of the Commons, who from this time onwards genuinely controlled taxation, was much increased in the reign of Edward III. The most brilliant days of English chivalry were, however, only slightly clouded by the reluctance of those who paid the price in taxation. The age of the greatest political power of the medieval Commons was still in the future and the social conflicts resulting from the Black Death had only begun.

PART TWO

1361–1485

CHAPTER SEVEN

LAY SOCIETY

(1) SOCIAL CHANGE

SOCIAL change is generally gradual and scarcely perceptible. Sharp breaks, like the Soviet Revolution of 1917 or, on a smaller scale, the Dissolution of the Monasteries by Henry VIII, are rare and even they sometimes turn out on investigation to be less decisive than they appeared. But most of us are aware that the distribution of power and wealth and the common opinions of people are different from what they were in the time of our fathers, and the cumulative effect of this continuous change over the centuries makes one age very different from another. One of the purposes of history is to define and explain these long changes, and this is partly what we shall be attempting in this chapter and in Chapters 8 and 12.

Before embarking on this attempt there are some preliminary observations to be made. Firstly we must distinguish the natural processes of economics and social evolution from revolutionary designs to change society in accordance with an ideal. The ideas which gained a brief fame in the days of the Peasants' Revolt of 1381 confronted the traditional view that society ought to be a hierarchy of graded ranks with the opposite belief in equality. John Ball told the rebels that John Miller and John Carter and John Nameless had been created equal with other men. The subversive ideas, encouraged by Wycliffe's theory of lordship depending on grace, 'that servants or tenants may lawfully withhold rents and service from their lords when lords be openly wicked in their living' may also have been widely held by the 'Lollards' who followed this English heretic.[1] The ideas of the Revolt and Lollardy are striking examples of the belief in equality and perfectibility which has threatened normal society at intervals in history. They are rare in England before the later fourteenth century,

1. See M. E. Aston, 'Lollardy and Sedition', *P. and P.* (1960)

when they erupted for a time with a sudden explosive force. They did not, however, gain a firm hold. To some extent they corresponded with natural changes which were going on at the same time: the powers of landlords, as we shall see, were seriously threatened by economic changes in the time of Ball and Wycliffe, and the ecclesiastical hierarchy, again partly for economic reasons, was losing some of its grip on laymen. But revolutionary ideology had little effect because its supporters had very little political power.

Secondly, when we come to the natural processes of social change, which move in directions largely unintended and unforeseen by the countless people whose struggles and ambitions contribute to them, we find that there are serious limitations to our powers of generalisation. Looking back through the long perspective of five centuries, it appears to us that the England of Henry VII (1485–1509) was substantially different in its distribution of wealth and power and also in some of its ideas from the England of Edward I. Magnates and bishops were somewhat less exalted compared with both kings and other men than they had been in 1300; parish churches were being built rather than cathedrals or abbeys; the world of ideas owed more to the writings of laymen, and the philosophy of the scholastics had long been in decay. The decline of the great seignorial estate, which had been so much the centre of medieval power, coming at the same time as the general standard of living was rising, meant that gradations of wealth between the freeman and the earl became somewhat less steep. In using these impressions we must remember that it is perilously difficult to generalise about the state of society in a distant period. Impressions may be wrong. There are many gaps in our knowledge. We have no figures of population or of production. The only major commodity for which we can guess at the scale of production is cloth, and even here we are almost entirely dependent on the figures of exports with very little information about production for the home market. We know something about wages and prices on which we can base theories of economic movements. But we know little about the incomes of people who did not live entirely on wages. We know even less about agricultural methods in 1500 than in 1300 because less agriculture was in the hands of lords who kept accounts and more in the hands of small farmers who did not. We know a great deal about the details of some departments of royal administration and justice, because their records have survived, comparatively little about the ordinary lives of ordinary people.

These warnings must be borne in mind as we go on to pick out the social changes of the fourteenth and fifteenth centuries. Changes of two broad kinds appear to have taken place. In the first place there are the economic changes which tended to level some classes and to elevate others. The growth of the cloth industry and the prosperity of commerce, compared with the relative stagnation of incomes from land, and especially from manors, in the fifteenth century, tended to make the merchant more important economically and socially. Of course there had always been wealthy traders, and William de la Pole (whom Edward III elevated to the rank of banneret in 1339 because he had 'made and procured to be made such a supply of money that by his means our honour and the honour of our followers, thanks be to God, has been preserved'), was perhaps outstanding in the whole Middle Ages. In the fifteenth century, however, the gap was very gradually closing. The merchant who called himself a 'gentleman', and was often a landowner as well, was common. In 1523 Thomas Spring, the clothier of Lavenham, was reckoned the richest man in Suffolk after the Duke of Norfolk: an exaltation of industrial wealth hardly imaginable two centuries earlier. No merchant entered the peerage in this period but it was not uncommon for fifteenth-century merchants to take knighthood, or for their daughters to marry into the landed gentry. The decline of demesne cultivation (to be described later) gave opportunities for the more prosperous peasantry to acquire more landed property. Chaucer's Franklin (i.e. a wealthy 'freeman', neither gentle nor serf) was evidently a type of farmer who was common in the fourteenth century. The economics of agriculture gave greater opportunities to men of this type and those below them and perhaps tended eventually to blur the distinctions between gentry and peasantry. There must always have been a large stratum of landless men living at a low material level, but the economic situation was certainly more in their favour in 1500 than in 1300.

Secondly, there is the relative decline in the importance of the clergy. Medieval men assumed the distinction between the laity, whose business was to work and fight, and the clergy, who enjoyed the monopoly of religious wisdom and of learning. This idea was challenged by Lollardy and imperceptibly dissolved by social change. In the twelth and thirteenth centuries the Church had commanded enough landed wealth and international prestige to divide the world with kings and magnates. It probably suffered more, however, than any other part of society from the relative decline in landed income in the fourteenth and fifteenth centuries, and its international loyalties decayed beyond recall. It was inconceivable that an archbishop of the late fifteenth century, a Bourgchier or a Morton, should stand up to the king like Pecham or Winchelsey.

By this time also the Church had long lost the monopoly of education which had once been so naturally assumed. That monopoly had not been complete. No judge of King's Bench was a cleric after the reign of Edward II. Cathedrals, abbeys, and colleges maintained grammar schools which might be attended by the laity, and there were parish schools at a lower level. But in the fifteenth century the supply of education for laymen seems to have been expanding. The first of many schools founded by citizens of London seems to have been that endowed by the will of the grocer, William Sevenoaks, in 1432 to provide 'a Bachelor of Arts but by no means in holy orders to keep a grammar school in Sevenoaks to teach and instruct all boys whatsoever coming there for learning'. The introduction of printing at the end of the fifteenth century satisfied an increasing demand for books. William Caxton, the first English printer, who had been a merchant in the Low Countries, learned the art at Cologne. In 1477 he printed at Westminster 'The Dicts or Sayengs of the Philosophres', translated by a layman, Earl Rivers. His printing of 'Tullius of Old Age' (a translation of Cicero's *De Senectute*) in 1481 was designed 'for noble wyse and grete lordes, gentilmen and marchauntes that have ben and dayly ben occupied in maters towchyng the publyque weal'. In the fifteenth century there were flourishing Inns of Court at London (Lincoln's Inn and Gray's Inn and the Inner Temple and Middle Temple), which provided a lay education in the common law for those who

134

intended to practise in the royal courts, quite independently of the universities. Estate administrators and royal officials in the reign of Edward IV were commonly laymen, and laymen took an increasing part in the administration of Church estates. Even religion, in the days of the Lollards and Margery Kempe, and after, was less a preserve of the clergy.

Another considerable and rather mysterious change was the replacement of French by English as the language of the nobility and of the law-courts in the fourteenth century. Not until then can we regard English as the language of all Englishmen. In the fifteenth century many official documents were still written in Latin but it was much diminished in importance and French was nearly ousted. Chaucer and his successors produced a cultivated courtly literature in English, the Lollards a Bible and popular religious writings. In England, as in some other European countries at the same time, the vernacular had become supreme, and this no doubt helped to break some of the barriers between classes.

The outstanding figure in the literary side of this development was of course Geoffrey Chaucer (c. 1343–1400). Chaucer was an esquire in the household of Lionel, Duke of Clarence, and then of the King in the later part of the reign of Edward III and the reign of Richard II. He was rewarded with the post of Controller of Customs in the port of London and went on several diplomatic missions abroad. On this business he visited Italy at least twice (probably for the first time in 1372–3) and possibly found some literary inspiration there. His long poem *Troilus and Criseyde* retells an old story partly in imitation of Italian authors and with a courtly sophistication of style that was new in English literature. The *Canterbury Tales* obviously owe much to a long and acute observation of manners by one who had done business with Englishmen of many different classes. Their *Prologue* is the most famous of all descriptions of English society and, since it was written in the middle of our period, it is worth recalling for a moment the individuals whom Chaucer assembled at Southwark on an April morning in the reign of Richard II. Gentle society was represented by the Knight, a chivalrous man of war who had fought against the heathen Slav, like Henry Bolingbroke before he became King Henry IV, and against the Turk in the East.

His son was a Squire who had been in a *chevauchée* in Flanders. They had a servant Yeoman who was a Forester. In Chaucer's cruelly realistic picture of the Church, the good side was represented by the conscientious and devout Poor Parson, a village priest who did not press his parishioners for their tithes or run off to work in a chantry saying prayers for payment, and the Clerk of Oxford, completely absorbed in his Aristotle; the bad side by the Prioress, a cheerful lady of accomplished manners, the hunting Monk, the worldly Friar, the lecherous and corrupt Summoner—an official of the bishop's court—and the Pardoner, selling indulgences from Rome which promised pardon for sins. Rural society was present in the Franklin, a prosperous landowner who had been knight of the shire and sheriff, the Wife of Bath who knew about cloth-making, the wily Reeve, the Miller, and the Ploughman. From commerce came the rich Merchant, who traded with the Low Countries, and the Shipman, who knew all the harbours from Denmark to Spain. There was also a Serjeant of the Law and a Manciple, who was a household official. This is a good cross-section of society. We have to investigate the fortunes of these classes in the century after the Black Death.

(2) PLAGUE AND THE PEASANTRY

A few single events in English history have been both sudden and enormously important. English history without the battle of Hastings and the consequent imposition of a new Norman aristocracy, or without the battle of Saratoga, and the consequent loss of the American colonies, would be unimaginably different. The Black Death of 1349 is a turning-point of a different but equally decisive kind. It initiated a long period in which the basic material forces working on society were different from what they had been in the central Middle Ages, and this change had profound effects on almost every aspect of history in the century after. The first plague of 1349 was unmatched in its ferocity but it began a long period, ending only with the Great Plague of London in 1665, in which pestilence frequently recurred; during the centuries of the Renaissance and Reformation men lived in terror of this common scourge. The age of plague began quite suddenly with the Black Death and it quickly altered the climate and tendencies of English history.

The bubonic plague, which was carried by black rats and had already ravaged much of the continent of Europe, probably appeared at Melcombe Regis in the summer of 1348. In that year and the next it spread through England like a forest fire, killing large numbers of people in every part of the country. Though we are suspicious of the hysterical entries of chroniclers, in this case they were justified; monasteries were sometimes nearly wiped out. In the diocese of Lincoln, which stretched from the Humber to the Thames, just over 40 per cent of the beneficed clergy died. In 1361 the scourge returned in the 'Second Pestilence', or 'Pestilence of the Children', as it was sometimes called, because it particularly attacked the young rather than those who had perhaps acquired an immunity in surviving the earlier plague; and it recurred in 1368 and 1375. After this it became increasingly frequent and also less severe, until in 1454 William Paston could write fairly calmly that he was retiring into the country to avoid an outbreak in London: plague had become one of the accepted hazards.

Apart from the catastrophic mortality of 1349 itself, the plagues caused a long decline in population. England in the reign of Edward II, we have seen, was a heavily populated country in which cultivable land was scarce. In the fifteenth century it was quite different. We do not know exactly how much of this change was due to the plague; the great floods and famines of the years 1315–17 had perhaps been the turning-point which ended the medieval expansion of population. In the over-populated England of 1315 many people must have lived on plots of land which could barely support them, or on barely adequate wages, so that they were very vulnerable to any natural calamity. Population growth may have been halted by the natural limits of subsistence. But there is little doubt that plague was the main factor in causing a steep fall in population. No one compiled population statistics in the Middle Ages, but we can tell from the changes in wages and prices that men must have been scarcer in the fifteenth century.[1] And there are also the tangible evidences of abandoned villages.

1. M. M. Postan, 'Economic Evidence of Declining Population', *Econ.H.R.* (1950)

137

It is quite likely that a population of about $3\frac{1}{2}$ millions in the early fourteenth century had been reduced to $2\frac{1}{2}$ millions by the sudden and then gradual fall lasting into the mid-fifteenth century. After that the population probably began to grow again, but only slowly; soon after 1500 a Venetian visitor was struck by the fact that 'the population of this island does not appear to bear any proportion to her fertility and riches', and it was probably not before the reign of Elizabeth I that as many people lived in England again as had done in the reign of Edward II.

It would be a great mistake to suppose that English society was quickly crushed by this series of disasters. On the contrary there are many reasons for thinking that in the reign of Richard II (1377–99) it blossomed in a profusion of original activity such as it had never known before. Chaucer and Langland were writing the masterpieces, the *Canterbury Tales*, *Troilus and Criseyde*, and *Piers Plowman*, which made English a great literary language after its centuries of obscurity. The naves of Winchester and Canterbury, the choir of York, and Westminster Hall were being built. The Wilton Diptych, perhaps the most beautiful medieval English painting, was made for Richard II. Wycliffe and the Lollards were attempting to resurrect apostolic religion. The cloth industry was growing and English merchrants, masters of their own trade as never before, were thrusting into the Baltic. In almost everything from perpendicular architecture to cloth export the civilisation of this country was more distinctively English, less bound to the common hierarchy and heritage of Christendom, than it had been for centuries.

But, while the break-up of Christendom continued, the artistic and cultural blossoming of English civilisation did not. The wider diffusion of wealth and education in fifteenth-century England probably meant that a higher proportion of the population could read books and buy works of painting and sculpture than in 1300. The music of John Dunstable, who served in the household of John, Duke of Bedford, in the minority of Henry VI, the beautiful bronze effigy of Richard, Earl of Warwick, set in his memorial chapel at Warwick later in the same reign, or the chapel of King's College, Cambridge, begun by Henry VI, would be outstanding in any period.

But these are almost the only aesthetic peaks and they do not equal the achievements of the age which saw the rebuilding of the octagon at Ely and the choir at Gloucester, or those of the reign of Richard II. Fifteenth-century art was more widely spread but also less impressive in individual examples. The churches of Somerset and other flourishing wool and cloth areas reached a new level of general excellence and lavishness in parochial architecture. The commonest sculptural remains are the alabaster reliefs of religious subjects and the funeral brasses which were produced in large quantities and tended to become monotonously standardised. Most English painting after the Wilton Diptych is both derivative and unexciting. Social explanations of art history are full of pitfalls, but it is worth while speculating about these changes. The old centres of patronage and inspiration, the court, the cathedrals, the monasteries, and the noble households, were all weakened in their relative economic power, and there were thus fewer incentives of the kind which produced the really aspiring enterprises of the central Middle Ages. The wider diffusion of wealth meant probably more art but also less art of superlative quality. Great things of course were being accomplished on the Continent, some of them not far from England, in the age of Donatello and the Van Eycks, contemporaries of Henry VI. But English social change reduced the old sources of patronage without replacing them by new ones comparable with the Florentine merchants of the Medici period, the contemporary Flemish merchants, or the court of the Dukes of Burgundy. If Florentine humanism and the Florentine and Flemish art of this period had so remarkably little impact on England it cannot have been because they were inaccessible: the two worlds existed side by side with much political, ecclesiastical, and commercial intercourse. It must have been because there were few people with the initiative or the power to take a serious interest in them. It is impossible to escape the feeling that England in the fifteenth century was culturally dull, flat, and unenterprising and had less to compare with the inventiveness of the Italian cities than in the lifetime of Edward I.

The interest of this later period consists, then, less in its few immediate cultural achievements than in the profound and gradual evolution of society and politics which was turning medieval into Tudor England. In most aspects of society we shall notice these two phases, both of which are intimately connected with the changes brought about by the plague: firstly, the atmosphere of crisis, social conflict, and lively self-consciousness which characterises the end of the fourteenth century; secondly, the stability and sleepiness of a society which had quenched the fires of upheaval but was gradually changing in its essential character.

In many parts of England today there are deserted villages, places which we know from the records to have been villages in the Middle Ages and where the outlines of the houses and streets can sometimes still be seen (Plate 2). They are not rare; in Lincolnshire, which was one of the counties where medieval rural expansion most overreached itself, there are over a hundred discovered sites. Probably there were two different periods in which this depopulation took place and two different reasons for it. In the decades following the Black Death many villages, especially those where the land was less suited for agriculture, must simply have died out. At Woodeaton near Oxford, for instance, soon after the Black Death, the Abbot of Eynsham could persuade the few remaining tenants to stay only by reducing their rents. Later, some time in the fifteenth century, a new kind of depopulation started. Landlords, affected by the scarcity of labour and the demand for wool and meat, began to destroy villages deliberately by putting an end to arable cultivation and turning the land over to grazing for sheep or to parks for deer. In the reigns of Henry VII and Henry VIII this was regarded as a scandal and legislated against, but most of the damage had probably been done before 1485. In 1506 it was said that 'about eighty years before, Pendley [in Hertfordshire] was a great town [the word means "village" in medieval English]. . . . There were in the town above 13 ploughs beside divers handicraftsmen, as tailors, shoemakers and cardmakers with divers other. The town was afterwards cast down and laid to pasture by Sir Robert Whittingham who built (Pendley Manor) at the west end there as the town sometime stood. . . .'[1] As early as 1459 a chantry priest of Warwick called John Rous

1. M. W. Beresford, *The Lost Villages of England* (1954), pp. 147–8

was agitating against the destruction of villages that he had observed in the country around. 'The sons not of God but of Mammon', who caused it, found wool and meat more profitable to produce than grain. The basic cause behind it was that there were many fewer people in the English countryside than there had been in the thirteenth century, and many places which had once been busy villages either naturally became, or could profitably be turned into, fields or wastes. Much of England had relapsed into economic decay, but the same factors gave new opportunities to the grazier and the enclosing landlord.

These were the long-term material results of the fall in population. The plagues also had important effects on the structure of rural society because they altered the relationship between land and labour. The seignorial society of the central Middle Ages had thrived on an abundance of men and a shortage of land which kept people bound to their plots and subjected to their landlords. It was now undermined. The most immediate effect of the Black Death, as it appeared to the seignorial lord, was to make labour scarce and wages high. In parliament the Commons, representing people of the gentry and 'franklin' classes, complained bitterly of the hardships resulting from this and sought measures to counteract them. Their main weapons were the Statutes of Labourers, which from 1351 onwards prescribed maximum wages and insisted that all able-bodied landless men must work. For some years the legislation was enforced by special Justices of Labourers in whom the Commons took a particular interest, as they did in urging increased severity in the penalties. Some of the cases show that there was competition between lords for labour and, though wages were kept lower by these statutes than they would otherwise have been, they still rose.

At Theydon Garnon in Essex about 1390 'Simon Jakeboy withdrew John Pretylwell from the service of Thomas Mason into his own service in the occupation of maltmonger giving him 26 shillings and eightpence and food and clothing every year excessively contrary to the statute, which John Pretylwell formerly was a ploughman'.[1] The period of panic and

1. N. Kenyon, 'Labour Conditions in Essex in the Reign of Richard II', *Econ.H.R.*, 4 (1934), p. 433

desperate measures, marked particularly by the statutes of 1351 and 1388, was succeeded by a long period in the fifteenth century when most wages were substantially higher than they had been in the early fourteenth century and the fact was accepted.

The changed conditions were manifested more seriously in a shortage of tenants. The pressure on land had been so great that many landlords found it easy to fill up the vacant holdings after the plague of 1349. By the end of Edward III's reign, however, the continued shortage was beginning to have its effects. Most manors had some houses and plots which were empty 'by reason of the pestilence'. This made things difficult all round for the manorial landlord. His tenants could now find alternative accommodation or employment and therefore he could not keep up his rents. At the same time he now had fewer villeins to perform labour services and so became even more dependent on the expensive wage labour. On top of this the tendency at this period was for agricultural prices to keep low (because fewer people were buying food), while the prices of imported things and manufactures went up. Landlords, and especially manorial landlords, were hard hit. The reaction of many of them was to make the most of their ancient rights of manorial jurisdiction. Villeins, at least, could legally be compelled to stay on the manor and even to pay rent for holdings they did not want. The steward of the Earl of March wrote to a reeve of a manor in 1391 ordering him to look after the villeins lest the lord should be 'disinherited of their blood'. The Abbot of St Albans on his extensive estates insisted that no land should pass between his tenants by their simply making charters granting it to each other outside his manorial courts, lest he should lose control of it. The manorial system became more resented as the tenants became more conscious of their scarcity value. In the first parliament of Richard II's reign (1377) the Commons complained at length of villeins conspiring together to withdraw their services. This evident conflict of interests was lifted directly into the political sphere by the 'poll taxes' of 1377–81. These were levied on everybody by head, instead of falling more heavily on the wealthy and hardly at all on the mass of the population, as did the traditional lay subsidies. The last

142

and most obnoxious of them provoked the first social revolution in English history.

The Peasants' Revolt began at the end of May 1381 with risings on each side of the Thames at Brentford in Essex and Gravesend in Kent. The two bands of rebels converged on London and entered the city on 13th June 1381. For two days the aldermen were cowed, the court besieged in the Tower, and the city given over to the mobs. Many houses were plundered and burned; they destroyed John of Gaunt's manor of the Savoy (he wisely slipped across the border into Scotland when the revolt started); Simon Sudbury, Archbishop of Canterbury and Chancellor, was captured in the Tower and killed. For the time being the court could survive only by negotiating, and so there took place the two extraordinary interviews between the fourteen-year-old King Richard II and the rebels. The meeting at Mile End, at which he conceded the abolition of villeinage, probably took place while the rebels were entering and sacking the Tower. The next day he went to Smithfield to meet another gathering headed by the Kentish leader Wat Tyler, who presented the most extreme of the proposals. When these demands had, with what seems now a pathetic irony, been granted, the Mayor of London, William Walworth, who was riding with the King, pulled Tyler from his horse and the rebel captain was immediately slain. Miraculously Tyler's followers accepted the King's order to disperse. Whether they believed they had really won their dream, whether the death of Tyler took the heart out of them, or whether they were tired of the rebellion, at any rate the crisis at London was virtually at an end.

In both Kent and Essex the original risings were directed at least partly against the hated poll tax, but it soon appeared that the aims of the rebels were more fundamental. The charter which they extorted from the King at Mile End abolished villeinage and laid down that the annual rent of land should be no more than fourpence an acre. This probably represented in an abbreviated form the hopes of the mass of the rebels. It does not appear to have been essentially a revolt of landless men but rather of tenants wishing to be rid of the irksome burdens of villeinage and the manor. William atte Marsh of Mose in Essex, who was fined along with the

143

other tenants of the manor for his part in the revolt and had to pay twenty shillings to get back his villein holding plus his other twenty acres, was typical of thousands of men of substance in the village communities of south-east England who took part in the great 'Rumor' (Plate 11). Another set of demands, which are said to have been presented to the King by the rebels at Smithfield, are quite different.

> 'And then . . . Wat [Tyler] rehearsed the points which were to be requested and asked that there should henceforward be no law except the law of Winchester [probably the police regulations of Edward I's Statute of Winchester] and that there should be no outlawry in any process of law henceforward, that no lord should have lordship but that there should be proportion between all people, saving only the lordship of the king; that the goods of holy church ought not to be in the hands of men of religion, or parsons or vicars, or others of holy church, but these should have their sustenance easily and the rest of the goods be divided between the parishioners; and there should be no bishop in England but one, no prelate but one and all the lands . . . of the possessioners should be taken from them and divided between the commons, saving their reasonable sustenance to them; and that there should be no villein in England or any serfdom or villeinage, but all to be free and of one condition.'[1]

This proposed a total subversion of the hierarchy of society, not the ordinary villein's demand for release from the disabilities of his condition. It is clearly connected with the famous couplet of John Ball, the preacher who was condemned after the revolt.

> When Adam delved and Eve span
> Who was then a gentleman?

Each of these social aspirations had a long ancestry. The desire to abolish villeinage had been foreshadowed in many village disputes between lords and tenants trying to establish 'ancient demesne' (that the estate in question had been held directly by the king at the time of Domesday Book), which

---

1. *The Anonimalle Chronicle, 1333–1381*, ed. V. H. Galbraith (1927), p. 147

was commonly held to free a manor of some of the burdens of unfreedom. The egalitarianism of Ball is foreshadowed in earlier sermons. The combination of the two made a particularly explosive mixture, the fight for material advantage fired with religious enthusiasm. The social circumstances—intensified conflict of interest between lords and tenants—were ideal; so was the political situation of a boy king hedged about by suspected counsellors, an unsuccessful war, a tax thought to be monstrously unjust.

The original movements in Kent, Essex, and London inspired others. In Hertfordshire, where the great abbey of St Albans covered much of the county with its manors and judicial liberties, a conscientious abbot, Thomas de la Mare, had caused much resentment by his careful guarding of the abbey's rights. On the day of the meeting at Smithfield a body of his tenants marched to London, secured from the King a charter of their rights, and marched back the same day to present it to the abbot. For some days the abbey was in a state of siege. The tenants believed there was a lost charter of King Henry I which granted them all they wished. Since it could not be found—and indeed did not exist—they insisted instead on rights of way and of hunting the woods, fishing the river, the right to grind their own corn at home instead of in the abbot's mill, the right to buy and sell land amongst themselves and, of course, the abolition of villeinage. For a few days they lived in the delusion that their new liberty was permanent.

From Essex the revolt spread over the border into Suffolk and developed into a number of dispersed risings and plunderings which were loosely controlled by a priest called John Wrawe. The most serious episode in this area was another quarrel with a great abbey, Bury St Edmunds. Here again the tenants of the town and the surrounding manors had old grievances against their powerful landlord, and the approach of the rebels was the sign for them to rise in sympathy. They broke into the abbey and for a time extorted liberties from the abbot. Another wing of the revolt at the other end of Suffolk reached its climax in the plundering of the town of Ipswich. Apart from the movement of Wat Tyler and John Ball, the most idealistic or ambitious of the risings was in Norfolk, where a rebel army, led by a dyer, Geoffrey Lister, and a knight, Sir Roger Bacon, advanced on Norwich, plundered it, and killed a judge. Bacon then led part of the rebels off to commit atrocities at Yarmouth, but Lister's followers remained in force in the north of the county and tried to legitimise themselves by seeking the recognition of local magnates. Several knights were persuaded or compelled to join them. Lister assumed the title of 'King of the Commons' and accepted petitions of grievances from all over the county. The records of the manorial lords were systematically destroyed until the rebels were defeated by the warlike Bishop Henry Despenser of Norwich in a battle at North Walsham.

By the end of June the revolts were everywhere suppressed. Concessions granted to buy off the rebels were withdrawn and society had returned to its previous stable hierarchy. The rebels achieved practically nothing. Their deeds are interesting mainly for their drama and for their revelation of the acute tensions in society. The social crisis of the early part of Richard II's reign died down and was succeeded by the gradual changes of the fifteenth century.

The problems of manorial and village society remained after the revolt and continued to be intensified by the growing shortage of men. The villein who flees from his native village to throw off the shackles of serfdom and live in freedom and prosperity in a distant town is a familiar legendary figure in English history. In the reigns of Richard II and Henry IV he was no legend but a real and common type. It was possible for some villeins to live legally outside their manors by paying 'chevage' annually to the lords. Others simply disappeared, for the shortage of men was so great that they could easily find employment in a town or a free holding in another village, and rural society was so fragmented that it was generally impossible to recapture them. In 1387 at Wilburton in Cambridgeshire the court roll of the manor tells us that no tenant can be found for the lands which a certain villein 'abandoned in flight'. This was a common occurrence and its effects on the organisation of the manor were serious. Holdings had to be let to new tenants for smaller rents and often without the old labour services. The total value of the rents of most manors declined somewhat and the combined effect of high wages,

146

disappearing labour services, and low prices of grain was to make the working of the demesne lands relatively unprofitable except to provide food for home consumption.

Most of the great seignorial landlords reacted to these circumstances by giving up the direct cultivation of the demesne and leasing it to farmers. It was the accepted remedy for the difficulties of the times. The auditors of John of Gaunt said of two of his manors in 1388: 'The husbandry of Higham Ferrers and Raunds is of no value beyond the costs there which are so great each year that the said husbandry is a great loss to my lord, wherefore the demesne lands ought to and can be leased at farm as in other places.' In the reigns of Richard II, Henry IV, and Henry V (1377–1422) this was happening all over England. John of Gaunt's manors, which made up the great Duchy of Lancaster, had practically no land in demesne by 1399 when his son conquered the throne. The estates of the Bishop of Winchester were all farmed out in the early fifteenth century. By 1422 the old régime of the manorial lords was practically dead.

It is more difficult to say what replaced it. The elaborate organisation of the great estates of the thirteenth and fourteenth centuries produced a mass of written records, especially accounts and court rolls, which tell us much about the manors and about the countryside in general. In the fifteenth century when lords were no longer cultivating the demesnes themselves, their manorial accounts commonly became brief lists of rents paid by tenants, and this is an obstacle to our understanding of the countryside. There are, however, a few things which we can say about it with a fair degree of certainty. Firstly the class of substantial peasants or farmers flourished greatly and to a large extent the control of most villages was given over to them. At Forncett in Norfolk there were eighteen villein families in the manor in 1400. Six of them were still there in the early sixteenth century, of whom three continued to hold moderately sized lands while three others became big farmers: the villein family of Bolitout included one individual farming seventy-eight acres, a member of the Dosy family held two houses and a hundred and ten acres in 1500, and a Bole in 1477 farmed the whole of a neighbouring manor. Similar changes happened in most parts of England. The big farmers

147

inherited the position of the manorial lords. This happened partly because of the leasing-out of the demesne, which put much more land at the disposal of tenants, partly also because of the shortage of tenants which enabled the more energetic of those who remained to take over vacant holdings. The typical farmer of the fifteenth century held a patchwork of pieces of land; the symmetrical villein tenements, all of the same size and owing the same services, which had been common still in the fourteenth century, became rare. The extremes of wealth and poverty in the peasantry were stretched. At Frisby in Lincolnshire in 1381 there were sixteen families, all tenants, of whom the richest were reckoned to be two or three times as wealthy as the poorest. In 1524 there were only ten families of whom three had no land and two were wealthier than all the rest together.

The second thing which certainly happened was the gradual disappearance of villeinage. The reason for this was generally not deliberate manumission of individuals (Henry VII manumitted all villeins on Crown estates in 1485 partly because villeinage was by then becoming an anomaly) or commutation of services. It was firstly because many villein families died out and could not be replaced; secondly, because many fled and their villeinage was forgotten; thirdly, because the splitting-up of demesnes made labour services out of date. In this way both personal villeinage and villein tenure gradually died. The mass of descendants of the villeins were coming to hold their lands not by the old customary tenures but by copyhold, that is to say by an agreement with the lord of the manor, made in the manor court, to which the title deed was 'copy of court roll'. In the reign of Edward IV the common law-courts were beginning to hear cases about copyhold and the importance of the manorial court was evaporating with the rest of the manor.

(3) CLOTH AND COMMERCE

The changes in the character and direction of commerce were as remarkable as those in agricultural society. In this period there took place the fundamental change from England as an exporter merely of raw material, to England as an exporter of cloth which was to be the basis of her commercial and imperial power for several centuries after.

In 1437 the fashionable poet Lydgate could still write 'Of Brutus' Albion his wool is chief richesse'. The export of raw wool remained an essential part of the English economy. But there were changes. Wool-growing was not now concentrated so much in the great Cistercian and Benedictine estates or in the north-eastern parts of England. By the end of the four-teenth century Hull and Boston had lost their predominance as exporting ports to London and Southampton, because the chief centre of sheep-farming was now the Cotswolds. We do not really know why this change happened. One factor may have been the improvement in the quality of Cotswold as compared with Lincolnshire wool. Another may have been the decline of demesne farming by the great religious houses and the greater importance of small estates, which were common in the Cotswolds. Some of these Cotswold woolmen are still portrayed in the brasses over their tombs in churches which they built with the proceeds of their trade in Northleach, Chipping Camden, and Stow-on-the-Wold (Plate 16). We are given an unusual insight into the organisation of the trade in the fourteen-seventies and eighties by the surviving letters of a London family, the Celys. They rode out to the Cots-wolds to buy their wool, mainly from dealers in the towns and villages like William Midwinter of Northleach. The wool was then carried to London and packed by professional woolpackers for the crossing to Calais. Once it got to Calais it came under the jurisdiction of the Company of the Staple of which the Celys, like most English wool exporters, were members. Since its establishment at Calais in 1363 the Company of the Staple had continued with only brief intervals to dominate the export of English wool. Although the trade was now in decline from the great days of de la Pole, this had perhaps served only to strengthen the Staplers' monopoly and it was still active enough to be an important national institu-tion. It was a rigid monopoly controlled probably by the larger exporters. The Celys, who were not big businessmen, found its regulations irksome and attempted to evade them by surreptitiously changing the marks on their bales when they were being graded by the Company's officers. English wool seems to have been as indispensable as ever to the clothiers of Flanders and now to the growing cloth towns of Holland, like Leiden which regularly sent representatives to Calais to buy the year's supply for the town. So the monopoly of the Staple was effective. In the early part of the reign of Henry VI the Staplers even tried for a time to make foreign merchants pay for their wool in gold and silver on the spot, and to compel all native exporters to take part in an organised partition of profits. In the days of the Celys, however, the usual system seems to have been for the foreign buyer to fetch his wool from Calais and then pay the representatives of the exporter at a later time at one of the great fairs held in the towns of the Low Countries, probably Bruges or Antwerp.

The Staple was for several reasons an important political institution. Except during the period when much of northern France was controlled by the English, from 1417 to 1435, Calais was an outpost between France and the Duke of Burgundy's dominions in Flanders. It was heavily fortified and guarded by a permanent garrison. Wool itself was a source of great profit to the king through the customs, and the staplers were a source of loans. By the Act of retainer in 1466 the Company took over the farming of the wool custom in return for paying the wages of the garrison, which was by that time the only English force on the Continent.

But the Staplers controlled a declining trade. In the middle of the fourteenth century England exported over 30,000 sacks of wool a year. This figure sank gradually to about 15,000 by 1400 and about 10,00 by 1485. It was not the lack of a market that caused the decline. 'I have not bought this year a lock of wool,' Richard Cely wrote in 1480, 'for the wool of Cotswold is bought by the Lombards.' Not only the Flemings hungered for English wool; Venetians and Florentines still came to ride about the Cotswolds, seeking it for the industry of Italy. Italians who exported directly to the Mediterranean by sea had the privilege of exemption from the Staple and they carried quantities in their galleys from London and Southampton. For the explanation of the decline we must turn to the other most notable feature of English commerce, the rise of the cloth industry.

In the second half of the fourteenth century the export of

English cloth rose from small beginnings to a yearly average of over 30,000 cloths (each twenty-four yards by two yards), while the import of cloth practically disappeared. In the fourteen-forties the average rose to over 50,000 and, after a fall for two or three decades, this was roughly the level again in 1485. We do not know why the cloth industry made such strides just at this period and perhaps the lack of direct evidence will prevent us from ever knowing, but we can guess some of the probable factors. Firstly, a high level of customs, generally about £2 a sack or a quarter of the price, was levied on wool exports throughout this period, while cloth paid only a small duty. This must have given enormous advantages to the English manufacturer over his Flemish counterparts, who indeed complained at one time that the cost of the English finished product was no more than Continental clothiers paid for their raw material. Secondly, it is probable that the English industry, which, as a relative newcomer, did not suffer so much from old-established monopolies and gilds, had advantages over the industry of such old city centres as Ghent or Florence. Thirdly, it is possible that the declining profitability of agriculture encouraged more peasants, and even lords, to take an interest in cloth-making.

The most striking development of cloth-making in the fourteenth century took place in a group of towns, notably Coventry, Norwich, York, and Salisbury; but already in the first half of the fifteenth century they were losing their predominance to the country districts in which the industry was to have its future. Because water power was necessary for fulling-mills, cloth-making tended to be concentrated in three areas which were well supplied with suitable streams: the hilly country of the southern Cotswolds, the Mendips, and western Wiltshire; the Stour valley in Suffolk and Essex; and the West Riding of Yorkshire. Why the industry moved out of the towns at this period is again in part a mysterious matter, but it may be that the decay of tillage made weaving an attractive alternative, and that the small man had advantages over the large employer. In its early stages the country cloth industry seems to have been very much the business of small men. The clothing village which we know most about in its early stages is Castle Combe in Wiltshire where the lord of the manor, the soldier Sir John Fastolf, encouraged the industry to supply cloth for his soldiers in France. In 1435 a villein died there whose chattels were worth the large sum of over £200, who contributed £20 to bulding a church tower, and who had a stock of cloths and dye-stuffs and a fulling-mill of his own. At least fifty new houses were built in the village in the first half of the fifteenth century. Castle Combe is in the heart of the Wiltshire cloth area. Near by at Trowbridge and Bradford on Avon lived James Terumber who died in 1488, one of the first magnates of the country cloth industry, who must have organised the work of many weavers and spinners.[1] The most famous of them were perhaps the Spring family of Lavenham in Suffolk, where the church which they endowed, like other cloth churches in Suffolk, remains witness to the wealth of the industry at the end of the fifteenth century. In the West Riding the clothing industry spread up the valleys along the streams away from the old town centres of York and Berverley, and this is the only area where it has survived into recent times. In the others only a few lavish churches remain to remind us that England was the Japan of the later Middle Ages, exporting all over the Western world certain standard types of cheap, serviceable cloth, mostly plain, undyed stuff. In the fifteenth century, Englsish cloth was being sold by the Hansards to the Russians at Novgorod, and by the Italians at Byzantium.

Certain main arteries of commerce became particularly important. In the first place there was the trade with northern Europe and especially with the Baltic, traditionally the preserve of the Hanseatic towns of the North Sea and Baltic coasts. In the reign of Richard II, Englishmen from London and from the east coast ports, Lynn, Boston, and Hull, began to push into German territory. By the end of that reign they had organised themselves, elected a governor, and had warehouses at Danzig. The Hansards bitterly resented the intrusion and there was a long series of disputes lasting throughout the fifteenth century and beyond. The English regularly demanded the same generous privileges in the Hanse towns as the

1. E. M. Carus-Wilson, 'Evidences of Industrial Growth on some Fifteenth-century Manors', *Econ. H. R.* (1959); *Idem* in *Victoria History of Wiltshire*, iv, ed. E. Crittall (1959)

Hansards enjoyed in London; the Hanse demanded their exclusion from the Baltic. Fifty years of bickering and piracy preceded the treaty of 1437 in which the Hanse largely gave way and allowed English trade at Danzig. For a time English trade in the Baltic expanded greatly. Then came renewed conflicts culminating in 1449 when a great fleet of 110 Hansard ships, coming through the Channel from western France, was captured by an English pirate holding a royal commission. After another long period of bickering a regular war broke out in 1468, to be ended by a treaty in 1474 by which the Hansards retained their extensive privileges in this country and the English were largely excluded from the Baltic. These quarrels illustrate the conditions of medieval trade and its relation with politics. They were struggles between would-be monopolists. Piracy was close to trade. The victory of the Hanse, remarkable in view of the large privileges which it had in London, was presumably ensured in the long run by the fact that its merchants were useful, as importers of pitch and furs and exporters of cloth, to almost everyone except the exporters with whom they competed directly.

The second, and the most important, branch of English trade was with the Netherlands. Earlier it had been mainly the export of wool for Flemish textiles. Now it was increasingly the export of English cloth to be finished in the Netherlands or passed on unchanged into central Europe. In the trade with Middelburg, Antwerp, and Bergen-op-Zoom there began to develop the groups of English merchants who came to be known as the Merchant Adventurers. Organised groups of English traders with the towns of the Low Countries appear in the reign of Richard II, about the same time as in the Baltic. They received their first royal charter, the ancestor of all the privileges of the Merchant Adventurers, from Henry IV in 1407. From 1446, when they received an important grant of privileges from the Duke of Burgundy, they were particularly associated with Antwerp which became the main port of entry for English cloth into the Continent. It was a former Governor of the Merchant Adventurers, William Caxton, who introduced printing into England in the reign of Edward IV. Merchant Adventurers were also generally members of the Mercers' Company of London, that is to say dealers in cloth and 'mercery', miscellaneous luxury imports. They became increasingly the wealthiest groups of English traders overseas, as the artery connecting Rhine and Thames grew still more important.

The third big overseas connection was with Gascony, an old link which grew weaker through the interference of the Hundred Years' War with the wine trade, and the ending in 1453 of English political control.

Lastly there was the trade with the Mediterranean, especially the Italian cities, which remained important but acquired a new character. In the reign of Edward III the large-scale export of wool both declined and passed out of Italian hands with the withdrawal of the big Florentine firms and the growing dominance of the Staple. In the early fourteenth century regular voyages to England by Italian galleys were only beginning. In the early fifteenth century the Italians revived their trade and developed the galley system, Venetian galleys and Genoese carracks, much larger than the ships of northern Europe, visiting England in regular convoys of huge capacity. The Florentines did not begin to send galleys until the reign of Henry VI but they remained important in banking. They dominated the international exchanges of the north from their banks at Bruges and a subsidiary company of the Medici was bankrupted by lending money to Edward IV. The main articles exported to Italy were now cloth and tin. Tin for bronze statues was one small contribution from England to the art of the Renaissance. In the reign of Henry VI English merchants also made their first tentative efforts to break into the Mediterranean. In 1456 William Sturmy, who had been Mayor of Bristol, took a ship with cloth and tin as well as pilgrims and tried to bring back a cargo of spices. He was waylaid near Malta by the Genoese, who feared this new rivalry, and his ship was sunk. Native English enterprise in the Mediterranean made little progress in this period, but Bristol merchants traded extensively with Spain and Portugal and sometimes ventured farther. The two ships which left Bristol in 1480 'to seek and discover a certain island called the Ile of Brasile' foreshadowed the expeditions of the Cabots who sailed to America from the same port only a few decades later.

The total volume of English foreign trade seems to have declined during the period when the European economy was lengthily depressed by the fall in population after the Black Death; and it is probable that in the Lancastrian period (1399–1461) the quantity of trade was somewhat smaller than it had been in the early fourteenth century. It was also a period of great bitterness between English and foreign merchants struggling for the same business, of which the quarrels with the Hanse are an example. The Italians, who had considerable colonies in London, were particularly hated in the reign of Henry VI by rival Englishmen, and strenuous attempts were made to restrict their activities by imposing hosting laws which forbade them to trade except through English 'hosts'. Commercial jingoism was picturesquely expressed in a long doggerel poem called 'The Libel [little book] of English Policy', written about 1437 when English trade was temporarily handicapped by a war with the Duke of Burgundy who had just made an unsuccessful attempt to capture Calais. The 'Libel' took the view that foreigners, especially those of the Low Countries, could not do without our wool and cloth and would have to bend the knee or starve, and also that England should exploit her command of the Channel to strangle the trade of the Hansards or the Italians or any other merchants who were not amenable.

> Cherish merchandise, keep th'admiralty,
> That we be masters of the narrow sea.

On the whole English merchants agreed. They were aggressive and frequently successful in pushing their trade into new regions.

The age of depression was also an age of very great activity in which the general character of English overseas trade was fundamentally altered. Cloth replaced wool. The variety of luxury imports seems to have increased to meet a higher standard of living. The Merchant Adventurers not only took out cloth but also brought back more and more linen and silk and haberdashery. The Italians brought more spices, sugar, and silks than they had ever done before. Pepper, ginger, cinnamon, nutmeg, mace, black velvet, satin velvet, crimson velvet, a gold brooch, and eighty-four pieces of silk were listed

155

as the imports of one Venetian merchant in 1438. The 'Libel' called them 'nifles and trifles' but they were bought in increasing quantities by the English public. Far more of the silks and satins of Florence and Venice were seen here than ever before, and when Henry VI's queen, Margaret of Anjou, visited Coventry, she was given oranges by the mayor. When the renewed expansion of commerce began in the reign of Edward IV, one of the biggest changes in the pattern of English economic history had taken place and trade was already in general character, if not in quantity, what it was to be in the reign of Henry VIII.

(4) TOWNS

The Peasants' Revolt of 1381 was not an exclusively rural affair. At a few places, notably Beverley in Yorkshire, it inspired riots by mobs against the rulers of the town which remind us that the third quarter of the fourteenth century was also a period of crisis in urban society. In the towns as in the countryside the labourer was strengthened and the employer weakened by the shortage of manpower. This conflict of interest appeared very clearly in the attempts of the masters of crafts to prevent the formation of gilds by the journeymen, who were essentially their employees, and of the bigger merchants in the towns to safeguard their position against the mass of the people and against the industrial gilds. The ruling oligarchies were in general wholly successful, but not without some struggles which have left their marks in history. The Cambridge parliament of 1388, which renewed the Statute of Labourers, also empowered sheriffs to inquire into all gilds within their counties; and in 1437 a statute was passed by which the officers of gilds were required to register their royal licences with the Justices of the Peace or 'the chief governors of the cities, boroughs and towns where such gilds be'. These measures were no doubt taken because many gilds were thought to be dangerous and subversive institutions, as indeed they were. In the thirteen-nineties, for instance, the servants of the saddlers in London had an ostensibly religious gild in honour of the Virgin which the masters alleged to be in fact a conspiracy to raise wages and to have succeeded in raising them in thirty years to two or three times the old rates. There were many such unions in other towns.

The conflicts existed on a larger scale within the town as a whole. In the growing cloth city of Coventry the merchants united in 1364 into an all-powerful Trinity Gild. It owned the Drapery where cloth was sold, and a regular ladder of offices was established whereby the Master of Corpus Christi Gild regularly became mayor of the city two years after his mastership, and Master of the Trinity Gild two years after that. The members of the Trinity Gild were the mercers and drapers, the controllers of the cloth trade. The virtual identity between the merchants and the government of the city led in the fifteenth century to a series of quarrels between the corporation and the crafts of industries subsidiary to the cloth trade, especially the dyers, who several times tried to increase the price of dyeing against the opposition of the city, and eventually produced a leader of a real revolt against the oligarchy in 1494. The fullers and ironworkers were similarly repressed. In 1384 the city procured a royal inquiry into a gild of the Nativity on the ground that its real purpose was to resist the mayor and bailiffs. In the same year two journeymen tailors were accused of making a covenant to maintain their craft, and several times in the next few decades attempts to found a journeymen's gild of tailors were suppressed.

The most famous of these conflicts took place in London. There the leading aldermen and mayors, who governed the city, were nearly always substantial merchants who were also prominent in the export of cloth or wool; William Walworth (who dragged Wat Tyler from his horse) and Richard Whittington in the reign of Henry IV are good examples. For two years, from 1381 to 1383, a man from outside this group, a skinner called John of Northampton, was elected mayor as a leader of the crafts against the merchants. For two years he pursued an explicit policy of keeping the merchants out of power and keeping down the price of food. His success was temporary. As in rural society, the intense conflicts of the reign of Richard II subsided in the fifteenth century into a more peaceful divergence of interests in which the ruling classes held their own.

The fear of craft gilds and mobs is probably the reason why

many town oligarchies in the course of the fourteenth and fifteenth centuries gave a precise constitutional form to their government. At Norwich it was laid down in 1369 that the election of the governing four bailiffs should be made annually 'by the advice of the *bons gens* and the better of the crafts' and the same were to elect the council of twenty-four which was to meet regularly. In 1404 they secured a charter which made Norwich a county with a mayor and two sheriffs. After prolonged conflicts within the city, a charter of 1452 finally vindicated the oligarchy by giving complete power to the mayor and recorder and those aldermen who had held the office of mayor. Similar constitutional developments took place in many other towns. The select groups empowered to rule by royal charter were the ancestors of the modern corporations.

The general contraction of agriculture was not paralleled in the towns. Some contracted and others expanded according to the change in the whole economic structure of England. In general the towns which declined were the agricultural centres and the centres of the diminishing wool trade. Parts of medieval Oxford became so unoccupied that William of Wykeham could found his New College at the end of the fourteenth century on waste land where there had once been houses. It was said in 1450 that eleven streets 'be fallen down in the city of Winchester within eighty years past' and no services were held in seventeen of the parish churches of that city. Lincoln, the centre of a much decayed county and also a former commercial hub of the north-eastern wool trade, was another town whose economic basis was removed. A distinct class of towns now suffered the first stage of decline into the oblivion of the cathedral close and the weekly market which made them the Barchesters of modern England.

For other towns the economic changes of the later Middle Ages produced a great increase in wealth, activity, and importance. There were two main groups. Firstly, the cloth towns: Coventry, Salisbury, York, and Norwich. Secondly, the seaports of southern England which benefited from the reorientation of trade: Ipswich, Bristol, Exeter, Southampton, and, above all, London. London was, of course, a great city both as a capital and as a commercial centre. It was very small in area by modern standards. Its population was concentrated within the walls on the north side of the Thames from the Tower in the east, a royal fortress which also contained the Mint, to Temple Bar in the west. There were suburbs at Stepney; along the Strand, where John of Gaunt's manor of the Savoy stood; and at Southwark, from which Chaucer's pilgrims set out for Canterbury; but nearly all of modern London was country. A mile away at Westminster was the King's palace, where Edward II rebuilt St Stephen's Chapel and Richard II the hall with its remarkable new timber roof, where parliaments met and where the business of Chancery, Exchequer, and law-courts was done. Along the Thames were the wharves frequented by shipping from Italy, the Baltic, the Netherlands, and France. Inside the walls were the narrow streets with their hundreds of trades, shops, merchants' houses, churches, and, crowning all, the spire of old St Paul's. The hall of the Guildhall, the home of city government, was rebuilt on a grand scale in the early fifteenth century. Dick Whittington, the legendary embodiment of commercial success, was the mercer Richard Whittington who died in 1423 and, though he probably started with more capital than a cat, he certainly became a wealthy man—supplier of cloth of gold to the royal wardrobe, Mayor of the Staple of Calais, alderman of London, and lender of money to King Henry IV. In the fifteenth century London was drawing to itself an increasing share of national trade. It was as always ideally situated for contact with the Low Countries and it was nearer to the expanding cloth industries than it had been to the earlier centres of wool-production. All the Italian bankers and traders had their offices in London which, in the fifteenth century, was unquestionably the chief port for the export of wool and cloth and the import of luxuries.

The tower of St Michael's, Coventry, built in the reign of Richard II by two local merchants who were said to have spent £100 a year on it for twenty-one years, and the mystery plays, dating from around 1400, are witnesses of the blossoming of the most spectacularly rising town of this period. In 1345 it had achieved real independence for the first time with a royal charter. In the course of the fourteenth century the wool merchants in the town were superseded by the clothiers.

In 1397 about 75,000 yards of cloth were exposed for sale in the town and a single Coventry merchant is reported to have had £200 worth of cloth in a ship in the Baltic. York and Norwich reached their height as cloth towns about the same time.

There is a story that in the reign of Richard II a trader from Genoa offered to make Southampton into a great port with royal assistance, but was prevented by the jealousy of English merchants. Whether or not it is true, that town flourished in the fifteenth century as the normal last port of call for Italian galleys visiting England and Flanders and, next to London, their chief exporting place for cloth, wool, and tin. After London the biggest port in England was Bristol and, being remote from the routes of the Italians and Hansards, it was more than any other controlled by native merchants. Towards the end of the fourteenth century there developed out of the drapers of Bristol a class of merchants who dealt entirely in foreign trade and shipping. The most famous of these merchants were the Canynges dynasty. The last and greatest of them, William Canynges, who retired from business in 1467, had owned, amongst others, a ship of 900 tons. He rebuilt the church of St Mary Redcliffe in that town after the fall of the spire in 1446.

(5) THE NOBILITY

The nobility and gentry of England weathered the storm of the Peasants' Revolt without yielding their place in society. The social and political movements of the fourteenth and fifteenth centuries caused changes in the distribution of wealth and power between the elements of lay society, king, magnates, gentry, townsmen, and peasants. We shall see in a later chapter how greatly the economic position of the Crown changed; the wealthier towns seem to have acquired a greater importance in the fifteenth-century kingdom, and the wealthier peasants in the village. At the end of it all, however, England was a country only slightly less dominated than it had been in the central Middle Ages by its families of magnates.

In the higher ranges of noble society the rise and fall of families continued to follow much the same pattern, or lack of pattern, as before. Some great houses survived throughout the ravages of plague and civil war, such as the Courtenays, earls of Devon, the Staffords, who became dukes of Buckingham, the de Veres, earls of Oxford. Some died out like the Mortimers, earls of March, of whom the last died in 1425, the Beauchamps, earls of Warwick for nearly two centuries, who rose to the pinnacle of their fortunes with the last earl, Richard (died 1439), and the Mowbrays, dukes of Norfolk, of whom the last died in 1475. New families rose to take their place, like the brood of John of Gaunt, the Beauforts, prominent throughout the Lancastrian period (see Table II, p. 259); the Percies, made earls of Northumberland by Richard II and surviving several revolutions in the fifteenth century; the Nevilles, who became great with the old Beauchamp and Montague lands in the mid-fifteenth century. Broadly speaking, each reign saw the extinction of some old families and the exaltation of new ones. The new might be the king's relations, like the dukes of York, descended from Edward III, or the Beauforts, the Woodvilles (see below, p. 222), and the Tudors, or the king's favourites and men who made their position by successful careers, like the Talbot earls of Shrewsbury, descendants of a soldier of Henry VI, or the Herberts, descended from a soldier of Edward IV. Some new creations lasted only a single generation, like the successive dukes of Gloucester (Thomas of Woodstock, son of Edward III, Henry IV's son, Humphrey, and then Edward IV's brother, Richard III). So far as we know a similar pattern of extinction and replacement, elevation by good marriage, successful soldiering or prudent business, existed throughout gentle society.

The economic movements of the period radically altered the relationship of seignorial landowners with their estates and probably made most estates less profitable than they had been in the thirteenth and early fourteenth centuries. Economic changes also offered opportunities. The Hungerfords, who became great as stewards of John of Gaunt and Lancastrian supporters, were also great sheep-farmers in fifteenth-century Wiltshire. Probably many gentry, like the Verney family in the Midlands, made profits out of enclosure for sheep. Other families rose by political association, like the Pelhams of

Sussex, descended from Henry IV's councillor, or by law and estate management, like the Pastons of Norfolk.

The most splendid opportunities for established families to increase their wealth or for new ones to rise quickly to fame and fortune were offered by war, and this was an important factor, not only in the moral code but also in the economics of the nobility. Most of the fighting in the Hundred Years' War was done by companies serving under contracts made by their captains with the king. The expenses of transport and the wages of the troops were met by the Exchequer and, though it was often dilatory in payment (Sir Walter Manny claimed in his will that Edward III still owed him £1,000, 'which he will pay me if it pleases him and if it does not please him let it be between God and him'[1]), it provided the essential investment necessary to fit out an expedition, leaving the commanders to make what extra profit they could. The profit could be very substantial. In the first place there were ransoms. Noble captives might be well treated, but they were expected to pay large sums for their freedom. War contracts commonly laid down how the profits of ransom were to be divided between employer and employee, and prisoners were sometimes traded from hand to hand like property or debentures at prices varying according to the size of the expected return. The Black Prince raised £20,000 by selling prisoners from Poitiers to his father. In the second place there was plunder. We know little of this in detail, for it did not generally enter into official records; but there is every reason to suppose that the opportunities were attractive. There was obviously a large element of risk in the business of war. The soldier might be killed or he might be ruined financially, like Lord Fitzwalter, who mortgaged a castle to Edward III's mistress, Alice Perrers, to pay his ransom. But, apart from the minority who suffered in these ways, the soldiering classes as a whole could hardly fail to gain considerably at the expense both of their fellow countrymen and of the enemy. A large part of the proceeds of taxation was available to meet their basic expenses and, since the wars were almost entirely fought outside England, the French losses by plunder were balanced by very little loss on the English side. Among the great

1. Lambeth Palace Library, Register of Archbishop Whittlesey, f. 121

magnates made wealthier by foreign war can be counted John of Gaunt, who returned from Spain with a large pension in return for the undertaking not to press his claim to the throne of Castile, and Richard Beauchamp, Earl of Warwick, commander in France under Henry V and Henry VI, who left the Warwick Chapel as his memorial and was credited by his biographer with the ambitious project of deepening the Avon for large vessels between Tewkesbury and Warwick. For many lesser men war was the sole source of fortune. The words attributed to Sir John Hawkwood, the Essex knight who commanded the armies of the city of Florence in the late fourteenth century, 'Do you not know that I live by war and that peace would be my undoing?' might have been echoed by many an English captain in France. Typical of them was William of Windsor, Alice Perrer's husband, who had commanded in France and Ireland and was described by a chronicler as an 'active and valorous knight rich with great wealth which he had acquired by his martial prowess'. The most famous, because of the records left by him and his executors, was Sir John Fastolf, hero of many battles in Henry V's conquest of France and after, who started his career as a humble squire and came home rich enough to build Caister Castle, buy manors all over England, and lend money to merchants.

Besides the long-term economic changes in the countryside the position of the magnates was affected, and perhaps more deeply, by the political changes of the later fifteenth century. The first of these was the changed attitude of the Crown to land. By uniting the Duchies of York and Lancaster and acquiring other great estates, notably those of the Nevilles, the king became already in the Yorkist period a greater landowner than before. Magnates were not so easily able to build up their lands by getting grants of estates which had escheated to the Crown or beneficial leases of royal property. Some new houses, notably the Hastings family, were endowed by the Crown, but on the whole the balance of landed wealth shifted perceptibly from nobility to king.

The second change was the ending of the Hundred Years' War. Throughout the Middle Ages, and perhaps never so much as in the reigns of Edward III, Henry V, and Henry VI, the nobility had drawn both profit and prestige from their leadership in war. After 1453 no major foreign war was fought by the king of England for over half a century and, apart from Calais and the Scots' Marches, no large garrisons were maintained. It was the longest period of external peace in English history. The nobility were thus deprived for a long period of the opportunity both to captain great armies paid for by royal taxes and to plunder the French. In the *Boke of the Noblesse*, written in 1475, when the renewal of war in France seemed for a moment to be a real possibility, Sir John Fastolf's former secretary, William of Worcester, bewailed the sad decline of English arms since the days of his master's exploits:

> 'But now of late days, the greater pity is, many one that be descended of noble blood and born to arms, as knights' sons, esquires and of other gentle blood, set themselves to singular practise, . . . as to learn the practise of law or custom of land, or of civil matter, and so waste greatly their time in such needless business, as to occupy court holding, to keep and bear out a round countenance at sessions and shire holding, also there to embrace and rule among your poor and simple commons of bestial countenance that lust to live in rest.'[1]

Even more than Worcester knew, the future lay with those who had been to the Inns of Court, were learned in the law, and could turn such skill to their own estates or the service of the king. The popular medieval stories of the adventures of King Arthur and the knights of the Round Table received their last and perhaps finest expression in the grave and simple prose of Sir Thomas Malory, an obscure knight, who had served as a young man with the Earl of Warwick at Calais in 1436, in his later life fought on both sides in the Wars of the Roses, and died, possibly in prison, in 1471. Although exercises in the tilting yard were just as popular and more elaborate in the later fifteenth century and remained part of aristocratic life down to the reign of Charles I, the real pursuit of chivalric glory and profit on the battlefield never offered the same opportunities after the end of the Hundred Years' War.

1. *The Boke of the Noblesse*, ed. J. G. Nichols (1860), p. 77

164

Caister Castle was one of many 'partly builded by spoils gotten in France', as the Tudor antiquary Leland said of Sudeley in Gloucestershire, built by Ralph Boteler in the reign of Henry VI. The later Middle Ages were a great period of castle-building to house the barons, sometimes *nouveaux riches* in the comfort of a higher standard of living, to serve as the headquarters of their wealth and influence, and to be defensible in time of trouble. The huge fortresses of the Edwardian age were not copied, for the idea of an impregnable castle to dominate a large territory around it was undermined by changes in warfare. Some of the new castles, especially those near the coast such as Bodiam in Kent (1386) and Caister, had gunports in the walls for the artillery which was coming into use at the end of the fourteenth century. Additions were made to the old castles, like John of Gaunt's great hall at Kenilworth and the towers added at Warwick by Earl Thomas Beauchamp in the reign of Richard II, but the characteristic new castle was somewhat different. Tattershall in Lincolnshire, built by Ralph Cromwell, Henry VI's Treasurer, might be taken as a pattern of the baronial ideal. It consisted of a great tower, gaunt but windowed on the outside, with battlemens, several fine rooms with elaborate fireplaces within, a hall beside the tower, and a moat around. Beyond the moat were the church, a college of priests to serve it, the stables, the fishponds, and the village. Sir Edward Dallingridge's Bodiam and the Earl of Northumberland's Warkworth in Northumberland are fine examples of castle-building at the end of the fourteenth century, and Roger Fiennes's Herstmonceux in Sussex (Plate 15) followed the courtyard plan of Bodiam in the reign of Henry VI. One of the last great baronial castles was Kirby Muxloe in Leicestershire built by William Hastings in the reign of Edward IV. On a lower social level the timber and brick house at Ockwells in Berkshire, built in the reign of Henry VI, with a hall, fine windows, living-rooms, a chapel, and farm buildings, represents the aspirations of the richer gentry.

It was said that Lord Cromwell had a hundred persons in his household at Tattershall. The magnificence of the household and the prestige of the lord were maintained by wealth and influence. Beyond the castle the nobleman had his estates which might be scattered over several counties. Though medieval demesne farming largely disappeared in the fifteenth century the estates still required a staff of receivers and stewards, and English society was enmeshed no less than before in the complicated networks of bastard feudalism. Some time after Sir William Oldhall, the Yorkist speaker in the parliament of 1450, had escaped from the attainder which his political activities brought upon him, the Earl of Warwick recalled in a letter 'how that of long time past for the good services that Sir William Oldhall knight had done unto us and shall do hereafter we gave him the office of steward of our lordship of Soham and restored him to it that he may rejoice it peaceably and have payment of such fee as other afore him have had and taken. . . .'[1] Great magnates like the Earl of Warwick maintained huge followings by their fees, some in permanent service as household officials, some in more tenuous connections retained as lawyers, as councillors, or as soldiers to come when they were required. In the Wars of the Roses armed retinues went into battle wearing the badges and crying the names of the nobility, but the permanent affinities which they maintained in peace time were yet more important. They assured to the nobleman a wide support in politics and law from below and they riddled the society of lesser men with connections which were influential in practical affairs. 'Good lordship' was one of the important needs of the yeoman or the gentleman to make his way in the world: it helped him at law and in business. From the standpoint of a healthy-minded modern society it seems a mass of wasteful bribery and corruption; and the ideal of a supreme impartial royal justice was sufficiently developed even at that time for its excesses to be denounced occasionally by aggrieved contemporaries. 'That is the guise of your countrymen,' said a complaining lawyer in Norfolk in 1454, 'to spend all the good they have on men and livery gowns and horses and harness and so bear it out for a while and at the last they are but beggars.' About the same time the Earl of Northumberland was spending more on his retainers than his estates could bear.

1. P. B. Chatwin, 'Documents of "Warwick the Kingmaker" in possession of St Mary's Church, Warwick', *Transactions of the Birmingham and Midland Archaeological Society*, 59 (1935), p. 3

The parliaments of the period heard several petitions against the misuse of liveries and indentures and made Acts against them and against the practice of corruptly supporting friends by 'maintenance' in suits at law. On the whole, however, the affinity, whether in the formal relationships of councils, stewardships, fees, and liveries or in the less definite manner of influence, was part of the normal fabric of society. It was not the cause of the Wars of the Roses, nor was it cured by the new despotism which followed. William Hastings, a new magnate under Edward IV, quickly built up a large following of indentured retainers, and English society continued to respect the household and following of the nobleman long after Henry VII had endeavoured in the spirit of the early parliamentary petitions to restrain its abuses with his Statute of Livery and Maintenance.

CHAPTER EIGHT

THE CHURCH

(1) HERESY

THE thirteenth century had been one of those periods, like the later ages of Renaissance and Romanticism, when a new intellectual impulse gave rise to bold and original speculation and the construction of dazzling systems of thought. England had participated fully in this European movement, and in the early fourteenth century Oxford was still the centre of an active and original school of philosophers with an influence throughout Christendom. Apart from their theological and logical works, the scholars at Merton College, in that period for instance, are important in the history of science for the advances which they made in the theory of motion. But the later Middle Ages after this was a period of philosophical decay in England. Thinkers quarrelled over the difficulties of the old systems and did more to destroy than to create. The new ideas which excited the humanists of the Italian cities in the fifteenth century gained no more than an occasional foothold in a country which could only be described at that time as intellectually backward. A few visiting humanists were patronised by Cardinal Beaufort and Humphrey, Duke of Gloucester in the reigns of Henry V and Henry VI. Humphrey should perhaps rank as the greatest patron of literary art and scholarship in the fifteenth century. The 'pleasaunce' which he built at his castle at Greenwich was in the fourteen-thirties a haven for Italian classicists and English poets after the fashion of Italian princes and merchants. He founded Duke Humphrey's Library, still the core of the university library at Oxford, encouraged the study of the classics there, and presented many manuscripts. A number of later churchmen imported humanistic manuscripts and ideas from Italy, and before 1485 the master of Magdalen College School had produced a new kind of Latin grammar which was to be influential in the schools. But on the whole, in scholarship as in art, England was very much on the margin of the Renaissance.

For the germination of religious heresy and reformation, however, the English thinkers of the fourteenth century were of the first importance. The generation which died about the time of the Black Death had turned philosophy into different channels. The most outstanding of them was William of Ockham (died 1349), who had developed his metaphysical ideas before he left Oxford in 1324, and his importance was that he criticised radically the Thomist synthesis of faith and reason. He argued that religious belief was entirely based on faith, which could not be supported by reason because it was concerned with matters which were beyond the scope of rational argument. Neither the existence of God, nor His attributes could be proved by reason, which could deal only with abstract concepts. Man's only knowledge was an intuitive knowledge of individual things, which did not depend upon reason. Ockham was not attempting to modernise theology, rather to withdraw God and the whole of theological belief from the structure of rational proof and explanation which had been developed to support it in the thirteenth century; but his views had important theological implications. He played down the rational, comprehensible aspect of God's actions and emphasised the irrational, incomprehensible omnipotence of God's Absolute Power, which lay behind them. In the relationship between God and man he emphasised the free will of both. Neither was predetermined and God accepted man into grace on the strength of his meritorious acts of free will. The ideas of Ockham and his followers smacked of 'Pelagianism'—the belief that men can perfect themselves by their unaided free will. They were answered by an Oxford contemporary, Thomas Bradwardine, later Archbishop of Canterbury (died 1349), who also paid little attention to the philosophical basis of theology but emphasised that the whole of creation was an emanation of divine will, and reinstated grace by insisting on the priority of God's help rather than man's free will in every human action. A later writer, Richard Fitzralph, Archbishop of Armagh (died 1360), developed the theory that the lawful exercise of all lordship depended on grace.

It was in the intellectual climate engendered by these debates that John Wycliffe grew to be the leading Oxford philosopher of his generation. By 1372 he was a Doctor of Divinity and had already written most of the philosophical works in which he defended the importance of 'universals' and showed some sympathy with Bradwardine's views on grace and predestination. The later development of his thought is inseparable from his involvement in politics. Whether this was due to an early reputation for anti-clericalism we cannot say; probably it was, but in any case it was not unusual for scholars to be employed by kings on diplomatic and ecclesiastical business. In 1374 he was a member of a diplomatic mission to Bruges to negotiate with papal envoys about ecclesiastical taxation. In 1376 he sprang into prominence as John of Gaunt's agent in his quarrel with the bishops, and in February 1377 was summoned to answer charges, resulting from that activity, in St Paul's, where Gaunt accompanied him with armed men and broke up the trial. In 1378 he was summoned again and again saved from condemnation, this time by the King's mother, Joan of Kent. In the same year he appeared in the Gloucester parliament to defend the violation of the sanctuary at Westminister Abbey. Then, his usefulness to the politicians at an end, he disappeared from the world of affairs. He was already regarded as a very dangerous thinker. Propositions drawn from his books on Civil and Divine Dominion, in which he developed Fitzralph's idea of the necessity of grace to justify lordship, had been condemned by the Pope in 1377 and they were indeed subversive of ecclesiastical authority. It was in 1378, and after, that he produced the books which were to stamp him as the great heresiarch of later medieval England and Europe, and it is difficult not to believe that the excitements and disappointments of politics helped to inspire them. His book *On the Church*, written in 1378, developed a view of the Church as the community of believers rather than the ecclesiastical hierarchy. In 1379, in the book *On the Eucharist*, he touched the very heart of the medieval Church by denying the doctrine of transubstantiation. He left Oxford in 1381, but continued from the rectory at Lutterworth, where he was probably protected, though no longer employed, by John of Gaunt, to pour forth a stream of increasingly virulent heretical literature until he died in 1384. Wycliffe's earlier ideas on the nature of universals and the importance of grace, derived from Oxford learning, probably supplied some of the preconditions of his later heresy. By the end of his life, however, they had been lost in a mass of heretical doctrine, which denied authority to the pope and the hierarchy, and overthrew the accepted notions of monasticism, excommunication, the mass, and the priesthood—in short, of the whole structure of the medieval Church. In place of the authorities of tradition, reason, and the hierarchy, Wycliffe placed an extreme reliance on the dictates of Scripture and of the individual conscience. There may have been little in Wycliffe, as in most reformers, that was entirely original, but his doctrine was as a whole impressively destructive and his ideas were to be the touchstone of heresy—not only in England—for some decades.

Heresy of one kind and another was common enough in many places in the Middle Ages and anti-clericalism was fashionable in many more. But there had never been an important heretical movement in England, and the hierarchy had slumbered in easy indulgence, allowing Oxford philosophers to treat fundamental dogmas as debating-points and popular preachers to lampoon clerical vices. The events between 1377 and 1382 were a rough awakening, which threw the Church briefly into an uproar and changed the atmosphere of ecclesiastical thinking. The essence of the new situation was, firstly, that the most eminent living philosopher had put his weight behind completely subversive doctrines, hitherto confined to ignorant eccentrices; secondly, that he had done this in a time of mounting anti-clerical feeling at several levels of society, which had had some prospect of serious political support. The abuses of clerical wealth and absenteeism, which critics attacked, were not new at this period. It is true that the Church, especially the papacy, was making more use of indulgences (remissions of sins in return for the penance of a payment in money) to supplement its falling income, and that the Pope had invented the device of exacting annates (the first year's revenue of a benefice) from bishops when they were appointed. But these were minor alterations in the structure of ecclesiastical finance, and there is no reason to suppose that there was more to condemn in the reign of Richard II than there had been a century before. Still, the fact that the three classical scathing criticisms of the clergy, from the different standpoints of Wycliffe's scholarly analysis, Chaucer's worldly wisdom, and Langland's offended piety, were all written about the same period, is probably not an accident. There was a crisis of anti-clerical feeling.

Later commentators, either revelling in the literary abuse or mesmerised by the continuity of the Church's imposing organisation, have not explained why this was so. We can only offer a few guesses. In the first place, some weight must be given to the simple decline of enthusiasm. There must have been a great many honest and even saintly men in the Church in 1377 as at all periods, but there had not been for a century an innovation like Cîteaux or the Franciscan Order or an intellectual awakening like that of the age of Grosseteste to canalise religious impulses. It was easier to see the Church as a rich, self-satisfied organisation, for ever guarding its property without offering new religious inspiration and even anti-spiritual in its effects. Secondly, there are the complex effects of the fall in population. Though one might think from the anti-clerical literature that the Church was growing richer, it was in fact poorer by the fall in landed income. In clerical as in lay society the Black Death caused friction between employer and employed. It was necessary to fix maximum rates of pay for the scarcer unbeneficed clergy, vicars, and chaplains. The very strong feeling in Wycliffe's age against the 'possessioners', the abbeys and cathedrals supported by great landed property, was no doubt given weight by the mass of priests who lived on stipends which they were struggling to increase. John Ball, the ideologist of the Peasants' Revolt, is the obvious example of the common priest who would have liked to overturn the organisation of the Church; and a number of priests took part in the attack on the abbey of Bury St Edmunds in the same year. It is possible too that the common hardships of landowners in this period stimulated that jealousy of propertied laymen for the Church, which found expression in the Statutes of Provisors (1351) and Praemunire (1353) and the suggestions of confiscation of Church lands made in parliaments. Thirdly, there was the new friction in relations between king and Church, which came to a head in the thirteen-seventies. It is clearly visible in the parliament of 1371, which tried to impose a tax of £50,000 on the Church, where the Bishops of Winchester and Exeter were removed from Chancery and Exchequer to be replaced by laymen, and someone invented the fable of the ecclesiastical owl whose feathers had been given to him by lay birds who could properly demand them again in time of need. A few years later the collector of one of the infrequent papal subsidies in England was hampered by royal regulations, and the amount to be collected was restricted in the negotiations at Bruges, in which Wycliffe took part. Resentment was voiced in the Good Parliament (1376) and shortly afterwards friction reached its climax when John of Gaunt instigated the seizure of Wykeham's temporalities for the Crown and defended Wycliffe at St Paul's. King and Pope were in fact competitors in their urgent need to tax the clergy (Edward III for his war in France, and Gregory XI for his war in Italy), and the lay commons were wholeheartedly on the side of the King. In 1380 they demanded that the clergy should pay one-third of the taxes because they owned one-third of the land, and in 1388 they rejected a new papal request for a subsidy.

Reformation, however strongly backed by anti-clerical sentiment and theological justification, was impossible without political support. For a brief period around 1377 all these motives worked together and the threat to the Church was more serious than at any other time before 1529. It was removed by the abandonment of John of Gaunt's anti-clerical policy; and this turn in affairs was probably assisted by the beginning of the Great Schism—the division of authority between two rival popes—in 1378. The Schism, though it did great injury to the prestige of the Church in the eyes of many people, made political relations easier by giving the English government the assurance of an ally in one of the two popes. By the time the Hierarchy in England began its serious rooting-out of Wycliffite heresy, the real danger had passed. There remained the problem of widespread doctrinal error, encouraged by Wycliffe's teaching and other recent events, which was to exercise the Church for many a year. Both the origins and the personnel of Lollardy, as the heretical movement was called from this time, are obscure. Wycliffe himself had contributed in two ways. Firstly, he gathered about him at Oxford a substantial group of scholars in agreement with his views (they included some of the abler intellects of the time, for instance Philip Repton, later Bishop of Lincoln), and started a tradition of thought which, in spite of attempts to stamp it out, survived in the university into the early fifteenth century. Another and much more influential movement of Reformation was started in Bohemia by John Hus, who was burned at the Council of Constance in 1415. One of the most prominent theologians of the Hussite movement was an English Wycliffite, Peter Payne, who had been Principal of St Edmund's Hall before he fled from Oxford. Even apart from Payne, the doctrines of the Hussites would have been very different if they had not swallowed much of Wycliffe's teaching and been influenced by contacts with Oxford. Secondly, Wycliffe assisted the wider dissemination of his views by his encouragement of the religious use of English. He wrote some of his works in English and sponsored the translation of the Bible, which was begun by his disciples in his lifetime. Apart from the scholars a certain amount of Lollard sympathy was to be found in fairly high places in lay society. Several eminent knights, including some in the royal household, were suspected of Lollardy under Richard II. Sir Thomas Latimer was summoned to the king's council for possessing heretical books in 1388, and Sir John Oldcastle, the leader of a revolt in 1414, was a successful career soldier. Though the movement owed something to the dispersion of heretic scholars from Oxford, most of the Lollards, however, both priests and laymen, were humble men, and it is impossible to distinguish the ancient tradition of puritanical criticism from the new influence of serious heretical doctrine. The most famous of the humble men, William Swinderby, had been a censorious hermit at Leicester long before he was touched by the doctrines of the heresiarch. Lollardy was in part the continuation of an old stream of religious feeling, which was only enriched by Wycliffe and revealed to history by the new persecution which the anxiety of the bishops unleashed. However that may be, Lollards were common in the decades of the late fourteenth and early fifteenth centuries in several parts of

England, notably the Midlands, the Welsh border, and the Chilterns.

The counter-attack began with the condemnation of Wycliffe's teachings on the Eucharist at Oxford in 1381. In 1382 William Courtenay, Archbishop of Canterbury, to whom more than any other man the Church owed its strength in this time of crisis, convened a council at Blackfriars in London, which condemned twenty-four propositions from Wycliffe's writings. The leading Oxford heretics recanted, though not all permanently. The status of Wycliffe's teaching was now clear and it needed only to be stamped out. The machinery for bringing heretics to justice was tightened up in Richard II's reign and the period of active persecution by the bishops began, soon reinforced by the Statute on the Burning of Heretics in 1401. The need for severe measures was shown in 1395 by a Lollard manifesto nailed to the doors of Westminster Hall during parliament, and again in 1410, when the Commons seriously considered the possibility of confiscating ecclesiastical property. By this time Courtenay's role had been taken over by Archbishop Thomas Arundel, who had the weight of royal sympathy on his side. In 1411 he carried out a visitation at Oxford to ensure that the University fully accepted the official condemnation of Wycliffe's views. This was virtually the end of learned heresy in England until the Reformation. Two years later, however, Arundel faced another serious challenge. In 1413 Sir John Oldcastle escaped from prison, after being convicted of Wycliffite opinions. In January 1414 a small army of his followers from various parts of the country were rounded up by the King's men when they were on the point of assaulting London. This was not the end of Lollardy. Many heretics, with opinions varying from 'the pope of Rome is a great beast and a devil of hell' to 'it is no better for a layman to say *pater noster* in Latin than bibble babble' were investigated by fifteenth-century bishops. In 1431 there was a substantial, though abortive, conspiracy led by one who called himself 'Jack Sharp of Wigmoreland', and Bishop Reginald Peacock's elaborate argument against Lollard theories, 'The Repressor of Overmuch Blaming of the Clergy' was written towards the end of Henry VI's reign. Lollard ideas, obscurely handed down in various parts of England, came to the surface again at the time of Henry VIII's Reformation. Courtenay and Arundel, however, had broken the force of the movement and for a century orthodoxy was safe.

(2) ORTHODOXY

In the same generation as Wycliffe and Chaucer, another Englishman, William Langland, set down a vision of human life, in which the weaknesses of contemporary religion were exposed with no less cruelty, but Holy Church was accepted still as the only hope of salvation. As a poor London cleric in Minor Orders, who made a living by saying prayers for money, but also a man of some learning with the insight of genius, Langland was fully aware of the corruption of his superiors, and a great part of *Piers Plowman* is taken up with satire of clerical vices and with the disillusionments experienced by the honest seeker after truth in the company of the scholarly theologians. The friars were particularly singled out for attack as money-grubbers and easy confessors. The bad influence of Rome and the uselessness of pilgrimages were emphasised. Learning was presented as a gluttonous and fastidious scholar, who could not stand the plain fare of sound ordinary doctrine and was deeply suspicious of those who sought to rely on the simple power of love. At the same time, however, it was Holy Church that first revealed the truth about the world to the dreamer and, at the end of the book, the honest and conscientious Piers Plowman, representing the best in humanity, was identified with St Peter, the founder of the Church, which had received the power from Christ, in spite of the clerical vices which assailed it from every side, to continue the work of salvation. Langland was a moralist; the sacraments, the hierarchy, and the contemplative life play relatively little part in his vision of the Church as it should be, and there was an apocalyptic element in his last picture of the Church's struggle with the power of Antichrist. He was certainly no admirer of the Church as it was, and he probably set much less value than the ordinary churchman on the orthodox establishment. Still, he was a moralist who wished to purify rather than subvert, and his book is the most splendid example of a tradition of spirituality, expressed in the English tongue, within the Church.

It is by no means alone. The anonymous *Cloud of Unknowing* and *Scale of Perfection*, and the *Revelations of Divine Love*, by the anchoress, Juliana of Norwich, were all written in the late fourteenth century. These are works of unusual power dealing with the individual religious life and, together with the writings of the earlier Richard Rolle (died 1349), form an important group of mystical treatises in the orthodox tradition. Perhaps the most extraordinary literary production of the later Middle Ages, both for the light it sheds on common religious beliefs and for the revelation which it gives of the self-consciousness of ordinary people, is the *Book of Margery Kempe*. This is the autobiography, written in the early part of the reign of Henry VI, of the wife of a burgess of Lynn, who abandoned her married life to devote herself to religion. She knew some of the English mystical writings, indeed she once visited Dame Juliana at Norwich, and she travelled on pilgrimage to Jerusalem, to Rome, and to Wilsnack in Poland. She had visions, and her life was dominated by an intense spiritual awareness and an outspokenness, which made her several times suspect of Lollardy and got her into trouble with the Archbishop of York. She was orthodox but completely unawed by the hierarchy. 'Almighty God,' she once said to no less a person than Archbishop Arundel, 'has not given you your benefice and great worldly wealth to keep His traitors and them that slay Him every day by great oaths swearing.'

The diocesan organisation, the monasteries, and the friars continued to control religious life as before. It is noticeable, however, that the outstanding examples of spirituality in this period were less intimately connected with ecclesiastical institutions than their predecessors of the twelfth and thirteenth centuries. There is no one to compare with Abbot Ailred or Bishop Grosseteste, and it is impossible to avoid the conclusion that the institutional Church, for all its continuing magnificence, had lost its spiritual leadership and was in slow material decline. The notable abbots tend to be great managers in the tradition of Henry of Eastry: Thomas de la Mare, Abbot of St Albans from 1349 to 1396 and a powerful defender of his house, is perhaps the most famous example. The religious

Orders did not attract their old share of pious endowment. With the exception of two religious houses set up by Henry V at Sheen and at Syon, there were few new foundations at the end of the Middle Ages, and a certain amount of property, taken from 'alien priories' (daughter houses of French monasteries) during the Hundred Years' War, was transferred by Henry VI to the colleges at Windsor and elsewhere. Monasticism tended to remain static in a world where new sources of wealth and new religious interests were growing, and so to become relatively less important.

The European Church was split at the centre by the Schism in 1378, which left one pope at Rome, accepted by England, and another at Avignon, dividing Christendom between them. The council at Pisa in 1409 introduced a third pope. Unity was restored by the great council which was held at Constance from 1414 to 1418 but the papacy was never the same again. The Roman court had bowed, however unwillingly, to the authority of an assembly representing the whole Church, and it was to be harassed again by the long council which sat at Basle intermittently from 1431 to 1449. The popes of the fifteenth century withdrew into the cultivation of their Italian patrimony much more than their predecessors had done, and were less influential in both the politics and the ecclesiastical administration of northern Europe. In England the second Statute of Provisors in 1390 and the third Statute of Praemunire in 1393 reinforced anti-papal legislation. The attempts of Martin V to persuade first Henry V and then the lords of the council, during the minority of Henry VI, to repeal the Statute of Provisors failed. An agreement between Richard II and Pope Boniface IX in 1398 formally reserved control over appointments of bishops jointly to king and pope. In practice the king's candidate generally won and papal intervention, though sometimes important, was less successful than it had been in the past. The system of papal provisions continued but the nomination of foreigners to English benefices was again less frequent than it had been in the central Middle Ages. Papal taxation of the clergy was bitterly resisted by the laity in 1375 and 1376, refused by Richard in 1388 and 1391, and by Henry VI in 1427 and 1446, though it was partially replaced by the custom that newly appointed prelates should pay the first-fruits—the first year's revenue of their benefices—to Rome. In the fifteenth century Englishmen looked altogether less to Rome than they had done at the height of the Middle Ages and, although a bishop would have to pay considerable sums to the papacy for his provision, he nearly always came into office as a nominee of the king. The famous prelates of the fifteenth century were therefore strikingly more conformist and more involved in English politics than those of the thirteenth. Archbishop Arundel of Canterbury (1396–7 and 1399–1414), the scion of a great noble house, and Cardinal Beaufort, the King's half-brother, will be seen in a later chapter on the political stage. Henry Chichele, Archbishop of Canterbury, 1414–43, the son of a London grocer, was a conscientious administrator of his province concerned to keep up reasonable relations with the secular arm, and more reluctant than helpful to Pope Martin V's desire to maintain provisions and tax the English clergy for war against the Hussites. John Kemp, Archbishop of York from 1426 to 1452 and of Canterbury from 1452 to 1454, was an old friend of Beaufort and another ecclesiastical statesman deeply involved in the politics of the king's council, and he paid little attention to his faraway diocese during his long tenure of it. Thomas Bourgchier, Archbishop of Canterbury from 1454 to 1486, is again more remarkable for his long connection with lay politics through many twists of fortune than for his ecclesiastical career.

The great age of medieval cathedral-building continued into the late fourteenth century with undiminished splendour. The rebuilt naves of Winchester, begun about 1360, and Canterbury, begun in 1379 by the mason Henry Yevele who also collaborated in Richard II's new hall at Westminster, continue on a larger scale the tradition established at Gloucester. The rebuilding of York began in 1361, with the east window introduced at the very beginning of the fifteenth century. But, with the exception of the towers, notably those of Canterbury and Gloucester, the fifteenth century, after its first decades, is not a great age of cathedral building. The impulses and money were directed elsewhere.

The commonest types of ecclesiastical buildings at the end of the Middle Ages were chantries, colleges, and parish churches. Chantries and colleges were built by wealthy men

179

partly to perpetuate their own memories and to ensure that prayers should be said for their souls for ever. To do this a patron had only to build a chantry chapel in an existing church and bequeath enough money to pay priests to say the masses in perpetuity. The will of Richard Beauchamp, Earl of Warwick, made in 1435, directed that 'when it liketh to God, that my soule depart out of this world, my body be enterred within the Church Collegiate of Our Lady in Warwick, where I will that in such place as I have devised ther be made a Chappell of Our Lady, well, faire and goodly built, within the middle of which Chappell I will that my Tombe be made. . . . Also I will that there be said every day, during the Worlde, in the aforesaid Chappell . . . three masses.' The result was the chapel at St Mary's, Warwick, which still contains the superbe bronze effigy of the founder. An earlier example is the chapel built in Tewkesbury Abbey, in accordance with the will of Edward Lord Despenser (1375), with a kneeling effigy of a knight above it.

Colleges were more elaborate foundations, including buildings to house a group of clerics who would maintain the services in the chapel and also perhaps do educational work. Lord Cromwell's new castle at Tattershall was embellished with a nearby college of seven priests and six choristers. Arundel College, founded by the Earl of Arundel in 1406, and Fotheringay College, founded by Edmund, Duke of York, in 1412, are other examples of a common type. Some of the finest were intended especially as learned foundations. They greatly enriched the resources of English education and established a new pattern in schools and universities. New College, Oxford, founded in 1379 by William of Wykeham, Bishop of Winchester, and designed by the mason William of Wynford who also did the new work at Wykeham's cathedral, was a new departure, lavish both in buildings and in maintenance for scholars. It was imitated by Archbishop Chichele's All Souls in 1438 and Bishop Waynflete of Winchester's Magdalen in 1448. Magdalen has one of the finest of English towers. In 1446 Henry VI began the building of King's College, Cambridge, whose huge chapel is in some ways the fullest expression of the late perpendicular style. Wykeham also founded a new kind of school, Winchester College, on a collegiate basis, with provision for seventy scholars (Plate 14). This again was imitated in Henry VI's Eton and in other foundations.

Finally the end of the Middle Ages saw the building and rebuilding of parish churches on a more lavish scale than ever before. These depended less on the beneficence of individual magnates and bishops and more on the common wealth of parish communities. Church wardens' accounts occasionally survive to show how the money was raised from parishioners' contributions. There are many fifteenth-century churches up and down the country. Some of the finest are concentrated in two rich cloth and wool areas: Suffolk in the east and Gloucestershire and Somerset in the west. St Michael's in the cloth town of Coventry, St Mary Redcliffe in the port of Bristol, the churches at Northleach, in the heart of the Cotswold wool country, and Lavenham, the centre of the Suffolk cloth industry, are all examples of building on a grand scale supported by rich communities, which had benefited, as the cathedrals and abbeys had not, from the economic changes of the later Middle Ages.

CHAPTER NINE

RICHARD II AND HENRY IV

(1) THE AGE OF JOHN OF GAUNT

THE thirteen-sixties were an unusually peaceful time in English politics. Edward III, rich with the spoils of war and with the ransom of John of France flowing into his treasury, was undemanding and the new danger that was to come at the end of his reign from France had not yet made itself felt. In 1362 the King's sons, Lionel of Antwerp, John of Gaunt, and Edmund Langley, were made Duke of Clarence, Duke of Lancaster, and Earl of Cambridge, and liberally endowed, like the Black Prince, with grants of land to maintain the lustre of the royal family. Relations with parliaments were on the whole peaceful. The King was enjoying the rewards of prowess. But the thirteen-seventies were quite different. The revived French monarchy under Charles V recovered most of the territory ceded to Edward at Brétigny, and England was on the defensive for most of the rest of the century (see ch. 10). The death of Queen Philippa in 1369 was also an important factor in the collapse of morale at the court. Soon Edward was not only too old to fight or lead but also dominated by Alice Perrers, the most ambitious and unscrupulous of royal mistresses. The group which scandalously controlled the court in the last years of the reign was led by Alice and by William Latimer, an old soldier who had become Chamberlain after making his reputation and his fortune in Brittany. They were befriended by John of Gaunt, now the chief prince of the blood after the early death of Clarence in 1366 and the sickness of both Edward, and the Black Prince who died in 1376, a year before his father.

As the military and financial situation deteriorated, the court made strenuous efforts to get more money out of the Church. It is difficult to know how far the distinctly anti-clerical policy of these years (see above, p. 173) was designed

182

to win favour with the Commons in parliament; how far it reflected enmity resulting from heavy taxation of the clergy and financial jealousy; how far it was a matter of personalities. It first appeared clearly in the attitude of Lords and Commons in the parliament of 1371, when William of Wykeham was dismissed from the Chancellorship. Wykeham, later to be the founder of New College and Winchester, was the greatest of royal clerks, the most successful of all those in medieval England who followed the road from the office desk to high prelacy. Rising through his judicious administration of the rebuilding of Edward III's much-loved Windsor Castle, he had eventually become Bishop in 1366, Chancellor in 1367, and the most trusted of advisers. His fall was a break with the old order of things. In 1374 and after, the court was negotiating hotly with the Pope about their respective rights to tax the English clergy, and it was at this time that John Wycliffe entered the service of John of Gaunt as an anti-clerical propagandist.

Apart from the great men of the land it is probable that many others resented the scandal and waste at court in the context of military failure. The materials of political crisis were at hand. The scandal blew up in what was known as the 'Good' Parliament of 1376. The Commons, led by the Speaker, Sir Peter de la Mare, attacked the court party openly, though without mentioning Lancaster, on the two counts of conspiring to lend the King money at high interest rates and criminally losing English territory in Brittany. It seems probable that the courtiers had in fact borrowed money on behalf of the King for high premiums which they shared themselves, that they had sold licences for evasion of the Staple, and that they had negotiated with the French behind the backs of English soldiers fighting in Brittany. There was also a mass of general and personal resentment. It was a dramatic moment when the mere knight, Peter de la Mare, stepped up before the magnates, including John of Gaunt, in Westminster Hall, to accuse the King's evil councillors, but it seems probable that he was securely backed by many of the magnates, some bishops, and London merchants who had been offended by the court's manipulation of the wool trade and their association with the financier, Richard Lyons. Latimer

183

and Lyons were condemned by impeachment—indicted by the whole Commons before the Lords as judges—and Alice Perrers was driven from the court.

The Good Parliament initiated a period, from 1376 to 1381, in which, more clearly than at any other time in the Middle Ages, social conflicts found expression in high politics, against a background of military failure and divided leadership. Conflicts of interest, intensified by the social upheavals following the Black Death, were strong enough for a time to break into the world traditionally dominated by courtiers, bishops, and magnates. Several factors conspired to keep the country on the brink of radical divisions. The landed gentry, now feeling the full force of the population decline, were less willing than ever to pay taxes and more anxious to shift the burden on to the clergy or the peasantry. The war was consistently dangerous and seemed badly handled. During the minority of Richard II there was no adult king to give a lead and no one statesman who commanded enough respect to take the place of a king, so politics were a matter of conflicting factions. John of Gaunt, orthodox as he was in doctrine, flirted dangerously with Wycliffe and might have caused a Protestant reformation if he had not ceased to use Wycliffe after 1378. Lollardy and the Peasants' Revolt had little lasting effect, but they must be seen in part as products of a general ferment which deeply affected politics and was not far from causing a total upheaval of the kind that occurred later in Hus's Bohemia or Luther's Germany. The English magnates, disputing for influence at court and command of military expeditions, were playing on top of a minor volcano and they were lucky to escape an eruption.

The purge effected by the Good Parliament lasted only a few months, for as in the reign of Edward II it proved impossible to control the court from without. By the end of the year the scoundrels were all back, Wykeham's lands were confiscated, and Alice Perrers was at the King's bedside to slip the rings from his fingers when he died in June 1377. John of Gaunt dominated a parliament at the beginning of 1377 in which the first poll tax was granted. At the same time a clerical convocation was being held, in which Wykeham was defended and Wycliffe attacked, and, when the latter came to answer charges against him in St Paul's, supported by John of Gaunt's armed men, the London mob were incited to march on Gaunt's manor at the Savoy. It is difficult to disentangle the confused passions of anti-clericalism and hatred of the court in these proceedings.

The King's death affected the pattern of influence at court more radically than a parliament could. Most of those courtiers whose positions had depended on his friendship now disappeared. John of Gaunt remained the most powerful individual, because of his rank, as the new king's eldest uncle, claimant to the throne of Castile, and the possessor of the huge Lancastrian inheritance. Richard II, the Black Prince's son, was a boy; and the most influential person in his court, until her death in 1385, was probably his mother, Joan of Kent. Court offices were filled by knights from the Black Prince's household, such as the King's tutor, Sir Simon Burley. Gaunt found his position somewhat weakened. A council representing various parties and not dominated by Gaunt was set up for the King's minority. Gaunt had to contend with the opposition of bishops, especially Wykeham and William Courtenay (Bishop of London 1375–81, Archbishop of Canterbury 1381–96), who emerged as a formidable defender of the Church, and effectively prevented Wycliffism from gaining a serious foothold. There were powerful magnates who were jealous of Gaunt's desire to control military policy, especially his brother, Thomas of Woodstock (Earl of Buckingham, created Duke of Gloucester in 1385) and the wealthy Earl of Arundel. Finally the leading merchants of London took more than their usual interest in politics during this period of naval threats, and their control of customs and loans enabled them to exert some influence. The first parliament of the new reign in 1377 took the unusual step of insisting that the taxes it granted should be put into the hands of two merchants as treasurers of war (William Walworth and John Philpot, both prominent in the politics of this period), to ensure that the money was spent for the proper purposes. In 1378 a parliament was held at Gloucester, probably, as at other times when it met outside Westminster, to keep clear of the influence of the Londoners. A body of men from the court had broken sanctuary at Westminster Abbey to recover a prisoner, and

185

Wycliffe appeared in parliament to defend the lay power against the argument of the bishops that sacrilege had been committed by the violation of sanctuary and the shedding of blood in the abbey. The conflicting aims of various groups, without a clear lead, made the politics of the early years of the reign particularly confused. Two themes, however, stand out. Firstly, there was the overriding necessity of defence against France; secondly, the need to extract money for the expeditions from a series of unwilling parliaments. In 1377, 1379, and 1380 the Commons, instead of the usual lay subsidies and customs, which were being fully exploited, voted poll taxes at a fixed rate on individuals instead of on their property. The last of these provoked the Revolt of June 1381.

After the Revolt, magnates and parliaments returned to the old intractable problems of war. The dispute between those who wished to attack France directly and those who wished to go with Gaunt to Castile ('The way of Flanders' and 'The way of Portugal') was acute before and after the Bishop of Norwich's crusade. But now the King was growing up. In 1382 he was married to Anne of Bohemia, a happy marriage though it was made to cement an alliance. Soon Richard's personality began to dominate the political scene.

(2) RICHARD II

Richard II made no formal announcement of his majority until 1389 but, long before that, his personality had become the most important factor in English politics. This much is clear. Just what his personality was is much more difficult to determine. Richard is the most enigmatic of the kings of England. He was certainly one of the many kings unfitted to rule; he was hated and unsuccessful. But he was not predominantly either a capricious tyrant, like John, or an unrealistic aesthete, like Henry III, or a lover of unworthy favourites, like Edward II, though he had streaks of all these in his character. It is possible, and perhaps right, to discern a constant policy in his actions, a policy of abandoning the endless war with France and exalting the independent power of the king at home above his magnates, and he has sometimes been regarded as a benevolent despot before his time. It is also true that he was sometimes impulsively violent, as in his quarrels with John of Gaunt in 1384 and 1385, his murder of Thomas of Woodstock in 1397, or his bitter anger in striking Arundel in the face at Queen Anne's funeral; and what must impress the historian most of all is the extraordinary lack of political realism in a man otherwise so intelligent and sensitive. A love of peace, a disdain for the crude and brutal magnates, though they were his natural counsellors by all accepted tradition, and a tenacious preference for his own circle of friends whom the nobles despised, might seem amiable enough characteristics in a man; but in a king, unless he was supremely powerful and efficient, which Richard was not, they necessarily led to strife, and, if he was vindictive into the bargain, to political suicide.

The most important and offensive of the King's friends in the early years were Michael de la Pole and Robert de Vere, Earl of Oxford. Pole, the son of the great merchant, became Chancellor in 1383. He may have climbed to this position as the associate of Lancaster, but later his connection with the King was closer, and he was made Earl of Suffolk with a large estate in 1385. De Vere was a young man, a close personal friend of the King who showed his love by giving him the novel title of Marquess in 1385, then by making him Duke of Ireland in the next year. As Richard grew towards manhood he kept increasingly to the circle of the court and made enemies outside. At the beginning of 1385 we hear rumours of a plot by the King and his friends to do away with John of Gaunt. About the same time Richard was rebuked by the Earl of Arundel for his bad advisers, and by Archbishop Courtenay for his high-handed ways. He had been exhorted to lead an army in war, but his only venture of this kind for many a year was the expedition which he led with Gaunt to Scotland in 1385, the last summoning of the feudal host. When the army reached a deserted Edinburgh, Richard turned on Gaunt for wishing to lead them on into starvation, and took them back. In 1386 Gaunt at last went off on his long-awaited expedition to Spain. The King was left alone with his courtiers and magnates and the first reckoning came in the 'Wonderful' Parliament of October that year. Since 1383 little or nothing had been done to counter the threatening power of Philip the

Bold of Burgundy and the parliament met under the shadow of a recent invasion scare. A French fleet had massed at Sluys and only bad luck and dissension had prevented it from sailing, and the English defences had been bungled. Soon after the opening of parliament, Lords and Commons, with menacing references to Edward II, demanded the removal of Pole, and eventually he was replaced as Chancellor by Thomas of Arundel, Bishop of Ely and brother of the Earl of Arundel. Then the Commons proceeded to an impeachment of Pole, chiefly on the grounds of corruptly using his office for profit and neglecting defence against France. He was imprisoned and a continual council, including Thomas of Woodstock, the Earl of Arundel, and several bishops, imposed upon the King.

Richard had no intention of submitting for long to this indignity. Soon after the parliament Pole was restored to favour. The King set off on a long perambulation of the Midlands, which occupied most of 1387, and at Nottingham in August he questioned his judges about the validity of the parliamentary proceedings. He got from them the reply that the imposition of the council and the impeachment of Pole without his permission were contrary to his prerogative, and that the authors of such actions or of any other interference with his prerogative were criminals. In the political context these opinions seemed near to an assertion of absolute royal power. By November Richard had collected an army in Cheshire with the intention of proceeding against his enemies, while Thomas of Woodstock and the Earls of Arundel and Warwick had also assembled retinues near London to defend themselves. But they met the King in Westminster Hall to demand the impeachment of the offensive favourites and Richard had to agree to the summoning of a parliament for February 1388. In the interval before the parliament de Vere raised an army in the royal earldom of Cheshire (attempts to raise support in many other shires had met with the sheriffs' reply that the Commons stood with the Lords) and marched towards London. He was intercepted by the rebels, now joined by the Earl of Nottingham and Henry Bolingbroke, Earl of Derby (John of Gaunt's son, called 'Bolingbroke' after his father's castle in Lincolnshire, where he was born), and defeated in battle at Radcot Bridge in Oxfordshire. The rebels then returned to London and demanded satisfaction from the King. Frightened by threats of deposition, he was forced to imprison or banish a number of his favourite courtiers and replace them with officials appointed by the rebels. When the 'Merciless' Parliament met in February 1388 the King found himself defenceless and the rebels were able to proceed to their main purpose. This time they abandoned the method of impeachment by the Commons and used the more direct procedure of 'appealing' the accused in parliament of treason. The 'appellants' were Thomas of Woodstock, Bolingbroke, Arundel, Warwick, and Nottingham. Their victims included, besides Pole and de Vere, the Archbishop of York, several of the King's justices, Nicholas Brembre, a leading London merchant who had been in league with the court, and the King's old tutor, Simon Burley. Brembre and Burley were executed, Pole and de Vere died in exile. Richard's circle of friends was finally shattered.

The nine years from 1388 to 1397 were relatively peaceful. The appellants had done their worst and Richard was for the time being cowed. He allowed them a place in government and Thomas of Woodstock in particular took a large place. For many years there was no sign of serious strife. Richard seems gradually to have built up a circle of supporters wider and more moderate than the court faction of earlier years. The return of John of Gaunt from Spain in 1389 brought back a stabilising factor in politics. Richard remained on good terms with him and with Bolingbroke. Gaunt's rights as Duke of Lancaster were even enlarged and in 1396 his bastard children by Katherine Swynford, the Beauforts, destined to play a momentous part in history in the fifteenth century, were legitimised. The King was also on good terms with Thomas Mowbray, Earl of Nottingham, and with his half-brothers, John and Thomas Holand. But, though no deep divisions were apparent, there were some incidents which suggested Richard's restive discontent breaking through the calm. In 1389 he suddenly declared himself of full age and free to exercise his kingly rights without restraint. In 1392 a quarrel with London over the refusal of the city to lend him money ended in his annulling its liberties, to restore them for a large fine. The death of Queen Anne in 1394 contributed greatly to his melancholy and introspection and, when Arundel, his most implacable enemy, arrived late at the funeral at Westminster, Richard struck him down for the insult.

It is impossible to know exactly what dreams of grandeur and revenge the King had in these years, but some of the evidence suggests that he was moved by unusual fantasies. He appealed to the Pope for the canonisation of Edward II, whom he must have imagined as a king similarly wronged. The invasion of Ireland, the plans to help his new ally, the King of France, in an invasion of Italy, the plans for his own election as King of Germany, which led him to spend considerable sums in bribing the electors—all these were outside the usual policies of the kings of England at this period. The desire for complete revenge is clearer, because the King's actions in 1397 and 1398 seem like the execution of a plan to reverse completely and artistically the wrongs which had been done him in the 'Merciless' Parliament. He began quite unexpectedly in July 1397 with the arrest of the three chief appellants, Woodstock, Arundel, and Warwick. In a parliament in September they were 'appealed' and condemned in the same way as they had treated the King's friends in 1388. Woodstock had already been murdered at Calais, Arundel was executed, Warwick banished, Thomas of Arundel, now Archbishop of Canterbury, likewise banished. It is important not to underestimate the enormity of this sudden outburst. Woodstock and Arundel were among the very greatest men and the banishment of the Primate was a rare offence. Many estates fell into the King's hands and were largely redistributed amongst new earls, whose creation greatly altered the English peerage: Thomas Despenser, Earl of Gloucester, Ralph Neville of Westmorland, Thomas Percy of Worcester, and William Scrope of Wiltshire. Others, whom he regarded as his best friends amongst his relations, became new dukes: Bolingbroke, the Holands, and Edmund Langley's son, Edward, while John Beaufort was made Marquis of Dorset.

The next stage was carried through at a parliament at Shrewsbury in January 1398. Richard had been impatient of parliamentary criticism a year earlier, when he had imprisoned Thomas Haxey, who was acting as proctor for the Abbot of Selby, for criticising the expenditure of the royal household.

Now he seemed to be aiming to free himself entirely from parliament. The definition of treason was extended, customs were granted for life instead of the usual period of one or two years, and a committee appointed to continue the business of the parliament after its dissolution. In September 1398 a quarrel between Bolingbroke and the Duke of Norfolk (Nottingham in 1388) gave the King an excuse to banish both of the remaining appellants. Lately they had been honoured as his friends, but now Bolingbroke accused Nottingham of plotting to avoid the fate of the other appellants. For whatever reason, Richard chose to be rid of them both. The revenge was complete.

In the last two years of his life Richard moved rapidly towards political madness. He strengthened his permanent army of Cheshire archers. He tried to wreak revenge on the commons of the shires by fining them, since they had failed to support him in 1387. He went further in his assault on the nobility, and it was this last step which cost him the throne. When John of Gaunt died in February 1399, Bolingbroke, his eldest son, was his rightful heir, but the whole of the vast Lancastrian inheritance was taken into the King's hands. In the same summer, while Richard was making his second expedition to Ireland, Bolingbroke landed in Yorkshire with the avowed intention of recovering his inheritance by force. He was quickly joined in the north by Henry Percy, Earl of Northumberland, and Ralph Neville, Earl of Westmorland, and, as he came south, the Duke of York, uncle to the King and keeper of the realm in Richard's absence, came over to the rebels. At what stage Bolingbroke revealed his full intention we do not know, but it must have been clear in August when Richard, who had come back from Ireland, only to find himself deserted, surrendered at Conway. The King's abdication was presented to a parliament at Westminster on 29th September. It is hard to say how enthusiastic the Commons were, for they had little choice in the presence of Bolingbroke's armed men. The next day the King was deposed on the strength of a long list of his misdeeds. Bolingbroke then stood up and claimed the crown by right of descent as Henry IV. Richard died in prison early the following year, though legends of his survival encouraged rebels for some years after.

So began the sixty-one years of the Lancastrian dynasty. The glories of that line, as contemporaries saw them, were chiefly concentrated in the reign of Henry V. Bolingbroke was never again so successful as in the audacious stroke which won him the kingdom, and his reign, though we tend to forget this because of his son's unchallenged leadership, was troubled and insecure. His own character was a complete contrast with the high-handed unconventionality of Richard, but he inherited some of Richard's difficulties, particularly in relations with France, and acquired several new ones. Few people wanted to restore Richard II and the proceedings of the parliaments suggest that Lords and Commons were mostly content to have Henry IV as king. The only serious plot in favour of Richard, hatched by four of his favourites among the nobility, who had benefited from his seizures of other magnates' lands in the last years of the reign, was quickly suppressed and the leaders killed in January 1400. Richard had no children, but the fact that Henry was a usurper and that there were living representatives of the Mortimer family, whom Richard had declared heirs to the throne, gave a plausible excuse to rebels.

Serious trouble began, however, in an unexpected quarter. Some of the gentry of the Welsh Marches had suffered for following Richard II in his last years. One of these was Owen Glyndwr, a landowner in the valley of the Dee, descended from the ancient Welsh nobility, who turned his personal grievances into a revolt against English rule in the autumn of 1400, and assumed the title of Prince of Wales. The rebellion was astonishingly successful. The reasons for its success are probably to be found in widespread resentment against the English exploitation of Welsh tenants, carried on by the Marcher lords in their various lordships and similarly by the Crown in the Principality. In this sense it was perhaps partly the Welsh counterpart to the Peasants' Revolt. At any rate it spread rapidly to the greater part of Wales, Principality and lordships, and English control was either removed or reduced to the holding of isolated castles for much of the first decade of the century. The Glyndwr revolt was not in itself a serious threat to England, nor did it involve great military enterprises, but it was a running sore and an encouragement to other enemies for much of Henry IV's reign.

It began to have wider implications in 1402. An invasion by Henry himself, with the young Prince Henry and the Earl of Arundel, failed to put down the rebellion, and in the same year Glyndwr captured Sir Edmund Mortimer, the uncle of the Earl of March. Disgruntled by Henry's failure to ransom him, Mortimer joined the rebels. The worst trouble began in 1403. Henry's chief assistant in his own rebellion had been Henry Percy, Earl of Northumberland. Since 1399 Northumberland had become a great man in the kingdom, especially in the north, and added to his fame, and to that of his son Henry Hotspur, also a famous soldier, by defeating a Scots army at Homildon Hill in 1402. The King, however, had annoyed them by his refusal to ransom Mortimer, who was Hotspur's brother-in-law, by his demand that they should give up the Scots prisoners captured at Homildon Hill, and by his unwillingness or inability to pay all the money due to them as Wardens of the Scots Marches. They must also have hoped to repeat the success which they had had in the revolution of 1399.[1] In 1403 the Percies suddenly joined Glyndwr and Mortimer, agreeing with them on a fantastic scheme to partition England, and alleging Henry's usurpation as the justification for rising. The rebellion spread to south Wales and Cheshire. The King quickly took an army westwards and defeated them and killed Hostspur at the battle of Shrewsbury, a setback from which the fortunes of the Percy family did not fully recover until the Tudor period. This was not the end of the business, however. The war continued to go badly in Wales. In 1404 Glyndwr received encouragement and even a little military assistance from a French landing at Milford Haven. In 1405 Northumberland revived his treaty with Glyndwr and Mortimer. This time he was joined by a rising of some other northern magnates. They were defeated quickly at Shipton Moor, but Northumberland was still at large, though out of England, and it was not until 1408, when he was defeated and killed at Bramham Moor, that the danger in the north was really ended.

1. J. M. W. Bean, 'Henry IV and the Percies', *History* (1959)

These rebellions occurred against a background of persistent strife with France, which loomed larger in the frequent parliaments of the reign than the troubles at home. In the years 1403–6 the safety of English trade in the Channel and at Calais was threatened (see p. 200). This was really a much more important matter than the French league with Glyndwr. In most of the parliaments from 1401 to 1406 Henry was subjected to outspoken criticism on the two matters of naval defence and administration of money. The Commons, perhaps more active than ever before, were extremely insistent on their control of taxation and went to unusual lengths. They urged the king to restrict the expenses of his household, and to recover royal lands which had been granted away, and insisted on nominated councils with defined powers. This criticism was not based on any sympathy with Percy or Glyndwr, and the councillors appointed in parliament were mostly drawn from the King's own supporters, some of them administrators in the Duchy of Lancaster. There was no parallel with the opposition to Richard II. But it did mean that the Crown was harried on yet another front.

In the last years of the reign, from about 1408, the character of politics was affected by different factors. By this time the most urgent military dangers from France, Glyndwr, and the Percies had subsided. But Bolingbroke, now a broken man in health and spirit, declining towards his early death, was beset by the quarrels and opposition of his own relations. The most prominent was his son, Henry, Prince of Wales, already showing himself masterful and ambitious. Also becoming prominent were the Beaufort family, the legitimised progeny of John of Gaunt, represented in this reign by the King's three half-brothers, Henry Beaufort (Bishop of Lincoln, then of Winchester, and later Cardinal), John, Earl of Somerset (died 1410), and Thomas, Earl of Dorset. Apart from the Prince's ambition to take his father's place, the grounds of these quarrels are not clear. In 1409 the Prince assisted Oxford University to resist the inquisition into Lollardy proposed by the King's Chancellor and most substantial supporter, Archbishop Arundel. At a parliament in 1410 Arundel was replaced as Chancellor by Thomas Beaufort and a new council, headed by the Prince, was nominated. In 1411, while the

Prince was trying to seize the opportunity offered by divisions in France to intervene there, his father was trying to preserve peace. Henry IV seems, in that year, to have recovered control of his own government, but twice in 1412 the Prince came to London with a retinue, apparently aiming to assert himself by force. The power which Bolingbroke had usurped in 1399 was slipping from his hands before he died in March 1413.

CHAPTER TEN

THE HUNDRED YEARS' WAR 1361–1453

(1) ENGLAND AND FRANCE, 1361–1413

ENGLISH soldiers enjoyed two periods of overwhelming success in France under the warrior kings Edward III and Henry V in the years 1343–61 and 1415–22. The victories of these periods were separated by an even longer stretch of time in which the French kings recovered control of their country, forced England into a defensive attitude, and occasionally threatened invasion. The reason for these changes of fortune lies clearly enough in the characters of the kings. Henry V, like Edward III in his prime, had the gift of leadership which gave military strength and unity. Edward III in his senility and his grandsons Richard II and Henry IV had not. In Charles V of France (1364–80) and his brother Philip the Bold (Duke of Burgundy 1364–1404, and the effective military leader in France after Charles's death) they faced leaders with just the qualities of strength which they lacked. Military failure itself bred disunity in the world of jealous solider magnates and, throughout this period of the Hundred Years' War, English politics at home were deeply affected by the continual sense of military inadequacy which the continual kings were powerless to remove.

The gains of Brétigny melted like snow before the recovery of the French monarchy under Charles V. The process started seriously with revolts of Gascon nobles against the rule of the Black Prince as Duke of Aquitaine. When the Prince had refused to appear in Paris to answer charges brought against him, Charles V was free to invade Gascony in 1369. The Black Prince was entering on the decline in health which ended in his premature death. Edward III was declining into old age. Neither was competent any longer to lead a military expedition and the English attempts to reply were all failures.

There was an abortive expedition from Calais into northern France under the great captain, Sir Robert Knollys, in 1370. In 1373 John of Gaunt led his army in an enormous march through France from one English foothold at Calais to another at Bordeaux, which did much damage but yielded no permanent political advantage. Worst of all, a fleet carrying reinforcements to Gascony, under the Earl of Pembroke, was defeated by Castilian ships off La Rochelle in 1372 and the Earl himself captured. By 1375, when a truce was made at Bruges, the French reconquest was largely completed; the English hold on France was reduced once more to Calais, a strip around Bordeaux, and some footholds in the harbours of Brittany which were held grimly for many years.

An important shift in English foreign affairs resulted from the Black Prince's last great expedition, his invasion of Castile in 1367 in support of Pedro the Cruel, who had been ousted from the throne by the French-supported Henry of Trastamara. Though the Prince won his last important battle at Najera, he did not succeed in restoring Pedro permanently. The expedition had two important results. Firstly, England faced for some years an alliance of France and Castile, which brought the formidable Castilian navy into the Channel, gave the French and Spaniards control of the seas, and made possible raids on the south coast, spreading fears of invasion which filled the period 1377–80 with alarm. Secondly, the Black Prince's brother, John of Gaunt, married Pedro's daughter, Constance, in 1371, styled himself King of Castile, and, for some part of the minority of Richard II, when he was the most important single individual in English politics, hankered after a great invasion of Castile to make good his claim. The plan was not much supported by other Englishmen but he eventually carried it out with some modest success in 1386–9.

These circumstances are important for our understanding of the gloom and division in the country which contributed to the crises of the Good Parliament (1376) and the Peasants' Revolt (1381). Paying for war was even more unpopular when war seemed to be mishandled. The activity of these years centred largely on the Channel and on Brittany, where the English still had some territory but the Castilian ships were based on harbours in French hands. The war was brought home to Englishmen, accustomed to view it with detachment across the Channel, when the French burnt Rye and Gravesend in 1377. In 1378 John of Gaunt retaliated by trying to capture St Malo. In 1379 another expedition to Brittany was shipwrecked before it arrived. The most ambitious of these efforts was a lengthy march, led by Thomas of Woodstock, Earl of Buckingham, in a great circle round Paris and back to Brittanny at the end of 1380. This was the immediate military background to the Poll Tax and the Peasants' Revolt.

Charles V died in 1380, and with him the active Franco-Castilian alliance, but the situation in France did not develop to England's advantage. Charles V was succeeded as England's main enemy by Philip the Bold, the leading figure at the French court for more than two decades and the creator of the Duchy of Burgundy, embracing the Low Countries and eastern France, which was to last until 1477. The beginning of the Great Schism in 1378 gave the opportunity for an alliance against the French-supported Clement VII, in which England played a leading part. The marriage of Richard II to Anne of Bohemia in 1382 was a part of this design. Ecclesiastical and secular politics were mixed, with scandalous and, as it turned out, disastrous indifference, in the Bishop of Norwich's crusade in 1383. The Flemish towns had risen again, as in the days of Artevelde, to resist French influence, this time in the person of Philip the Bold, claiming the succession to the last independent Count of Flanders. The English merchants, as in the thirteen-forties, were anxious to preserve their commercial link by keeping Flanders as far as possible an English rather than a French sphere of influence. A plan was evolved to send a crusade, paid for by ecclesiastical money and commanded by the warlike Henry Despenser, Bishop of Norwich, to defend Flanders against the supporters of the Avignon Pope. Commercial, political, and ecclesiastical aims could all be furthered at once. It was done, but the expedition broke up ignominiously owing to its divided aims and inefficiency. The crusade was the last serious effort against France on land for many years. Flanders capitulated to Philip the Bold.

Thereafter the war with France gradually petered out. There were fears of French invasion from Flanders in 1385 and 1386, which came to nothing. There was piracy in the Channel, in paricular an expedition by the Earl of Arundel in 1387 which acquired fame because he captured a wine fleet. There were no substantial expeditions on land. In 1386 John of Gaunt set off at last on his much-planned journey to Spain with royal blessings and royal money. He returned in 1389 without the crown, but bought off with pensions which enabled him to spend the last decade of his life in England, rich, honoured, and old. The English footholds in France continued to be precariously held, without much loss or gain of territory, for nearly thirty years. Relations with France were immediately and constantly important to two groups of people; to the merchants, who wanted to keep open the vital sea-links with Bordeaux and Flanders and were therefore anxious for naval defence and protection of Bordeaux and Calais, and to the magnates and soldiers, who hankered for profitable expeditions on the French mainland. Richard II and Henry IV, the former from choice and the second from necessity, failed on the whole to satisfy these groups. Richard, from 1385 effective ruler of England, seems to have adopted a deliberate policy of conciliating the dangerous power of France, preferring to be friendly with a court which dazzled him and attracted him more than his own circle of warlike nobility. Though there were expeditions at sea and constant haggling for the rest of his reign, the truces were in the main respected on land and in 1396, after the death of Queen Anne, Richard sealed a long-term peace and a contract to marry Isabella, the child daughter of Charles VI. He visited France in that year to indulge his tastes in an elaborate ceremonial meeting with Charles VI and to take home his new queen. Rightly or wrongly Richard preferred to fight in Ireland rather than in France. His expedition there in 1394–5, if not the most ambitious military enterprise of his reign, was the one in which he took the most interest, and he was in Ireland again when the fateful landing of Bolingbroke took place in 1399.

Bolingbroke's accession upset the *entente* with France, for it involved the deposition of the French King's daughter. As a somewhat insecure usurper Henry IV was anxious not to add to his enemies and it was the French who took the initiative in threats, even after Isabella had been honourably returned to her family. As Henry's troubles at home grew in 1403 and 1404, with the rebellions of Glyndwr and the Percies, the French harried him in the Channel. In 1403 Plymouth was burned. Next year the French landed on the Isle of Wight and made a formal alliance with Glyndwr, and in the winter of 1405–6 a small French force was landed at Milford Haven to give direct assistance to the Welsh rising. In 1406 an attack on Calais was expected. This phase of the Hundred Years' War which recalled the situation of the early years of Richard II, with its sense of national emergency created by the threats in the Channel and at Calais, ended in 1407 as the rift in France between the parties of Burgundy and Orleans grew. Towards the end of Henry's reign the forty years of French revival and ascendancy were closing and political fortune smiled on the newly established House of Lancaster.

(2) THE ENGLISH CONQUEST OF NORMANDY, 1413–22

In the peaceful latter end of the fifteenth century Englishmen looked back with wonder at the great feats of their fathers in the reign of Henry V, which followed with sudden glory the humiliations of Bolingbroke, and they regretted the decay of English arms. The achievements were indeed remarkable, but the circumstances were also very lucky. The English victory was won against a France which was split by a feud within its nobility, and the victor was a young, toughly ambitious soldier king, who happened to appear at just the right moment to take advantage of French weakness. France was ruled by an old, mad king, Charles VI (1380–1422). The leading personality in his reign until 1404 had been Philip the Bold, Duke of Burgundy, his uncle. The divisions at the end of Charles VI's reign resulted from a quarrel between the followers of Philip the Bold's son, John the Fearless (who was also the ruler of a large and wealthy state, including Burgundy, Flanders, and Brabant) and the followers of another royal prince, the Duke of Orleans (called Orleanists or Armagnacs). In 1407 Orleans was murdered by agents of Burgundy and thus began a ruinous feud in French politics, which crippled the leadership of the country for a whole generation, leaving it exposed to English invasion as it had not been since 1365.

At this time the English possessions in France were Calais and a reduced Gascony, all that had been retained through the misfortunes of the last forty years. By 1411 both sides in France were trying to get help from England. Henry IV was not anxious to interfere but Prince Henry, on his own initiative, sent a small force to help Burgundy, and this assisted in the capture of Paris. It was the beginning of the Prince's life-work of humiliating France. In 1412 his father was once again in control of affairs and responded to the overtures of the Armagnacs, who offered England restoration of losses in Gascony, by sending an army to their help under his second son, Thomas, Duke of Clarence. In 1413 Henry V succeeded to the throne and there was now no obstacle to the policy which he seems to have conceived several years earlier. He quickly revived the most extreme claims of his ancestors, demanding both the French throne and the English possessions as they had been laid down at Brétigny in 1360. France in that year was in such an upheaval, with revolution in Paris, that it might well have seemed suitable for a rapid attack. By the next year the rift was patched up somewhat, but there was in fact bitter hostility between the two factions. Henry was negotiating with both sides, secretly with Burgundy, openly with the Orleanist régime in Paris, for he proposed marriage to Charles's daughter, Catherine, even though he seems to have intended all the time to invade the country.

In April 1415 the intention was formally announced. French envoys came over in the summer in a last effort to hold him off, willing to grant the Princess's hand with a large dower and extensions of territory in Gascony, but not, of course, to come anywhere near satisfying Henry's demands for the throne or the frontiers laid down at Brétigny. While the negotiations were going on he was already at Southampton, preparing to take the army across the Channel. The crossing was put off for a time by the discovery of a plot amongst the most eminent rivals of the Lancastrian house to overthrow the King. The ringleader was the Earl of Cambridge, brother of the Duke of York, brother-in-law of the Earl of March, and the plan was to put March, the representative of the Mortimer claim, on the throne. This foreshadowed the serious Yorkist claim to the throne, which was to come to fruitition forty years later, when the son of the ringleader of 1415, uniting in himself the claims of York and Mortimer, began his bid for the throne. Luckily for the King, March quickly betrayed the conspiracy; it was nipped in the bud and the Earl of Cambridge was executed. Apart from the abortive revolt of Oldcastle in 1413, this was the only serious threat which Henry V had to meet in England. Nearly all the dukes and earls sailed with the King on his expedition, not only his brothers, Humphrey, Duke of Gloucester, and Thomas, Duke of Clarence (killed in 1421), but also such potential opponents as the Duke of York, the Earl of March, on the second occasion Northumberland (restored to his grandfather's title in 1416), and other great magnates, like Richard Beauchamp, Earl of Warwick, and Thomas Montague, Earl of Salisbury. The promise and fulfilment of the two great enterprises of 1415 and 1417 made the English nobility united as it had not been since the early days of the Garter.

In August 1415 the army sailed. It landed near Harfleur in Normandy, at the mouth of the Seine, and immediately settled down to a month-long siege of the town. After this bitter business, which cost the English a very large number of casualties by sickness, Henry set off, early in the autumn, to march, as Edward III had done seventy years previously, through Normandy to Calais. Meanwhile the French nobility were mustering their forces and gathered a very substantial army (not including the Duke of Burgundy, however) to pursue the invader. Henry was compelled to make a long detour to cross the Somme, and it was a depleted and exhausted English army which eventually met the French on 25th October at Agincourt, less than thirty miles from Crécy. In spite of the great disparity in numbers, the well-commanded English army, fighting on foot, with very few losses, inflicted a terrible and most damaging defeat on the disunited French nobility. Henry returned home in November, the greatest hero since the Black Prince after Poitiers, bringing the Duke of Orleans into a captivity which lasted twenty-five years.

The year 1416 saw a lull in the war. Henry was visited by the Holy Roman Emperor Sigismund, who was trying to unite the powers of Europe in support of the Council of the Church, now being held at Constance, and for defence against the Turks. In August there were negotiations with him and with France and Burgundy at Calais, which produced a short truce. In 1417, however, circumstances in France became again very favourable to England. The Duke of Burgundy was advancing against his enemies in Paris. This diverted French attention from Normandy and left it almost completely open to English attack. At the beginning of August Henry landed once more on the coast of Normandy. The system which he followed in this campaign, unlike the wide-ranging, mobile raids of his predecessors, was to reduce the chief fortified towns one by one and so to get a complete grip on certain areas of French territory. In eighteen months the capture of Caen, Falaise, Cherbourg, and Rouen gave him a fair hold on Normandy. Probably this would not have been possible if the Duke of Burgundy had not been simultaneously attacking the French capital on his own account. In 1418 the Duke captured Paris and with it the old King Charles VI. There were now virtually three powers controlling different parts of France: Burgundy in the north-east; Charles's heir, the Dauphin, later to be Charles VII, with the Armagnac party in the south; Henry V in Normandy.

Henry remained in France during 1419, carrying his attack in the direction of Paris, while there was a temporary reconciliation of the two native factions. The fate of France was sealed, however, in September 1419, when the Duke of Burgundy was murdered at Montereau by the Dauphin's people, in revenge for the murder of Orleans in 1407. Montereau greatly deepened the feud. It led to a rapid agreement between Henry V and the new Duke of Burgundy, Philip the Good, and was the basis of the English position in France for the next fifteen years. Having all the French royal family, except the Dauphin, under his control, Burgundy was able to give effect to the Treaty of Troyes, sealed in May 1420, by which Henry was to marry Princess Catherine and to succeed to the French throne on the death of her father, Charles VI. Henry V and Burgundy, now firm allies, spent the rest of the year in capturing Sens and Melun before entering Paris itself in December. Henry made a brief visit to England in 1421. He was back in France again in the summer of that year, determined to make his title to the French throne complete and effective by crushing the Dauphin's party, and he had begun that task successfully when he died of sickness in August 1422 at the early age of thirty-five.

(3) ENGLISH POWER IN FRANCE, 1422-53

At the time of his death Henry V had not succeeded to the throne of France, but his son did so a few months later, on the death of Charles VI, and for some years an English king ruled at Paris as well as London. The Duke of Bedford went into battle at Verneuil in 1424 with a 'banner quartered with France and England to signify the two conjoint realms'. His rule was effective over large parts of France, north of the Loire, and especially in Normandy, where the normal machinery of government was maintained, with the provincial 'estates' (the Norman parliament) meeting to vote taxes for the upkeep of the English forces. In the first years of the reign of Henry VI these extraordinary conquests were kept intact and expanded. With the revival of French power, the eventual French reconciliation with Burgundy and also the growing weakness of English leadership at home, Henry VI's inheritance was gradually wasted. The long and, from the point of view of the English nobility, dismal story of the decline of the English in France is a most essential part of the reign of Henry VI. It may be divided into four phases: firstly up to the relief of Orleans in 1429, secondly to the death of Bedford and the Treaty of Arras in 1435, thirdly to the marriage treaty of Henry VI with Margaret of Anjou in 1444, and fourthly to the final expulsion of the English in 1453.

The English government in France was entrusted to Henry V's brother, John, Duke of Bedford, who acted as regent and ruled from his castle Joyeux Repos at Rouen. He began in 1423 by securing the Treaty of Amiens with Burgundy, which confirmed Henry VI's position in France, and by himself marrying Burgundy's sister. The alliance with Burgundy was severely strained by the independent action of the other surviving brother of Henry V, Humphrey, Duke of Glouces-

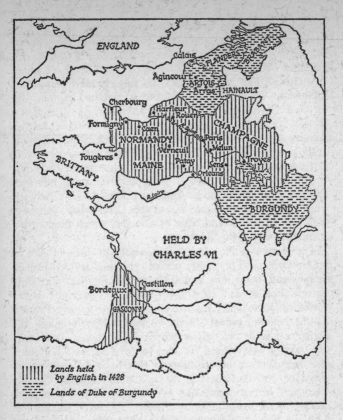

English possessions in France in 1428

ter, who accepted in marriage the heiress to the county of
Hainault, Jacqueline, although she had been married to a member of the Burgundian family whom she had abandoned.
Gloucester even carried out a brief invasion of Hainault on his
own account in 1424–5. But the personal enmity between Burgundy and Gloucester, which these events produced, did not
extend to the rest of the House of Lancaster, and the alliance
was the cornerstone of the English position for some time. The
Years 1422–8 were on the whole a period of English success, of

maintenance and extension of control in northern France. The victories were won by great nobles like Bedford, Thomas Montague, Earl of Salisbury, the most successful of the commanders, William de la Pole, Earl of Suffolk, Richard Beauchamp, Earl of Warwick, who was named Captain and Lieutenant-General in 1425; and by less exalted captains like Sir John Fastolf and John Talbot, later Earl of Shrewsbury. It was a time of great triumph and profit for the English nobility and of miserable disorder and depredation for many of the people of northern France. The English possessions were expanded in a series of campaigns culminating in Bedford's victory at Verneuil in 1424. In 1426 the advance was renewed. English and Burgundian government extended over nearly the whole of northern France above the Loire when Salisbury began in 1428 his fatal siege of Orleans, which might have opened the way to the South.

The turning-point was the appearance of Joan of Arc to relieve Orleans. The saintly peasant girl, who revived French morale and began the expulsion of the English, was only sixteen. For several years she had seen visions and heard voices which told her that she was destined to save France. At the beginning of 1429 she presented herself before the Dauphin and her incredible powers of persuasion convinced him that he was indeed the true son of Charles VI (doubts had been cast on his legitimacy), that he could recover his kingdom, and that she was the appointed instrument of his victory. When an army had been placed in her hands she quickly succeeded in relieving Orleans. Thereafter success was with the French. Fastolf had won his famous battle of the Herrings, defending a convoy of food for the besiegers of Orleans, but after the relief the English were driven northwards. In June the French triumphed at Patay, capturing Talbot himself. In July Charles VII was consecrated king in the cathedral at Rheims.

In the next year, 1430, Joan was captured by Burgundians at Compiègne; she was sold to the English and burned after trial for heresy, to which her visions and unwomanly pretensions gave some colour. But neither this outrage nor the coronation of Henry VI at Paris, also in 1431, helped to prevent the English position from gradually crumbling.

Money became harder to raise in Normandy. The English parliaments were unsympathetic and ungenerous. Worst of all the alliance with Burgundy broke down. Bedford's wife, the chief personal link, died in 1432 and Bedford himself in 1435. The Duke of Burgundy, feeling the change in the political climate, began to make friends with Charles VII. In 1435 a diplomatic congress of England, Burgundy, and France was held at Arras under the auspices of the Pope. The English delegates, after holding out for the extreme claim to the French throne, which was now becoming obviously unrealistic, walked out. In September the Duke of Burgundy made peace with France and recognised Charles VII. In 1436 the English had to leave Paris and in 1437 Charles VII made his ceremonial entry into the capital.

The dual monarchy was ended and the balance of power had changed. England was now fighting France and Burgundy, though Burgundy's Duke took little action against England after his unsuccessful attempt to capture Calais in 1436. In the next few years a number of expeditions went out from England to hold the remaining territory, and much fighting was done by these armies under Richard, Duke of York, who succeeded Bedford as Regent and then Lieutenant-General, under Richard Neville, Earl of Warwick, Edmund Beaufort, Earl of Dorset, later Duke of Somerset, and under John Talbot. But they could not stop the gradual infiltration of the French into the country between Paris and the coast. From 1438 onwards the French were also attacking English territory in Gascony. Meanwhile at home the feeling began to grow amongst the group which controlled the council that peace must be made. This movement was especially associated with the Earl of Suffolk, who had been instrumental in procuring the release of the Duke of Orleans in 1440 to return to France and act as a mediator. Finally Suffolk was able to lead an embassy to France in 1444, which made a truce and arranged the marriage of Henry VI with Margaret of Anjou, niece by marriage of Charles VII. They were married in 1445.

From 1445 to 1449 there was an uneasy truce, marred by the agreement to cede Maine to the French, which was for a long time resisted by the English forces in that area under

Dorset. In 1449 an attack by mercenaries under English command from Normandy on the town of Fougères in Brittany gave Charles VII what was probably a welcome excuse to start the war again, and this last phase began on French initiative. Rouen, the capital of Normandy, was quickly taken and Somerset's command there destroyed. The last English relief force, sent out under Sir Thomas Kyriel in 1450, was defeated with enormous losses at Formigny, Somerset himself was captured at Caen, and the last vestiges of English occupation of Normandy disappeared. Then Charles VII turned his attention to Gascony. Bordeaux itself fell in 1451 and, after reoccupation with the help of the veteran Talbot's last expedition which ended in his death at the battle of Castillon in 1452, fell finally to the French in 1453. The centuries of government by the kings of England in France—the Duchy of Normandy, the Angevin Empire, the Duchy of Aquitane, the claim to the French Crown—were at an end. Henceforth, except for the one town of Calais, which was retained for another century, kings of England ruled only on this side of the Channel.

The destruction of English power in France was in part a matter of military efficiency. The victories of Agincourt and Verneuil had been won by the superiority of English archers meeting the oncoming French knights and men-at-arms in the open field, in a manner not very different from that used at Crécy and Poitiers. In the later stages of the war the French did not allow that situation to arise again and the English were less effective in close fighting around a town as at Formigny. Artillery was beginning to be important and, though Henry V had used guns to good effect in the siege of Harfleur, the French seem to have been far superior in that arm by the middle of the century. But the main reasons for English failure were political and moral. Charles VII not only had a new spirit in himself after Orleans; he was also creating a more centralised and powerful monarchy which contrasted with the divisions and the crippling jealousy of noble factions under the weak Charles VI. This happened just at the time when the English monarchy in its turn was declining to its lowest ebb. England was ruled by magnates and bishops who gave no clear lead in policy, and parliaments refused to pay as they had paid for the victories of Henry V. Henry VI of England was the grandson of Charles VI of France. Perhaps his intellectual and physical weakness, which lost the inheritance in France, owed something to that other legacy.

CHAPTER ELEVEN

THE WARS OF THE ROSES

(1) THE AGE OF BEAUFORT AND GLOUCESTER

WHEN Henry V died his only son was a baby of nine months. The longest minority in English history was then followed by one of the most tragic reigns. During the minority it was natural that the kingdom should be ruled by the leading magnates, but it was most unnatural that the ending of the minority in 1437 should make no difference to this state of affairs. Henry proved to be the exact opposite of his father, a pious well-intentioned recluse and, later in life, weak-minded. His best memorial is King's College Chapel at Cambridge. He hated war and had no capacity for politics, and he was managed from beginning to end, first by his uncles and then by his domineering and clever wife. He reigned negatively for nearly forty years and spent another decade in exile and imprisonment, seeing the complete ruin of the dynasty which had been the mightiest in Europe at his birth. We shall have little to say of his own actions, but his complete nonentity as a king was the leading factor in English politics in the mid-fifteenth century.

The later part of his reign was an age of revolution, but the greater part of it was relatively free from violent internal upheavals. Perhaps the most important reason for this was that the best energies of many of the most able and powerful of the English magnates, such men as Richard Beauchamp and Richard Neville, Earls of Warwick, and Richard, Duke of York, who might otherwise have taken a disruptive part in politics at home, were absorbed by the war in France. Political conflicts were relatively peaceful and circumscribed. The first part of the reign was dominated by three forceful noble-men of the royal blood. John, Duke of Bedford, the King's uncle, was the most respected, an efficient soldier and administrator, who maintained English power in France for most of the minority. Humphrey, Duke of Gloucester, his other uncle, on the contrary, was an adventurous soldier and a great patron of literature, lacking in political finesse and no match in this respect for his more solid relations, but a powerfully turbulent figure in English politics for a quarter of a century. Henry Beaufort, Bishop of Winchester, the King's great-uncle and a son of John of Gaunt, is a more baffling character. Henry V prevented him from becoming cardinal but he achieved that ambition later. He showed great interest in the ecclesiastical diplomacy of Europe—in the wars against the Hussites for which he tried to raise an English army in 1428, and in the Council of Basle. Perhaps he would have preferred to spend his life in the ecclesiastical councils or at the papal court. But, though it is doubtful whether the lay politics of England were his chosen career, he had an unrivalled experience in them dating at least from 1404, when he had first been Chancellor, to his death in 1447. His enigmatic figure broods over English history for a great part of the reign of Henry VI. He exercised a laborious and skilful devotion in the duty which was thrust upon him by his eminence in the royal family. The great wealth placed in his hands by his long tenure of the see of Winchester enabled him to make indispensable loans to the Crown over a longer period than any other medieval financier. It is difficult to know whether he stayed in power because it allowed him to arrange his loans so profitably for himself, or whether he lent money because there was no other way to keep the ship of state afloat. Perhaps both explanations are true.

The constitution, within which the government was to be carried on during the minority, was settled in the November parliament of 1422. The title of Regent was refused to Gloucester, whom nearly everyone mistrusted; he was to govern under a nominated council of lords, bishops, and ministers and was to be Protector of the realm only when Bedford was out of England. Bedford was the most acceptable ruler, but his continual absence in France left English politics to the other councillors and to the long duel between Beaufort and Gloucester. Beaufort had been Bishop of the rich see of Winchester since 1405; he was also one of the trustees of the Duchy of Lancaster. He was therefore in command of vast sums of money which were urgently needed for the carrying-on of the government in a period which saw a sharp decline in the willingness of parliament to make grants. Gloucester was poorly endowed with lands and always short of money himself, and in the long run the combination of Beaufort's financial indispensability with his superior political skill always won. Gloucester's violent actions, however, caused him to be a repeated source of trouble to the council between 1422 and 1440 and there were several major crises in relations between him and Beaufort. While Beaufort consistently supported the war with France with his money and diplomacy, Gloucester's personal hatred of the Cardinal was supported by a difference of policy based on his desire to pursue his own feud with the Duke of Burgundy. It is possible that the anti-Flemish feelings of many English merchants gained him some popular support. The first serious crisis began in October 1425 when Gloucester, fresh from his expedition to Hainault, challenged the council's financial arrangements and, when refused admission to the Tower on Beaufort's orders, enlisted the armed support of the Londoners, who were annoyed by the council's protection of foreign merchants. Bedford hastened to England to restore order. At the so-called 'Parliament of Bats' at Leicester in 1426 the two enemies were reconciled with difficulty, and at last, in January 1427, Gloucester was persuaded to follow Bedford's example in promising to act only with the guidance of the council. Another crisis developed at the end of 1431, when Beaufort was away in France with the King. Gloucester brought a charge against him, under the Statute of Praemunire, relating to the Cardinal's dealings with the Pope, and followed this up at the beginning of 1432 by making a wholesale replacement of ministers by his own supporters. Beaufort came back to England and cleared himself of the charge against him in parliament, but he was not able to regain his position in the council until Bedford came over again in 1433 and restored the status quo. Once again in 1436 Gloucester came temporarily to the fore. The Burgundian siege of Calais in that year gave him the opportunity to lead a royal army into Flanders and to become briefly a national hero, championing the anti-Burgundian policy of the mercantile interest against Beaufort.

After these episodes Gloucester was no more than a thorn

in the flesh of the Beaufort faction. After Bedford died in 1435 and the King came of age in 1437 control by the faction became more complete; the real power slipped more and more from the formal council into the hands of the clique which dominated it and, more important from this time, dominated the adult King and his court. Apart from Beaufort himself the notable members of the faction included William de la Pole, Earl of Suffolk; Adam Moleyns, Bishop of Chichester; John Kemp, Archbishop of York; and the other members of the Beaufort family, the Earls of Somerset and Dorset. In 1440 Gloucester attacked the peace policy of direct negotiation with Burgundy and negotiation with Charles VII through the Duke of Orleans. He accused the council of wholesale corruption in finance and betrayal of English interests. But he was powerless, and his impotence was fully demonstrated in 1441 when the bishops revenged themselves by convicting his wife of witchcraft and condemning her to an humiliating public penance in London.

As Beaufort aged and gradually withdrew from his long involvement in politics, the controlling power was inherited by his henchmen. The chief amongst these was Suffolk, Steward of the Household since 1433, Chamberlain in 1447, Marquis in 1444, and Duke in 1448, who rose finally to pre-eminence by carrying through the King's marriage with Margaret of Anjou, making himself all-powerful at court, and acquiring a great array of lands and offices. When Gloucester's objection to the cession of Maine, which was part of the marriage agreement, threatened to be dangerous, Suffolk decided to silence him finally by impeachment in a parliament at Bury St Edmunds at the beginning of 1447. Gloucester died under arrest before the trial had begun. Beaufort died in his bed only a few weeks later.

(2) THE ORIGINS OF THE WARS OF THE ROSES, 1447–61

The first part of Shakespeare's *Henry VI* contains a famous scene, set in the lifetime of Joan of Arc, in which the Duke of York and the Earl of Somerset pluck red and white roses in the Temple Garden to signify their implacable opposition to each other. The traditional name 'Wars of the Roses' for the revolutions and battles between 1455 and 1485 is, like 'The Hundred Years' War', rather misleading. The white rose was indeed the badge of the House of York, but the red rose of the Tudors did not appear until the Tudor claim to the throne came to the fore at the very end of the period. Another invention of the sixteenth century was the idea that England declined in the late fifteenth century into a state of disorder, from which it was only rescued by the Tudors. Writers of the Tudor period thought that the victory of Henry VII in 1485 had ended a series of disasters produced by the evils of usurpation which had begun with Bolingbroke in 1399. The usurpation of Henry VII himself—as shameless as any—had to be glossed over by the argument that he united all claims to the throne by his marriage with the Yorkist heiress and that he was descended through his Welsh forebears from the ancient kings of Britain. Much of this propaganda is familiar to us nowadays because it was an important part of the material out of which Shakespeare constructed his history plays. In these plays Richard II appears as a weak king, who failed in his duty to maintain the ancient monarchy, but also a king wrongly deposed. Henry IV's was an unhappy reign because he was a usurper. The dissipated and cheerful Prince Hal, the bane of his father, who turned into the splendid Henry V, could be presented by Shakespeare as a happy warrior and a fine king because he was not himself a usurper.

The modern historian would wish to modify the Tudor picture in many ways, both in detail and in general. Richard III was presented as a hideous tyrant, and the story that the 'Princes in the Tower', Edward V and his brother, were murdered at his command was eagerly elaborated by Tudor historians from Thomas More onwards. Though it is very likely true, since there is no contemporary evidence that they died in any other way, and it would certainly have been in Richard's interest to dispose of better claimants to the throne, there is also no conclusive evidence in its favour and, as has often been pointed out, it would also have been in Henry VII's interest to have them out of the way.[1] The period from 1455 to 1485, moreover, was not outstandingly

1. The evidence is judiciously presented by A. R. Myers, 'The Character of Richard III', *H.T.* (1954)

turbulent in comparison with earlier medieval history. As a whole it was perhaps less packed with bloodshed than the anarchy of King Stephen's reign or the reign of Edward II. The 'wars' really amounted to a small number of battles separated by long intervals of peace. The prudent measures by which the first Tudor, Henry VII, consolidated the monarchy after 1485 had nearly all been initiated by the policy of Edward IV, in re-establishing effective central control by Crown and Council and restoring the government's financial solvency. If there is a break in the history of kingship it comes in 1461 rather than in 1485. What is true, however, about the idea of the Wars of the Roses is that in this period there was more uncertainty about the rightful succession to the throne than there had been since the twelfth century, and that this uncertainty gave good excuses for a series of rebellions aimed at usurpation, of a kind which had been absent in the thirteenth and fourteenth centuries. Though Shakespeare was already remote from the period he was writing about, he could feel the importance of personal kingship and of inherited legitimacy better than we can.

One of the roots of the Wars of the Roses was therefore Bolingbroke's usurpation in 1399. After 1399 it was always arguable that the Lancastrian claim to the throne was no better than the claim of the descendants of the Earl of March, whom Richard II had chosen as his heirs, the claim which was inherited in the mid-fifteenth century by the powerful Richard, Duke of York. When the Lancastrians showed themselves unfit to rule in the fourteen-fifties there was an alternative claimant to the throne, with a plausible claim, ready to hand. This uncertainty, however, would not have mattered much to a strong king. The cause of the Wars is to be found in the personal rivalries within the magnate class, which the withdrawal of Henry VI allowed to fill the political stage, and in the circumstances of the English expulsion from France, which embittered feelings and transferred warlike energies from the old outlets on the Continent to new ones at home. The factions which fought in the battles from 1455 to 1461 first appeared in, and partly sprang from, the events of the years 1443–5. The French advance in Gascony was thought by the council to require a special defensive effort in that area, which would necessarily divert men, money, and command from Richard, Duke of York. York was actually operating in Normandy but held the position of Lieutenant of the whole of France. With full realisation of the affront which was being offered to York, John Beaufort, Duke of Somerset, was sent out as Captain-General of France and Gascony, with an independent command in the south. He had little success and died in 1444. By this time Suffolk was replacing Beaufort as the active leader of the council, and it had become clear that the English, apparently unable to stem the tide of French reconquest, had to seek peace. Suffolk was particularly fitted for the peace embassy, with which he was entrusted, by his friendship with both the Beauforts and the Duke of Orleans, and he arranged the betrothal of King Henry to Margaret of Anjou. He accepted as part of the bargain the French demand for the cession of Maine, which was still in English hands. Henry and Margaret were married in April 1445. York was superseded as Lieutenant of France by Edmund Beaufort, Marquis of Dorset, brother of the dead Duke of Somerset and soon to succeed to that title. In spite of much resistance from the soldiers on the spot, Maine was actually ceded to the French.

The results of these manoeuvres were important. Margaret of Anjou, a new force in English politics, proved to be masterful and ambitious, accumulating property and favours for herself and her friends, providing the centre of a real court party for the first time in the reign and well able to lead it if necessary. Naturally she allied herself with the Beauforts and Suffolk who had brought her to England. Secondly, though the most obvious opponent of peace and the cession of Maine, Gloucester, was removed by his death in 1447, there was plenty of feeling against the humiliating settlement both in the country and among the commanders in France, and the effect was to realise the latent division between the great royal houses of York and Beaufort. For the time being the Beaufort interst and Suffolk (by 1448 not only elevated to a dukedom but also the King's Chamberlain and Captain of Calais) were supreme at court, while York was removed out of danger as Lieutenant of the King in Ireland. The theme of the politics of the rest of the reign is the deepening cleavage between the two parties, leading through military disaster in France, growing poverty of the Crown, and increasing disorder in England, to revolution and the overthrow of the Lancastrians. For most of the period the Lancastrians retained control of the machinery of government and the support of the majority of the magnates, but they were very much hampered by the weakness and failure of their government at home and abroad. On the other side, Richard, Duke of York, was the greatest individual landowner in the kingdom, a man of experience, descended from Edward III's sons through both his father and his mother and therefore in a good position eventually to claim the throne (see Table III). He was supported by two great magnates of the Neville family, which had risen greatly by good marriages in the last half-century: Richard, Earl of Salisbury, inheritor of the Montague estates, and his son, Richard, Earl of Warwick, who inherited the Beauchamp estates in 1449 and began the career which was to win him the nickname of Kingmaker. Both sides included experienced soldiers and the families were closely connected by marriage. Nor was there any clear division of policy to explain their enmity. The conflict was in essence a return to the situation which had been seen before in the reigns of Edward II and Richard II, the response of powerful and disgruntled magnates to their exclusion from a weak and corrupt court.

Down to 1454 the Lancastrians retained control of the government and avoided open war with York, but not without bitter opposition and violent crises. The worst of these began at the end of 1449 as a result of the court's failure on the new war in Normandy and its need to plead again for financial help from parliament. At the beginning of 1450 Bishop Moleyns was assassinated and Suffolk impeached in parliament, chiefly on the grounds of his responsibility for the disasters overseas. Suffolk had been protected by the King from parliamentary attack in previous years, but this time the outcry was too strong to be resisted. He was banished and mysteriously murdered while crossing the Channel.

Close upon this came one of the rare outbreaks of popular revolt. Jack Cade's Rebellion in June and July 1450 was a rising of the men of Kent. Its avowed aims included the overthrow of the court party, the ending of the financial corruption and oppression of the King's officials, resumption into

217

royal hands of Crown lands which had been granted away, and the abolition of the Statute of Labourers. Its social aims and origins are much less clear than those of the Revolt of 1381, and it appears to have been inspired by the desire to reform politics and administration rather than by dreams of social upheaval. The rebels included substantial landowners and were Yorkist in sympathy. For several days they terrorised London and some courtiers were executed, but the rising did not develop into a civil war between magnates. Soon after the rebellion had been put down, the hostility between York and Somerset became more bitter and open. In the parliament of 1450–1, York, newly returned from Ireland, was outspoken and dominant, while the Commons called for the banishment of Somerset and his supporters from the court, and one member dared to petition that York be recognised as heir to the throne. In 1452 York was arrested for a time after denouncing Somerset and raising troops.

Events in the second half of 1453 somewhat changed the situation. Several subsidiary quarrels between magnates contributed to the main conflict between York and Lancaster, and one of these, between the Percies and the Nevilles, led to a pitched battle at Stamford Bridge in August. In the same month Henry VI had his first attack of madness, which lasted sixteen months. This rather weakened Margaret's control of the court, but the birth of her only son in October, securing the future descent of the Crown in the Lancastrian line, both strengthened her position and probably increased the jealousy of her rivals. In the parliament of 1453–4 Somerset was again violently attacked, and in spite of the reluctance of the court York was declared Protector of the Realm during the King's madness. In the period from 1454 to 1456 Yorkists and Lancastrians alternately controlled the court. While York was Protector, Somerset and the Duke of Exeter were imprisoned. After Henry VI recovered his wits in December 1454 York had to lay down his protectorship and Somerset recovered power, but the manoeuvring of the two parties after this led in May 1455 to the first battle of St Albans (usually regarded as the beginning of the Wars of the Roses) in which the Yorkists were victorious and Somerset and Northumberland were killed. At the end of the year York

The Wars of the Roses

was again given the protectorship, apparently through the urgent pressure of his supporters in another parliament, and this lasted until the beginning of 1456.[1]

The years 1456–9 were a period of relative quiet. Margaret had recovered control of the court and the government with the exception of Calais. At Calais the Earl of Warwick could not be dislodged from the captaincy, which he had secured in 1455 and which gave him command of the only royal standing

1. J. R. Lander, 'Henry VI and the Duke of York's Second Protectorate, 1455–6', *Bulletin of the John Rylands Library* (1960)

army and the best possible refuge to prepare for a future attack.[1] York returned to Ireland. In 1459 each side was arming again and apparently preparing for a final enforcement of its will. In October, York's army was defeated at Ludford and he and his followers condemned in their absence at a parliament shortly after. They were still at large; York returned to Ireland and Warwick remained poised at Calais. It was from Calais that the decisive attack came. In June 1460 Warwick crossed the Channel with his father, Salisbury, and the Duke of York's young son, Edward, Earl of March, the future Edward IV. They occupied London and then advanced to Northampton, where they defeated the courtier army in July and captured the King himself. York's party now controlled the government, and in the autumn the Duke came over to a parliament in which he for the first time claimed the throne instead of Henry VI. The claim met with much resistance and in the end he agreed to accept the protectorship during Henry's lifetime, with the succession after. At the end of the year he marched out to destroy the Lancastrian forces in the north but was himself killed at the battle of Wakefield. The country was now hopelessly divided between the two warring parties. After the new Duke of York had defeated one Lancastrian army at Mortimer's Cross in Herefordshire, Margaret brought her main forces down from the north and released Henry VI from Warwick in the course of the second battle of St Albans. In March, however, Edward IV assumed the Crown and confirmed himself in possession of it by leading an army northwards to win a bloody victory at Towton. Margaret and Henry fled into Scotland leaving the new King in control.

(3) EDWARD IV AND THE EARL OF WARWICK, 1461–75

The politics of the first decade of Edward IV's reign were unusually confused. Independent and effective man of action as he was, the new King never during this period won the full leadership or confidence of the nobility or even of his own brothers, George, Duke of Clarence, and Richard, Duke of

1. G. R. Harris, 'The Struggle for Calais: an Aspect of the Rivalry between Lancaster and York', *E.H.R.* (1960)

Gloucester. The backbone of Edward's support amongst the nobility was provided by his own creations, such as his father-in-law, Earl Rivers, his brother-in-law, Lord Scales, William Herbert, and Humphrey Stafford, whom he made Earls of Pembroke and Devon, the Percies, whom he restored to the earldom of Northumberland, and William Lord Hastings who was made into a substantial magnate. Many of his opponents were at large and there were frequent rumours of treachery, with or without foundation. Moreover the prevalence of disorder in the country, the outbreaks of private warfare, on the fringes of the main political conflict or unconnected with it, continued as in the later years of Henry VI. Edward was faced by the avowed Lancastrians, and later by a new body of opponents led by Warwick the Kingmaker. This triangle in the English nobility complicated the triangle of relations between the three powers of western Europe, England, France, and Burgundy, for the rivalry of the Hundred Years' War still smouldered and the parties at home competed for support abroad. For the first few years the King and Warwick were in agreement in their efforts to stamp out the remaining Lancastrian opposition in this country. Pembroke and Exeter remained at large in Wales. The Earl of Oxford was executed in 1462 for an attempted landing on the east coast. The most substantial forces retired with Margaret and Henry VI to the Scots border, attempting to hold on to such border castles as Alnwick and Bamborough, and to get what support they could in the rear in Scotland itself. This entailed several Yorkist expeditions to the north country and it was not until 1464 that the border castles were firmly in Yorkist hands. In the same year the Duke of Somerset, after changing sides twice, was captured and executed. Meanwhile, from her base in the north, Margaret had begun her policy of trying to enlist the help of her relations at the French court. Starting in 1462 she made several perilous journeys to seek the help of the new French King, Louis XI, who had succeeded to the throne in 1461; though Louis was far too cunning to put his weight behind such a hopeless enterprise for the present, the connection was dangerous.

The moderate pacification achieved by 1464 might have endured, however, if it had not been for the deep rift in the

Yorkist camp itself which began that year. The first clear manifestation of it was Edward's secret marriage to Elizabeth Woodville, without the consent and against the wishes of the Kingmaker. The Queen's relations, not hitherto of the first rank of nobility, quickly became a new and important element in the royal circle, and the estrangement between Edward and Warwick grew into enmity. For the next five years the King and the Earl were both seeking helpful alliances abroad, but in different camps. Edward maintained the Yorkist friendship with Burgundy. In 1468 he married his sister Margaret to Charles the Bold who had become Duke of Burgundy in the previous year. The friendship had been celebrated in 1467 by a ceremonial deed of arms at London, famous in the annals of chivalry, between Antony the Bastard of Burgundy and Lord Scales, from which the Nevilles were absent. Warwick was in fact negotiating on his own account with Louis XI, perhaps to turn the friendship of England in that direction, perhaps simply to forward his own personal plans. In spite of the mediation of another great Neville, George, Archbishop of York, the rift grew.

In July 1469 a marriage alliance, which the King had earlier tried to prevent, was made between Warwick and the King's brother, Clarence. In the security of Calais they declared themselves against Edward for his oppressions, though not as yet for any alternative king. About the same time another Neville rising began in the north with the obscure rebellion of Robin of Redesdale. The Yorkist forces were quickly defeated at Edgecote in Northamptonshire, Rivers and Devon executed and the King captured. In the next few months an apparent reconciliation took place between the two sides, but both Warwick and Clarence were in fact planning to continue their efforts. The fire of war was started again in 1470 with another local dispute in Lincolnshire, which turned into a rising against the King. Warwick finally completed his change of sides by allying with Margaret in France, and in the autumn he and Clarence landed in Devon to proclaim Henry VI king. Edward, without sufficient troops to meet the invaders, fled to the Netherlands. The old King Henry was brought out of the Tower, where he had been kept since Edward's men had had the luck to capture him in 1465, and for a few months a Lancastrian reigned again in London. However, the war which began at this time between France and Burgundy made it easier for Edward to raise troops and money from his brother-in-law, the Duke, against the Lancastrian allies of Louis XI. In the spring of 1471 he was able to land on the Humber. Clarence changed sides again to join him on the way to London, and in April and May he defeated both his main enemies in two battles which ended this phase of the Wars of the Roses. Warwick was defeated and killed at Barnet. Henry VI was also captured there and survived only a few weeks in his second captivity. Margaret was defeated and captured, and her son killed at the battle of Tewkesbury.

After he had weathered, by good luck and good generalship, the revolutions of the years 1469–71, Edward's possession of the throne was not seriously threatened again. The Nevilles' power was destroyed for ever, even the Archbishop of York taken into captivity, the Lancastrian king dead, and the Lancastrians scattered. A few years later Edward was able to settle his international position in an extraordinarily satisfactory way. Having several times proclaimed his intention to invade France like his predecessors, Edward at last made a firm agreement with Charles the Bold in 1474 for a joint invasion in the following year. The money was raised, a great army collected, and the King crossed to Calais. But before a blow had been struck Edward met Louis XI and, at the Treaty of Picquigny in August 1475, agreed to withdraw his army for a large payment and a pension. Charles the Bold and his Duchy were destroyed in 1477, but Edward IV was able to spend his last years on the throne, tolerably secure at home and abroad, at peace, and increasingly rich.

(4) THE END OF THE YORKISTS, 1475–85

Apart from the irreconcilable Lancastrians in exile, the only danger in Edward IV's later years came from the rivalry of his own brothers, George, Duke of Clarence, and Richard, Duke of Gloucester, and the treacherous ambition of the former. One of the chief results of the King's victory had been to put at his disposal the immense landed inheritance of the Neville family. His two younger brothers were rivals for the larger share of it, and Edward's determination, recorded by Paston 'to be as big as they both and to be a stifler atween them', was exercised until the final partition of 1474 when, roughly, the old Beauchamp and Despenser properties went to Clarence, and the Salisbury and Neville estates to Gloucester. Clarence's unrest, which had been so useful to Edward's enemies in the crises of the reign, continued. It seems to have been stimulated by Edward's refusal to support his bid for marriage to the heiress of Burgundy. In 1477 the court took action against him. After the condemnation of some of his followers for practising necromancy against the King, he was arrested. In 1478 he was impeached in parliament and died mysteriously, whether or not in the traditional butt of malmsey is unknown.

When Edward IV died in April 1483, his successor, Edward V, was only twelve. The disastrous train of events, which was to end in two years in the final ruin of the Yorkists, stemmed essentially from the difficulties of a minority. The boy King and the court were controlled by the Queen Mother, her relations, Earl Rivers and the Marquis of Dorset, and other close associates of the dead King, notably William Lord Hastings and Thomas Lord Stanley. They doubtless intended to maintain their position with the Queen as Regent. The most powerful man in the kingdom and the person whom Edward IV had intended to control the regency was, however, Richard, Duke of Gloucester. In recent years he had spent most of his time in the north, where he had wide estates and had been granted large regalian powers in return for his successful warfare against the Scots. He acted quickly to assert himself against the court. Moving south, he joined forces with another substantial Yorkist magnate, Henry Stafford, Duke of Buckingham, encountered Rivers bringing Edward V to London at Stony Stratford, and seized them both. Dorset fled the country, the Queen retired to sanctuary at Westminster, and, within a month of Edward IV's death, Richard was in control at London and able to assume the protectorate.

It was not long before he went much further than this in revealing a determination to make his rule absolute by removing all possible opposition. In June, Hastings, the most prominent layman of Edward IV's intimates still in power, was suddenly arrested at a council meeting and executed. Less than a fortnight after this and less than three months after the old King's death, Richard set forth in parliament the novel argument that Edward IV's marriage had been invalid, Edward V was therefore a bastard and he himself was the rightful successor. He immediately took the crown as Richard III. Rivers was executed and Edward V and his younger brother placed in the Tower, where they were probably murdered soon after.

Richard's seizure of the throne was the most sudden and ruthless of all the revolutions of the Wars of the Roses, but his reign lasted only two years. He was threatened almost immediately in the autumn of 1483 by a revolt in the west, led, for reasons which are not at all clear, by the nobleman whom he had most trusted, Buckingham, with the support of the Woodvilles and the Lancastrian Courtenays. This collapsed and Buckingham was executed. If it had been successful this rebellion would have installed as king Henry Tudor, Earl of Richmond, and it was he who finally was going to succeed on his own account. Henry's dubious claim to the throne was based on his close kinship with the Lancastrians. His father, Edmund, had been the son of Henry V's widow by a Welsh gentleman, Owen Tudor, and had been made Earl by Henry VI. His mother, Margaret Beaufort, Countess of Richmond, who was still living, was the heiress of the Duke of Somerset who died in 1444. Henry had fought at Tewkesbury and then fled to Brittany and France to await his chance. In 1484 he wisely withdrew quickly, when the rebellion collapsed, but in the next year he tried again. Landing with an army in Pembrokeshire, of which his uncle Jasper was Earl, he advanced quickly through Wales and the Marches to meet Richard in battle at Bosworth in Leicestershire on 22nd August 1485. And there, partly by the help of Margaret Beaufort's third husband, Thomas Lord Stanley, who betrayed the Yorkist cause at the last moment, Richard III was slain and the Tudor dynasty founded.

'Oh God! what security are our kings to have henceforth, that in the day of battle they may not be deserted by their subjects?' wrote the Prior of Crowland, soon after Bosworth. In fact the storms of the age of York and Neville and

Woodville, released by the infirmity of Henry VI and carried on by the momentum of ambition, uncertainty, and disloyalty, were to be ended completely by a king who was luckier and cleverer than his predecessors; but no one could be sure in 1485 that the Wars of the Roses were over. Two nephews of Richard III, not to speak of pretenders, survived to trouble Henry Tudor for many a year. The treachery and division within the nobility, the shameless proclamation of one rightful title after another by the usurpers of the past thirty years, might seem to have undermined kingship for ever.

CHAPTER TWELVE

GOVERNMENT

(1) THE KING'S FINANCES

IT IS doubtful if any century in the varied history of English monarchy has seen changes more remarkable than those which took place between 1400 and 1500. At the beginning of the fifteenth century royal power was deeply influenced by, and in important respects dependent on, the parliamentary system which had grown up during the thirteenth and fourteenth centuries; by the end of the century the king had become to a large extent independent and free of obligations to consult systematically the will of his subjects. Henry VII has been called a despot and there is much to recommend the description, not of course in the oriental sense, but certainly in the sense that he was much less trammelled by parliaments and councils than Edward III or Henry IV. Our main business in this chapter is to discover how much of this development had happened by 1485 and to explain the paradoxical emergence of stronger and more self-sufficient monarchy from the nadir of kingship in the Wars of the Roses.

The taxation system which had been set up by the mid-fourteenth century, consisting of lay subsidies and customs duties voted in parliament, and clerical subsidies voted in convocations, continued into the early fifteenth century. There were ups and downs according to the demands of wars and the popularity of kings, but the general character of taxation and its potentialities remained much the same up to the end of the reign of Henry V. Like the last great soldier king, Edward III, Henry V was able to persuade his subjects to grant him an average of over £100,000 a year at a period of extensive and successful campaigns in France; and the money came, broadly speaking, from the same kinds of taxes.

Some changes had taken place in detail and there had also

been some serious conflicts. The first group to make a successful resistance to royal taxation was the clergy. It is very likely that they had suffered worse than anyone else from the effects of the Black Death, for their incomes came mainly from rents and tithes, which would be immediately affected by a fall in the value of land. When war broke out again in 1369, the King's lay councillors and the parliaments tried to keep the taxation of the clergy up to the high levels of the first phase of the Hundred Years' War, but this was bitterly opposed. The antagonism between the court and the clergy in the great decade of official anti-clericalism, the thirteen-seventies, seems to have sprung at least partly from this reisitance to taxation, though in fact the clergy went on paying heavily. From about 1383, under Archbishop Courtenay's leadership, the Church was more successful in opposing the principle that lay grants should be regularly paralleled by grants in convocation, and thereafter clerical subsidies, though still levied, were less frequent.

The years from 1377 to 1381 saw also the disastrous aberration of the poll taxes. They were voted by the Commons in parliaments. The first, in 1377, was at a flat rate of 4d charged on all laymen and clerics over the age of fourteen; the second, in 1379, graduated from 4d for ordinary people to £6 13s 4d for a duke or archbishop; the third, which inspired the Peasants' Revolt of 1381, at the rate of 1s a head on the average for all persons over fifteen except beggars. These taxes abandoned the principles of taxation according to property and taxation only of the more prosperous, which governed the lay subsidy. It is probable that they were a deliberate attempt by the Commons and their constituents to shift the burden from themselves to the population as a whole, but the Revolt frightened them out of making the attempt again. In 1404 (a tax of 1s in the pound on the rentals of lands), in 1411 (6s 8d on £20 annual rent), and in a few other years, there were feeble efforts to introduce new kinds of land taxes, which may have been aimed partly at the nobility, but there was no further revival of the poll tax and the large sums which the Commons contributed towards the wars of Henry V were in the old form of the lay subsidies. In fact, because the clergy were paying less, the lay subsidies formed a larger proportion of the royal income than they had in the early part of the Hundred Years' War. Also the gradual decline of the wool trade, which had gone a long way by this time, meant that the produce of the customs duties was smaller than under Edward III. The Commons were financially more important to the king than ever before. They were perhaps still more important because the great borrowing schemes, based on the wool trade, which had been essential to the finances of Edward I and Edward III came to an end. Wool was no longer exported on the same scale, the Italians had lost their position in the trade, the Staple was dominant. Borrowing from merchants still went on. The scandal which broke in the Good Parliament of 1376 was partly about the loans arranged by Richard Lyons, for which it was said that 50 per cent interest had been charged. London and the merchants lent money to the King in the naval crisis of 1377, when the coasts were threatened. Richard Whittington and other merchants lent money to Henry IV when the French were attacking again. But there was nothing like the borrowing of the twelve-nineties and thirteen-thirties. The scale of royal finance had contracted with the wool trade.

Though the Commons complained of the drain of money to France and withheld a grant in 1420, Henry V kept up the pressure of taxation to the end of his reign. His successor was never able to imitate him; in the reign of Henry VI the medieval system of taxation collapsed. For the first seven years the King was a minor and the English were at the height of their power in France, controlling so much of the country that plunder and taxation of the natives sufficed for much of the cost of fighting. After the tide had turned at the siege of Orleans in 1429, though money was often urgently needed, it was not granted on the old scale. The double subsidy which the Commons granted after the relief of Orleans was not equalled until the sixteenth century. In 1433 the Commons cut the conventional value of a lay subsidy by £4,000 to £32,000. In the same year the Treasurer, Lord Cromwell, produced a balance sheet of Exchequer finances to prove his difficulties, showing that the normal receipts, excluding subsidies, totalled about £65,000 annually, enough for regular expenses, but that the extra cost of campaigning in

France had to be met entirely by parliamentary grants. Moreover the Exchequer was £164,000 in debt.[1] Unimpressed by these arguments, however, the Commons gave little and rarely for the rest of the reign, although the decline of English power in France might have been thought to call for heroic measures. In the crisis of 1437, when Calais was threatened and the English had lately been driven from Paris, the Commons temporarily abolished the petty custom on exports by natives, induced 'by corruption of the merchants', as the Archbishop of York said. There were some attempts at new kinds of land or income taxes in 1428, 1431, 1435, and 1450, and some taxes on alien merchants, but on the whole the Commons were unsympathetic and ungenerous throughout the reign of Henry VI. Grants of lay subsidies over the whole reign averaged only about £12,000 a year. The subsidies voted by the clergy had sunk to almost negligible proportions. The only substantial source of taxation was the wool customs, which still brought in large amounts, though much less than in the fourteenth century. Apart from the decline in wool export, it is not clear why these changes took place at this particular time. The relation between the decline in clerical subsidies and the decline in the income of the Church is a possible hypothesis but no more. The collapse of lay subsidies is the most important and the most unexplained part of the process. Presumably it happened partly because the small landowners, who had been the chief payers, were fewer, though it is hard to believe that they were all poorer. The remissions introduced in 1433 were to be applied to 'every town, city and borough desolate, wasted, destroyed or to the said tax over greatly charged', and there is little doubt that the recession of population must have made some areas much less able and willing to pay the quotas which had been established early in the reign of Edward III. The government of the age of Beaufort and after, also had less power of persuasion and it is difficult to evaluate the respective importance of political and social factors. All that is certain is that the great collapse of the taxation system took place in the reign of Henry VI.

1. J. L. Kirby, 'The Issues of the Lancastrian Exchequer and Lord Cromwell's Estimates of 1433', *Bulletin of the Institute of Historical Research* (1951)

In these circumstances the other sources of royal income became more important, in particular the king's landed estates, which had been less exploited than they might have been because of the possibilities of parliamentary income in the fourteenth century. The revolution of 1399 added to the royal lands the biggest magnate inheritance of that time, the Duchy of Lancaster, with its many manors and lordships scattered over England. This made somewhat more plausible the cry, which grew as taxation fell, that the king should live 'of his own', that is from those revenues which were his by acknowledged right without special grant. During the fourteenth century royal lands had been commonly regarded as the natural spoil of courtiers. No sooner had estates fallen by escheat into the king's hands than they had been granted out again to friends and favourites, and the amount of property that remained in royal hands was relatively small. In the reign of Henry IV the Commons began to be more restive about the constant granting-away to noblemen of property whose yield could potentially have been used to reduce the need for taxation.[1] In 1404 a wild attempt by the Commons, in their most aggressive mood, to reduce their liabilities (including a suggestion, which Archbishop Arundel had to fight down, that the property of the Church should be sequestrated for a year) persuaded the King to appoint a commission to look into grants of Crown lands since 1366. This was one of the first signs of a policy which was to become important later in the century. The difficulty, now as later, was that the 're-sumption' of Crown lands, as it came to be called, would injure most severely those who were most influential at the court and therefore best able to resist it. To take back all their lands was an almost impossibly agonising operation. The call for it, however, became strong in the last decade of Lancastrian rule. Probably the régime of Margaret of Anjou and Somerset made the dissipation of royal property particularly glaring. It was one of the grievances of Jack Cade's Rebellion; and the parliaments of 1450 and 1453 were so insistent (and the court so weakened) that they did actually force the government to withdraw some of the holdings of royal lands from prominent

1. B. P. Wolffe, 'The Acts of Resumption of the Lancastrian Parliaments', *E.H.R.* (1958)

Lancastrians and induce the Exchequer to lease lands at rents nearer to their real values.

The economic weakness and corruption, which undermined the monarchy in the reign of Henry VI, appear most clearly in the history of the Duchy of Lancaster[1] and in the activities of the man who was both England's most influential statesman and the chief lender to the King for over twenty years, Cardinal Beaufort. After 1399 the Duchy of Lancaster, though owned by the king, was kept separate, as it still is today, from the rest of Crown lands. In practice, however, much of it did not remain under the direct control of the king or the council. After Henry V's death some was set aside to provide for his widow and then, in 1446, for the jointure of Margaret of Anjou. Much of the rest was put into the hands of a group of trustees (the 'feoffees' as they were legally called) so that the income could be devoted to the execution of Henry V's will. They retained their holding until 1443, after which a large slice of the Duchy was again transferred to feoffees for the execution of Henry VI's will. The feoffees included influential councillors like Beaufort, and, though the Commons agitated at various times for the return of the lands into royal hands, they were not very successful in hastening the mysteriously lengthy execution of Henry V's will. The feoffees had enough money in hand to lend large sums to the King at various times, but this was always done under arrangements for repayment out of other income, so that Henry VI was in the peculiar position of depending on loans made out of the income of the hereditary lands of his own family. A similar mystery surrounds the large loans made to the King over a long period by Beaufort in person. In the twenty years before his death he loaned to Henry V and Henry VI at one time and another more than £200,000. For much of this time he was in a political position to dictate the terms on which his own loans were made, and it is certain that for long periods up to his death he had Crown jewels of great value as pledges, and that for some time he had complete control of the customs of the port of Southampton. Owing to the ecclesiastical prohibition of usury, loans were often made in the Middle Ages in forms which concealed the interest payments. This among other things makes it

1. See R. Somerville, *History of the Duchy of Lancaster*, i, (1953)

difficult to discover what profit Beaufort made out of his transactions, but at least he died a very wealthy man.[1] It is curious that a bishop and cardinal should have been the nearest equivalent in the Lancastrian period to the Italian and English financiers who had oiled the financial machinery of Edward III. The fact emphasised both the reduced importance of large-scale commerce as a source of loans for the king and the extent to which the whole business of government in Henry VI's time became a great spoils system. Before the Wars of the Roses began, the royal financial system had reached a state of chronic and paralysing inadequacy. An income smaller than ever before was unequal to any serious military enterprise and the accumulated debt was said to be £372,000.

Fifty years later the King of England was not only a powerful but also a wealthy monarch, who could afford to lend money to other people. Though his wealth was based on a financial system significantly different from that of the medieval kings, this had not been created by any sudden reforms or new taxes. It was built up gradually, and substantial progress had already been made by 1485. The two chief ingredients of the new state of affairs were, firstly, peace abroad and, secondly, the accumulation of land. The absence of war in France is perhaps an even more striking feature of the Yorkist period than the revolution and violence at home. Edward IV's abandonment of traditional foreign policy, his failure to fight a single battle in France, was enough in itself to relieve him of a great part of the financial embarrassment of his predecessors, for war had been the main, almost the sole, cause of the need for parliamentary taxation. Edward was able to make his international diplomacy profitable without fighting. Nearly all the grants made by the Commons in his reign were intended to carry out the plan of an invasion of France, mooted in 1468 and revived after the restoration in 1471: a double subsidy in 1468, an income tax in 1472, a subsidy in 1473, and an extra large subsidy in 1474. When this expedition actually took place in 1475 it ended, as we

---

1. K. B. McFarlane, 'At the Deathbed of Cardinal Beaufort', *Essays in Medieval History presented to F. M. Powicke*, ed. R. W. Hunt, W. A. Pantin and R. W. Southern (1948); *idem*, 'Loans to the Lancastrian Kings: the Problem of Inducement', *C.H.J.* (1947)

have seen, at the Treaty of Picquigny, by which Edward accepted large grants from the French King, including a pension of £10,000 a year for six years. No parliamentary subsidies were raised under Edward V or Richard III.

While parliamentary grants remained relatively unimportant, the Yorkists began to revive interest in the Crown lands.[1] The important changes were not so much deliberate resumption, which remained a politically difficult manoeuvre. The escheats and forfeitures which followed the usurpation of power and the crushing of rebellion were, however, retained, to a larger extent than in previous reigns, in royal hands. In addition to old Crown lands, Edward IV was himself the inheritor of the Yorkist estates and the conqueror of the Duchy of Lancaster, which was not allowed again to pass out of direct royal control; he thus held the two largest magnate inheritances of the later Middle Ages. Another major inheritance was that of Warwick the Kingmaker, which came into Edward's hands in 1471, was then granted to Clarence, but returned permanently to royal hands in 1478. Edward thus made a serious start with the accumulation of Crown lands which reached such heights under the early Tudors.

Yet more important was the changed attitude to the King's estates. The medieval Exchequer was ill-adapted for estate management. Its officials sat in Westminster and received the money brought from the shires by sheriffs and escheators, keeping very exact accounts but not venturing into the counties themselves to make sure that the largest possible profits were being extracted from the estates. Seignorial landlords, on the other hand, employed staffs of stewards, receivers, and auditors, not simply to collect profits but to maximise them. Though estate management may have been an unrewarding business in the long agricultural depression of the Lancastrian period, in the later fifteenth century land began to recover its value and the Yorkists began to extend to all the Crown estates the active administration which already existed in the Duchy of Lancaster. Officials perambulated the estates, investigating how they could be made to yield more. In 1476, for instance, the councillors of the Duchy visited Pickering and decided that

1. B. P. Wolffe, 'The Management of the English Royal Estates under the Yorkist Kings', *E.H.R.* (1956)

certain pastures 'which Thomas Gower now occupyeth paying for them £10 by the year . . . be much more worth. Wherefore it is advised that the treasurer of the King's house shall have them and stuff them with the King's cattle'.[1] This sort of investigation was made all over England. After 1478 the old estates of Warwick were placed under a special commission to act like the councillors of the Duchy. Furthermore the administrators and recievers accounted directly to the King's Chamber, and in this way the whole administration of Crown lands was being separated from the cumbersome and passive control of the medieval Exchequer.

In the middle of Edward IV's reign, Sir John Fortescue, an experienced lawyer and a turncoat Lancastrian, well versed in the political misfortunes of his age, wrote a book called *The Governance of England*, which is one of the first practical political treatises in the English language. 'We hold it for undoubted,' he said, 'that there may no realm prosper or be worshipful under a poor king.' His recipe was that the king should build up a large royal demesne: 'If the king might have his livelihood for the sustenance of his estate in great lordships, manors, fee farms and such other demesnes, his people not charged, he should keep to him wholly their hearts, exceed in lordship all the lords of his realm and there should none of them grow to be like unto him, which thing is most to be feared of all the world.' Edward IV took important steps in this direction. His boast to the Commons in 1467 'that I purpose to live upon mine own, and not to charge my subjects but in great and urgent causes', was on the whole maintained. Firstly, he sedulously avoided 'great and urgent causes'. Secondly, he possessed, in addition to his growing estates and to the relatively small grants of the Commons, a substantial and unquestioned income from the customs in trade, ignored by Fortescue's analysis, and trade was beginning by the end of his reign to recover from the depression of the fifteenth century and to expand in total quantity.

1. Public Record Office, DL 5/1, f. 90 v.

(2) THE COMMONS IN PARLIAMENT

> 'Then came there a King with knighthood before him,
> The might of the commons made him to reign.'

So wrote Langland in the third quarter of the fourteenth century, when the evolution of the medieval parliament was largely complete and the Commons had assumed their place as an essential part of it. For more than half a century after this the parliamentary element in the English constitution was especially prominent, partly because parliament had become the acknowledged forum for consultation between the king and his realm, partly because of its comprehensive control of royal finance, partly because the recurrence of war and of royal weakness repeatedly placed the kings at the mercy of their subjects. Their financial responsibilities enabled the elected representatives of the communities to play a part in national politics larger than ever before.

Who were the Commons and whom did they represent? The first parliament of Henry VI in 1422, for instance, included 188 representatives of cities and boroughs and 74 knights of the shires.[1] During the fifteenth century there was a growing tendency for towns to be represented not by their own prominent citizens but by lawyers, gentlemen, and politicians, who wished for some reason to be in parliament. During the great period of parliamentary government this process had made some headway but was not nearly complete. A few of the town representatives were lawyers, acting for the boroughs though with little personal connection. Most of them were burgesses and probably actual members of the oligarchies which governed the towns; many were merchants or engaged in characteristic town pursuits. The knights of the shires were supposed to be resident members of the shires for which they sat. They were elected in the shire court by the 'county', that is by the more prominent freeholders. After the act of 1429, which governed county franchise until 1832, the electors had to be freemen with income from freehold land within the county of not less than 40s a year and, sometimes at least, quite a large proportion of the people of this class actually took

1. For details see J. S. Roskell, *The Commons in the Parliament of 1422* (1954)

part in the election. In 1454, 494 freeholders took part in the election for Huntingdonshire. Of the members elected for the shires many were not, strictly speaking, knights. All, however, were men of substance of the squire class. Some were essentially landowners, often of prominent families, some were lawyers, many were the retainers or estate managers of great lords, many had been sheriffs, some had been prominent in the royal service, even as councillors. There was not the continuity from one parliament to the next given by the preponderance of career politicians in a modern parliament but there was a weighty representation of powerful interests.

Legally the Commons were elected by the more prosperous freemen of towns and shires to represent their interests. It is more difficult to decide whether they actually did this or whether they were frequently retained men who paid more attention to the interests of some great lord who had secured their election. The easiest way to influence an election was through the sheriff, who was the returning officer and sometimes certainly returned a man who was not the one chosen by the shire. Since the sheriff was a royal official, whoever controlled the royal administration would be in a good position to secure his help. It is possible that John of Gaunt tried to influence the membership of the Commons in this way in 1377, and likely that Richard II did so in 1397, Henry IV in 1399, and Henry VI in 1459. They were sometimes successful, though the sheriffs were said to have reported to Richard II in 1387 that at that moment of crisis opinion in the shires was too strongly against the King for this manoeuvre. The frequent resistance which the Commons made to the Crown shows that they were often free of this influence. More insidious was the power of a great lord to use the weight of his influence in a county, by bribery and pressure, to bring about the election of a man favourable to him. The extreme was John of Gaunt's palatinate of Lancaster, where he returned the knights himself. In Yorkshire the elections seem to have been dominated by great local lords like Neville, Roos, and Percy. In most shires the influence of one lord was not sufficiently dominant for him to manipulate elections freely. When the Duke of Norfolk was trying to ensure the election of two supporters in Norfolk in 1450, his agent wrote to John Paston, 'I told my lord of Norfolk at London that I laboured divers men for Sir Roger Chamberlain and they said to me they would have him; but not Howard, in as much as he had no livelihood in the shire, no conversement, and I asked them whom they would have and they said they would have you.' In other words, the local magnate had influence, which must often have been considerable, but not an overriding influence, and the feelings of the shire freemen were of great importance.[1] Each election must have been a tangle of conflicting views. It is even less clear how the members behaved when they got to parliament. A poem written at the end of Richard II's reign describes the debates in the Commons like this:

'. . . to save appearances, and in accordance with custom, some of them falsely argued at some length, and said: "We are servants and we draw a salary, we are sent from the shires to make known their grievances, to discuss matters on their behalf and to stick to that, and only make grants of their money to the great men in a regular way, unless there is war. . . ."
'Some members sat there like a nought in arithmetic, that marks a place but has no value in itself. Some had taken bribes, so that the shires they represented had no advantage from their presence. Some were tattlers, who went to the king and warned him against men who were really good friends of his. . . . Some members slumbered and slept and said little. Some stammered and mumbled and did not know what they meant to say. Some were paid dependents' and were afraid to take any step without their masters' orders.'[2] [Translated into modern English]

Allowing for the satire, it is probably a fair enough description of the types in the Commons; the bumpkins who were at sea in great affairs, the wily politicians, the retainers under orders, but also the common awareness that they were supposed to be doing the shires' business. The Speakers, who presented the Commons' decisions to the king, were invariably knights, generally experienced men of affairs. Sir Thomas Hungerford in 1377 was John of Gaunt's steward; Thomas

1. K. B. McFarlane, 'Parliament and Bastard Feudalism', *T.R.H.S.* (1944)
2. H. M. Cam, *Liberties and Communities in Medieval England* (1944), pp. 230–1

Chaucer, thrice Speaker under Henry IV, was a prominent Lancastrian courtier; Sir Arnold Savage, who annoyed Henry IV by his outspokenness in 1401 and demanded redress of grievances before grant of supply, sounds a more independent man.

The role of parliament in constitution and politics was determined by the complex of influences at work on it and by the different issues which came before it. At times the genuine financial interest of the Commons was dominant and they were also willing to use their pressure in foreign affairs, labour legislation, or anti-clericalism. Other parliaments were caught up in the conflicts of great magnates and the Commons might be too frightened or indifferent to be more than the instruments of the mighty. Others were dominated by the king. All these possibilities are illustrated in the reigns of Richard II and Henry IV, when the Commons reached the height of their importance in medieval English politics. For a period in each reign the Commons exercised the most extreme control over royal finances and the most critical interference in politics. In the early years of Richard II, 1377–83, the Commons were incited to activity by a variety of factors: the instability at court during the minority, the dangers to English trade resulting at first from the French control of the Channel and then the French invasion of Flanders, the constant demands for money for war, and the hope of relieving themselves of taxation by placing greater burdens on the clergy and peasantry. We have already seen the effects of their anti-clericalism and the poll taxes. When they granted money for war in 1377, the Commons went beyond their accustomed right to control the grant of money and demanded control of its use too. The merchants Walworth and Philpot were appointed treasurers of war. In 1378 the Commons complained of the use of the money for purposes unspecified in the grant. In 1380 they again criticised official extravagance and demanded a new committee of fifteen bishops, magnates, and commoners to ensure proper use of their money. The agitation died down somewhat after the shock of the Revolt and the decline of French naval activity but they were still critical. In 1382 they took a positive line in foreign policy, successfully supporting the project for a crusade in Flanders and opposing

John of Gaunt's plan to intervene in Spain. In 1383 and 1385 they were still agitating for effective action in Flanders after the crusade had failed and insisting on the uses to which their money was to be put. The first part of Henry IV's reign from 1401 to 1406 found the Crown similarly at the mercy of the Commons, through the weakness of the usurper and the pressure of war both at home and abroad. It was in 1401 that Sir Arnold Savage spoke up. In 1404, after emphasising the French danger to Calais, the Commons told the King that his revenues from wool taxation and his lands should be adequate in themselves, insisted on a continual council appointed in parliament and a fixed annual allowance to the royal household to prevent waste, reluctantly granted a land tax, with the stipulation that all record of it should be destroyed so that it could not be used as a precedent, and appointed four treasurers of war to administer it. In 1406 the Commons again put forward their own plan for conducting the war at sea, demanded the expulsion of foreigners from the household, appointed a continual council, asked for the resumption of royal lands, and appointed their own auditors of the money for the war.

The members of the Commons who enjoyed the highest social standing and the best connections were knights, and, as representative of the shires, the knights also had the larger share of lay subsidies to consent to. Burgesses were more numerous but, though a few of them, especially the members for London (merchants such as John Philpot and Richard Whittington sat at one time and another for the city), were men of great wealth and influence, they could not be speakers and most of their fellows would be small men from small boroughs. It is a striking fact, however, that in the periods of the Commons' greatest aggressiveness in 1376–83 and 1404–6 mercantile issues played a very large part in their demands. One might even guess from a reading of the political issues involved alone that the mercantile issues were dominant. Either the mercantile interest could mobilise a great deal of support in the Commons or it had a more coherent and urgent objective than any group of knights.

Attempts to place restraints on the right of lords to have liveried retainers also showed that the Commons were not afraid, on occasion, of attacking powerful interests besides the king. But the fearlessness of Sir Peter de la Mare in 1376 and Sir Arnold Savage in 1401 contrasts strangely with the Commons cowering before Richard II in 1397 ('Where are the true Commons?' asked Arundel). Parliament was also attended by bishops and earls as well as Commons and it was also a tribunal for quarrels of great men, which were to some extent above the heads of the knights. Knights and burgesses were closely associated with some of these quarrels by the procedure of impeachment, fully evolved in the Good Parliament of 1376, which in a sense began the great period of the Commons. Impeachment was trial by the judgment of the Lords with the Commons acting as joint accusers. It was used against Latimer and his associates in 1376, against Michael de la Pole, Earl of Suffolk, in 1386, and against his grandson, William de la Pole, Duke of Suffolk, in 1450. Since the lords were the judges the Commons could not have used this procedure successfully unless they had powerful sympathisers amongst the lords, and probably on all these occasions they managed to overthrow the king's favourite partly because they really hated him and partly because they had help and incitement from the magnates. The procedure used by the appellants in 1388 and against them in 1397 was Appeal, straightforward denunciation of the accused for treason, in which the Commons needed to take no active part. The deposition of Richard II was carried through by an assembly of 'estates of the realm', which, if not a parliament in strict theory since the King had already abdicated and could not take part, was composed of the people normally summoned to a parliament. Its procedure was in many ways similar to the deposition of Edward II and expressed a like constitutional theory but, though the Commons were associated with the action, there is no reason to suppose that they took any more initiative in it than they had done in 1327.

The powers and prestige of a parliament were never negligible in the fifteenth century. It was there that the councillors of Henry VI were appointed, that Richard of York acquired the protectorship and that his sons, Edward IV and Richard III, sought and obtained confirmation of their titles to the throne. The Commons' control of taxation remained the same in theory. Their importance, however, declined from the heights it had reached under Henry IV to a level more like that of the reign of Edward II, when they had been occasionally summoned without holding a central place in the political arena. Under Henry V they were frequently summoned to make grants of money; so also in the fourteen-thirties, when the disputes between Henry VI's councillors took place partly in parliament. Thereafter the frequency of parliaments declined rapidly. In the early part of the fifteenth century they were summoned about once a year. After his majority Henry VI summoned only eleven parliaments in twenty-four years. The last serious outburst of activity by the medieval Commons took place in the years 1449–54, occasioned by the renewal of taxation for the last phase of the Hundred Years' War and the beginning of the strife between York and Lancaster. The government was both demanding and unpopular and in 1450 the Speaker, William Tresham, revived the traditions of his predecessors in leading the impeachment of Suffolk against strong resistance from the court. In the same parliament and again in 1453 there was strong pressure for the resumption of Crown lands as an alternative to taxation. In 1451 the Commons demanded the banishment of leading courtiers. Some of the important events of the next few years were played out in parliament, but it is often difficult to see where the Commons stood between the two armed camps gradually resorting to naked force. Edward summoned only six separate parliaments in his twenty-two years. There was indeed a tendency under Henry VI and Edward IV to revert to the thirteenth-century practice of holding Great Councils of magnates without the Commons. Such assemblies had been held occasionally throughout the parliamentary era without robbing parliament of its central political and constitutional position. It was natural that they should become more prominent when the main political issues were relations between king and magnates. Negotiations were held in assemblies of this kind every year from 1453 to 1458. Edward IV held more Great Councils than parliaments, announced his marriage in one of them, and called for advice on the crucial question of relations with Burgundy in several others. The immediate reason for the decline of the medieval parliament was the abandonment by Henry VI and Edward IV of the hope of obtaining the large and regular grants of lay subsidies which their predecessors had received. The customs were granted for life to Henry VI in 1453 and to Edward IV in 1465. In this way the Commons reverted to the position of the early fourteenth century, losing control of the customs and making less frequent grants of subsidies. The result was a very substantial change in the character of politics. Compared with earlier kings, Edward IV and Henry VII summoned parliaments rarely, asked little of them, and paid little attention to them.

(3) GOVERNMENT BY COUNCIL

The parliamentary era of the late fourteenth and early fifteenth centuries was also an age of government by council (that is the small group which remained continually in control of royal policy and its execution, not the occasional assembly of great men in a Great Council). The historical evolution of the two bodies is to some extent parallel. Parliament originated in the need of thirteenth-century kings for an occasion on which to consult with their magnates, to deal with judicial grievances, and to obtain taxes; it grew into a body which assumed large powers of interfering in government and checking royal independence until it was temporarily discarded by the kings of the late fifteenth century. Similarly the council was originally nothing more than an instrument of royal power, a group of men entrusted with authority as efficient and loyal assistants of the king. In the reigns of Richard II and Henry IV it became the means of imposing upon the king an unwelcome recognition of his subjects' power to participate in government. Like parliament it enjoyed a lengthy but transient phase of independent importance which dissolved in the political upheavals of the mid-fifteenth century.

In the central Middle Ages councils were imposed upon the king only in times of minority or at moments of extreme distrust of the court. Examples of such occasions are the minority of Edward III and the York Parliament of 1318. The imposition of a nominated council in a political crisis was both rare and largely ineffective. It was the growth of this expedient into something like a regular practice which gave the council its central importance in the government at the same time as parliament was asserting itself. A nominated council was the Opposition's way of securing future restriction when they had ousted the courtiers in the Good Parliament of 1376. Its effectiveness was short-lived. The minority of Richard II made a council of regency necessary for several years in the early part of the reign. In 1380 the Commons expressed dissatisfaction with it and demanded instead parliamentary appointment of the chief officers (Chancellor Treasurer, Keeper of the Privy Seal, and Steward of the Household), together with a committee, to control finance. The 'Wonderful' Parliament of 1386 set up what was in effect a council to control finance and administration and hear grievances, consisting of the Chancellor, Treasurer, Keeper of the Privy Seal, two archbishops, two bishops, one abbot, two dukes, one earl, and three barons. The peers were Gloucester, York, and Arundel. The appointment of this council amounted to an assertion of control of government by the magnates against the growing independence of the young King. The victory of the appellants in 1388 produced another council of a similar kind, whose members were to take an oath to maintain the acts of parliament. In 1389 Richard declared his will to 'call whom I will to the council', but in practice a largely conciliar régime continued for some time. The councillors were reappointed in parliament in 1390 and included earlier opponents of the King. An ordinance in the same year laid down that 'the king should give full credence to the council in all things touching the government and suffer them to govern duly, without commanding them by message or letter anything to the contrary', and gave them power over grants of royal property and matters of law. A minute book covering the years 1392 to 1393, the first real insight into the detailed working of the council, shows that the officers and clerks, occasionally reinforced by great lords, did indeed regularly debate and decide a wide range of business, including foreign policy. Gradually, however, by diluting the council with his own supporters and reasserting his individual power, Richard transformed the conciliar into the despotic government of his last years when the council reverted to its original type.

Outside control was firmly reasserted in the parliament of 1404, which set up a 'great and continual council', including, besides the Chancellor, Treasurer, and Keeper of the Privy Seal, the Archbishop, four bishops, the Duke of York, two earls, four lords, and seven other laymen. The motive in this period was much more the Commons' suspicion of the court than the desire of a group of magnates to assert themselves over the King, but the constitutional device followed the precedents of Richard's reign. In 1406 a similar council was even more aggressively thrust upon the King. The new councillors were obliged to take their oath in parliament and their powers were described in a series of articles, including the provision that all warrants for letters to be issued by the Chancellor, Treasurer, and Keeper of the Privy Seal must be passed by them. The King was constitutionally unable to control any part of the machinery of government without the consent of a council whose nomination had been imposed upon him. Parliament reasserted its power in 1410, but this time it was acting partly under the influence of Prince Henry, and the new council had a larger proportion of magnates. For the last years of the reign parliamentary authority receded in the dominant quarrels of courtiers, and in the strong rule of Henry V the council reverted to the position of a body largely dependent upon the King.

The long minority of Henry VI gave the council a new lease of life. The council which the minority demanded was appointed by the lords in parliament and included, besides the three great royal uncles (Bedford, Gloucester, and Beaufort), the chief officials, several bishops and earls, and four prominent knights. Although the uncles were the most powerful individuals and Bedford insisted in 1433 that no councillor was to be removed without his consent, the personal dominance of any one of them was hindered and the government of England for the fifteen years of minority was largely carried out by this body of men, meeting regularly round the council table. Fortescue's later statement that 'the king's council was wont to be chosen of great princes, and of greatest lords of the land, both spiritual and temporal, and also of other men that were in great authority and offices' is most clearly justified during these years, though the practice continued, for somewhat different reasons, the intermittent custom of proceeding reigns. The council perpetuated itself, co-opting new members without reference to parliament, and the relationship with the Commons was quite different from what it had been at times under Richard II and Henry IV. The end of the minority in 1437 did not bring a sudden end to the power of the council. It was reappointed by the King and the articles of 1406 restated as the authority for its action. For some years it continued to debate and act with almost as little reference to the King as before. It was undermined by changes in the early fourteen-forties, when Henry VI asserted his right to issue orders by the Privy Seal without reference to council. Gradually the power of action in great affairs shifted entirely from the council to the King, the court, and the individuals who controlled them. The Yorkist and parliamentary efforts to restore real authority to the council in 1451 and 1453 were again like the attempts of fourteenth-century politicians to control a court which had got out of hand; but, though there was some return to conciliar control in the old sense in the short periods of York's protectorship, the age of government by council was over.

(4) YORKIST GOVERNMENT

The Wars of the Roses were a series of struggles for power between individuals, struggles which were caused, like earlier and similar disorders, by the failings of a corrupt and suspect court. To regard them as the trough which separates medieval from modern government is in a sense a confusion of categories, for the situation which caused them was novel only in a dynastic and personal sense. It seems equally clear, however, that the government of England in the reign of Henry VII was different in important ways, which were not dynastic or personal, from what it had been seventy years earlier. The history of the years between 1440 and 1470 has the appearance of something more than civil war; rather of a general breakdown of a system of government from which a new system emerged. The point can be made by comparing these years with the reign of Edward II. The period from 1307 to 1330 also saw repeated civil war and the deposition of a king, but it does not appear that the government restored by Edward III was very different in essentials from that of his grandfather. On the other hand, the mid-fifteenth century seems to be a period in which government was changing markedly in character.

We have already seen some of the elements of the crisis in government at the end of Henry VI's reign and how they were related to the personal quarrels which developed into the Wars of the Roses. The taxation system of the Middle Ages was declining for reasons which are obscure but include both the obsolescence of the old methods of assessment after radical social changes and the weakness of the Crown in enforcing its demands. The king had less power to raise money than at any time since the reign of Henry III. The system of close consultation with the realm in parliaments and councils was being abandoned. The exploitation of the royal administration by influential individuals had never been absent from medieval government and favourites had always been able to expect rich rewards, but the spoils system was probably never so much the raison d'être of government as in these years, when council and court had not been checked by the hand of a strong king for nearly four decades. While royal lands were being enjoyed by feoffees and lesses, important commands, like the Wardenships of the Scots Marches (held by Percies and Nevilles) and the Captaincy of Calais (used to good effect by Warwick), were increasingly regarded as sources of personal profit and power. A further, and much more obscure, point is the Crown's apparent inability to control local disorder. It is an obscure point because the extent of disorder in different periods is impossible to assess for comparison. The great difficulty of obtaining impartial justice and prevalence of lordly influence in the later part of Henry VI's reign are undoubted. In 1440 Judge Paston advised a man not to go to law with another party, 'for if thou do, thou shalt have the worse, be thy case never so sure, for he is feed with my lord (the Duke) of Norfolk, and much he is of his counsel; and also thou canst no man of law in Norfolk nor in Suffolk to be with thee against him; and forsooth no more might I when I had a plea against him; and therefore my counsel is that thou make an end whatsoever the pay, for he shall else undo thee and bring thee to naught'. In 1450 Sir John Fastolf's concern for the state of his own neighbourhood moved him to bring to the notice of King and council, through the same Duke of Norfolk, 'how the country of Norfolk and Suffolk stand right wildly, without a mean may be that justice be had, which will not be but if a man of great birth and livelihood there be sheriff this year coming, to lead the people in most peace'. There is no good reason, however, to suppose that corrupt justice and local disorder were not equally common in earlier days, which have left no Paston Letters to illustrate them so vividly. They were essential features of a society in which great men had real local power, some inevitably had the king's ear more readily than others, and the machinery of royal government was far too primitive to ensure impartiality and security everywhere. In the middle of Edward III's reign the Folville family lived as robber knights in the county of Leicester and once held a royal judge to ransom. In Henry IV's time a judge admitted that he had ambushed Lord Roos with a body of 500 men. Complaints of the depradations of armed retainers are common in the parliaments of the fourteenth and fifteenth centuries. What appears to be novel in the later years of Henry VI is not the influence of great men but the extent to which they were allowed to take the law into their own hands in going to war against each other. There are earlier examples, notably the war between the Earls of Lancaster and Surrey in the reign of Edward II, but in general it was something that the King had not tolerated. Now he was either powerless or indifferent. The quarrel between Sir William Bonville and the Earl of Devon in the west country flared into war in 1441 and 1451 and a battle at Exeter in 1455. The strict injunctions of the council did not prevent the Percy and Neville families from fighting at Stamford Bridge in 1453. The weakness of the Crown seems to have paralysed the machinery of royal justice.

English government in 1461 therefore has the double aspect of a declining constitutional system and a collapsing royal authority and it is a debatable matter how the two were connected. The achievement of Edward IV was to restore royal government to supremacy and also to restore it in a somewhat different form. His most difficult task was to restore

248

effective government. It took three months after Towton to subdue Cornwall, where a Lancastrian faction, led by one who was called 'the great errant Captain of Cornwall', was dominant, and indeed the west country was never fully at peace in the first decade of the reign. The long struggles of the Paston family to recover their legal control of old Sir John Fastolf's inheritance culminated in 1469, after many years of recrimination and violence, which the law could not settle, with the Duke of Norfolk besieging Caister Castle with a large army. No doubt many other people less well known to us took the law into their own hands. The revival of civil war in 1469 was connected with local feuds. Nevertheless the last decade of the reign saw order largely restored and the King far more firmly in the saddle. This was partly due to the settlement of political troubles and partly to Edward's persistent efforts to make his authority felt in all parts of the kingdom. He went himself on judicial progresses in 1464 and 1475. He took a great interest in local politics. The squires of his household were 'to be of sundry shires, by whom it may be known the disposition of the countries'. He substantially increased his influence in some areas by endowing faithful supporters with large properties, for instance Lord Hastings in Leicestershire. In the Wesh Marches and the north, Edward and his brother, Gloucester, had large blocks of territory which allowed a new approach to the problem of local control. In 1476 the disorder in Wales and the Marches was tackled by entrusting the Prince of Wales's council (presided over since 1473 by Bishop Alcock of Ely) with a general judicial commission covering the counties of Shropshire, Hereford, Gloucester, and Worcester, which gave a much more effective control over that area. Supreme judicial authority north of the Humber was divided between the Earl of Northumberland and the Duke of Gloucester and, at the end of the reign, Gloucester's council was given a judicial commission covering Yorkshire. This arrangement was continued by Gloucester as Richard III when he set up a Council in the North Parts under his nephew, the Earl of Lincoln. Thus considerable strides were taken towards the permanent pacification of disturbed areas in a manner which was novel and foreshadowed the later councils of the Tudors.

249

Both Edward IV and Richard III assumed the throne as if it were a rightful inheritance and had themselves crowned before obtaining the confirmation of their titles in parliament. The parliamentary element in their inauguration was therefore less than it had been in the case of Henry IV.[1] Edward IV took great pains to emphasise the elevation of kingship by the magnificence of his person and his court. In contrast with Henry VI, whose appearances did not inspire loyalty 'for by this mean he lost many and won none or right few, and ever he was shewed in a long blue gown of velvet as though he had no more to change with', Edward IV showed himself 'clad in a great variety of most costly garments . . . the royal court presenting no other appearance than such as fully befits a most mighty kingdom, filled with riches. . . .' A widely travelled German visitor in 1465, who thought it 'the most splendid court that could be found in all Christendom', marvelled with what extraordinary reverence the King was treated by his servants. 'Even mighty counts had to kneel to him.' Edward was generous in grants of land to trusted supporters, but he did not allow the corruption of courtiers to divert money from its intended purpose of paying for royal magnificence. The proper organisation of the whole household was carefully described in the lengthy Black Book of the Household of the King of England about 1471–2.[2]

Sir John Fortescue's often quoted advice that the council should consist of twelve laymen and twelve clerics, taking no fees except from the king, reinforced by the ministers and by four spiritual and four lay lords to be chosen annually, was not far from the arrangement which actually existed in a less rigid form when he was writing in the fourteen-seventies. The council consisted of the King's servants and ministers, prominent bishops, and magnates. It met often and was entrusted with a wide variety of important business. It has been shown, for instance, that the protracted negotiations about the finances of Calais, leading up to the Act of Retainer in 1466, were carried out by consultation between the council and the Staple.[3]

1. C. A. J. Armstrong, 'The Inauguration Ceremonies of the Yorkist Kings', *T.R.H.S.* (1948)
2. A. R. Myers, *The Household of Edward IV* (1959).
3. J. R. Lander, 'Council, Administration and Councillors 1461–1485', *Bulletin of the Institute of Historical Research* (1959)

About 1475 anyone who wished to farm royal lands needed 'first to have a bill enclosed of the king, then to certain lords of the council, (for there is an act made that nothing shall pass from the king unto time they have seen it) and so to privy seal and Chancellor'. The council recovered some of the powers of jurisdiction which had slipped from it in the mid-century. A case was heard in 1482, for instance: 'In the star chamber at Westminster . . . Present my lords the Archbishop of York, Chancellor of England, the Bishops of Lincoln, Privy Seal, Worcester, Norwich, Durham and Llandaff, the Earl Rivers, the lords Dudley, Ferrers, Beauchamp, Sirs Thomas Borough, William Parre, Thomas Vaughan and Thomas Grey knights. In full and privy council was openly read the judgement and decree made by my lords of our said sovereign lord's council. . . .' Edward IV's councillors were both eminent and powerful. In constitutional and political function, however, they had largely reverted to the situation of Edward I's reign. Their proceedings probably had more regularity and formality, but they were once again a body of trusted men assisting the King without any constitutional dependence upon parliament. This change in the nature of the council was paralleled by a greater centralisation of official business in the royal household. Edward made much use of his Secretary for sending out important letters. The organisation of finance, as we have seen, came increasingly into the hands of the Chamber, which partially superseded the Exchequer. These tendencies towards a more centralised monarchy, clearly visible in the Yorkist period, were developed with great effect by the early Tudors.

The political changes of the fifteenth century inspired no great political philosophy. The current ideas, expressed by politicians and lawyers, were for the most part the dissolving wreckage of the systems of thought inspired by the evolution of the monarchy in the thirteenth century or borrowed at that time from the Continent. Fortescue's *Governance of England*, the most famous political treatise of the age, can be read as a commentary on the paradoxical state of kingship under Edward IV. The later part of the book advocates in an extreme way the withdrawal of the king into an isolated dependence on his estates and his privy council. This was the path which the Yorkists and early Tudors on the whole followed and it led to a different kind of monarchy from that of the Middle Ages. The early chapters are a restatement of the traditional medieval ideal of government by consent, 'dominion political and royal' as he calls it in distinction from 'dominion merely royal'. There was no theoretical contradiction between the two arguments, for the object of his practical suggestions was to rescue the monarchy from its subservience to great lords, not to make it despotic. The historical effect of the constitutional changes which he advocated, however, was to release the monarchy from much of its old obligation to consult with the community of the realm. This implication was not generally accepted by fifteenth-century theorists. Even the English despotism, never to achieve more than a stunted growth in comparison with the Continental examples, was in its infancy and was not to receive philosophical expression for many years. The sermon which the humanist John Russell, Bishop of Lincoln, prepared for the parliament of Richard III, in which he exhorted the avaricious enclosers and depopulators to think less of their own interests and more of the 'common and public body of the realm', foreshadowed the theory of a co-operative monarchial commonwealth, which became popular in the sixteenth century. In 1483 it was still unusual.

The chief political groups whose wishes the Crown had been bound to consult in the early fifteenth century were the nobility, the gentry, and the merchants. The abandonment of foreign war and the decline of parliament partially removed from the gentry and merchants their power, and perhaps their wish, to bring pressure to bear on the king. The end of the Hundred Years' War had been itself, as we have seen, one of the main elements in the internal crisis of Henry VI's reign— York and Warwick were both disappointed and disgruntled commanders. The new dynasties of York and Tudor could profit from the ending of the war without themselves incurring the odium of defeat. They escaped from the vicious circle of summoning hostile parliaments to satisfy the demands of magnate commanders who would in turn be made more dangerously wealthy by the wartime finance which was ruinous to the Crown. The circumstances which compelled Henry VI to give up the old pattern of war and finance eventually enabled his successors to withdraw for the time being from the parliamentary system which had been evolved in the Middle Ages, to depend more on their own estates and the councillors of their own choosing. The ultimate, paradoxical result of the collapse of Lancastrian government was that power was concentrated more closely in the king and his servants, and that he was exalted as never before above his subjects. The sphere of consultation was narrowed while the area of royal power was extended.

The structure of government set up by the Yorkists was maintained and developed with very little change of purpose or method by Henry VII. He too relied on incomes from the royal estates and the customs, both of which grew substantially. Having no troublesome close relations, he was even more successful than Edward IV in acquiring estates by forfeiture and escheat without granting them away again, and the rising curve of exports was steeper. He too summoned few parliaments and fought no wars on the Continent, ruled through a central council subservient to his will, and developed the Councils of Wales and the North. The period from 1461 to the early part of the reign of Henry VIII therefore has some unity as far as its political and constitutional tendencies are concerned. All over Europe richer kings were uniting their countries with stronger central institutions. Similar features are found in the kingdoms of Louis XI of France (1461–83) and Ferdinand (1479–1516) and Isabella (1474–1504) of Aragon and Castile. The peculiarity of later English constitutional development—the parliamentary system giving supreme power to the mercantile and landed gentry within a monarchy —appeared in the seventeenth and eighteenth centuries. In 1485 England was much more like its neighbours and we should have to look far into the future to discover why there was so sharp a divergence by the end of the seventeenth century. One can only speculate whether some of the features of the English monarchy in 1509—the heavy reliance on income from overseas trade, which would again later as before in the fourteenth century give a political lever to the merchants, and the weakness of local magnate power—were essential preparations for the constitution of the eighteenth century.

Like all historical phenomena, however, the new monarchies of 1500 were transient. Kingship in France was weakened again by the upheavals of the Wars of Religion, similar in some ways to the Wars of the Roses, in the second half of the sixteenth century. Elizabeth I faced poverty and troublesome parliaments like some of her medieval predecessors. The elements of the body politic which we have observed in this book—Crown, parliament, nobility, the possible methods of taxation—were transformed very gradually over the centuries while one part or another rose temporarily to prominence or sank temporarily into insignificance. The Middle Ages did not end with the victory of Edward IV or Henry VII or their reforms; it was not the first or the last time that kings tried to live without parliaments. In 1642 constitutional arguments were being used that would have been in place in 1327 or 1399, and the king was struggling with financial and political problems which had many similarities to those of the fourteenth and fifteenth centuries.

APPENDIX A

TABLE OF DATES

1272–1307	*Edward I*		
1274	Edward returns to England		
1277	Invasion of Wales, Treaty of Conway		
1278	Statute of Gloucester		
1278–92	John Pecham, Archbishop of Canterbury		
1279	Statute of Mortmain		
1282–3	Conquest of Wales		
1285	Statute of Westminster II	1285–1314	Philip IV of France
1291	Edward overlord of Scotland		
1294–1313	Robert Winchelsey, Archbishop of Canterbury	1294–1303	Pope Boniface VIII
1295	Battle of Maes Moydog		
1296	Invasion of Scotland		
1297	Expedition to Flanders Confirmation of the Charters Rebellion of Wallace		
1298	Battle of Falkirk		
1303	Peace with France		
1307–27	*Edward II*	1308	Pope moves to Avignon
1311	The Ordinances		
1314	Battle of Bannockburn		
1318	Treaty of Leek	1316–34	Pope John XXII
1322	Battle of Boroughbridge Execution of Thomas of Lancaster		
1323	Truce with Scotland		
1326	Invasion by Isabella and Mortimer		
1327–77	*Edward III*		
1328	Treaty of Northampton	1328–50	Philip VI of France
1330	End of Minority Condemnation of Mortimer	1329–71	David II of Scotland
1333	Battle of Halidon Hill		
1337	Beginning of Hundred Years' War		
1333–48	John Stratford, Archbishop of Canterbury		
1340	Battle of Sluys		
1344–8	Foundation of the Order of the Garter		
1346	Battles of Crécy and Neville's Cross		

1347	Capture of Calais		
1348	Death of William of Ockham		
1349	Black Death	1350–64	John II of France
1351	Statute of Provisors		
	Statute of Labourers		
1356	Battle of Poitiers		
1360	Treaty of Brétigny		
1362	First version of *Piers Plowman*		
1363	Company of the Staple at Calais	1364–80	Charles V of France
1367	Battle of Najera		
1367–1404	William of Wykeham, Bishop of Winchester		
1369	Death of Queen Philippa		
1376	'Good' Parliament		
	Death of Black Prince		
1377–99	*Richard II*	1378–1417	Great Schism
1381	Peasants' Revolt		
1381–96	William Courtenay, Archbishop of Canterbury	1380–1422	Charles VI of France
1384	Death of John Wycliffe		
1386	'Wonderful' Parliament		
1388	'Merciless' Parliament		
	Battle of Otterburn		
1394–5	Richard II in Ireland		
1396	Peace with France		
1396–1414	Thomas Arundel, Archbishop of Canterbury		
1399	Death of John of Gaunt		
	Deposition of Richard II		
1399–1413	*Henry IV*		
1400	Death of Geoffrey Chaucer		
1400–1408	Revolt of Owen Glyndwr		
1402	Battle of Homildon Hill		
1403	Battle of Shrewsbury	1404	Death of Philip the Bold of Burgundy
1405	Battle of Bramham Moor		
1408	Battle of Shipton Moor	1404–19	John the Fearless, Duke of Burgundy
1413–22	*Henry V*	1414–18	Council of Constance
1415	Battle of Agincourt		
		1419–67	Philip the Good, Duke of Burgundy
1420	Treaty of Troyes		

1422–61	*Henry VI*	1422–61	Charles VII of France
1424	Battle of Verneuil		
1426	Parliament of Bats		
1429	Relief of Orleans		
1431	Joan of Arc burnt	1431–48	Council of Basle
1435	Treaty of Arras		
	Death of Duke of Bedford		
1436	English withdrawal from Paris		
	Siege of Calais		
1437	End of Minority		
1444	Truce and marriage contract with France		
1447	Death of Humphrey, Duke of Gloucester and of Cardinal Beaufort		
1449–53	Last phase of Hundred Years' War		
1450	Jack Cade's Rebellion		
1453–4	Henry VI's madness		
	First protectorate of Richard, Duke of York		
1455	First Battle of St Albans		
1460	Battle of Wakefield		
	Death of Duke of York		
1461	Battle of Towton		
1461–83	*Edward IV*	1461–84	Louis XI of France
1464	Edward IV's marriage to Elizabeth Woodville		
1469	Rebellion of Earl of Warwick	1467–77	Charles the Bold, Duke of Burgundy
1470–1	Restoration of Henry VI		
1471	Battle of Tewkesbury		
	Death of Sir Thomas Malory		
1475	Treaty of Picquigny		
1477	Caxton prints first book in England		
1478	Death of George, Duke of Clarence		
1483	*Edward V*		
1483–5	*Richard III*		
1485	Battle of Bosworth		

TABLE I   THE PLANTAGENETS

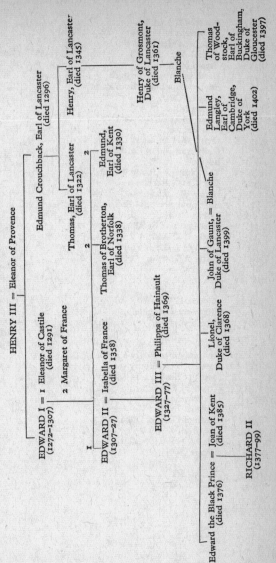

HENRY III = Eleanor of Provence

EDWARD I = 1 Eleanor of Castile (died 1291)
         = 2 Margaret of France

Edmund Crouchback, Earl of Lancaster (died 1296)

Henry, Earl of Lancaster (died 1345)

Henry of Grosmont, Duke of Lancaster (died 1361)

Thomas, Earl of Lancaster (died 1322)

Edmund, Earl of Kent (died 1330)

EDWARD II = Isabella of France (1307–27) (died 1358)

Thomas of Brotherton, Earl of Norfolk (died 1338)

EDWARD III = Philippa of Hainault (1327–77) (died 1369)

Lionel, Duke of Clarence (died 1368)

John of Gaunt, = Blanche Duke of Lancaster (died 1399)

Blanche

Edmund Langley, Earl of Cambridge, Duke of York (died 1402)

Thomas of Wood-stock, Earl of Buckingham, Duke of Gloucester (died 1397)

Edward the Black Prince = Joan of Kent (died 1376) (died 1385)

RICHARD II (1377–99)

TABLE II   THE DESCENDANTS OF JOHN OF GAUNT

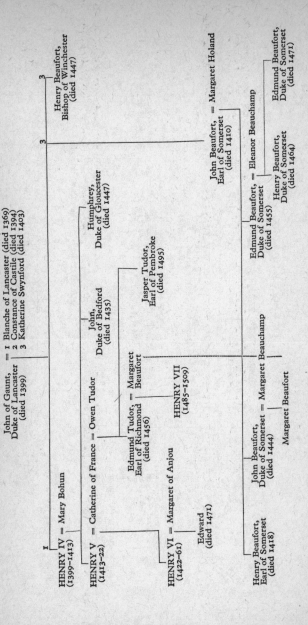

TABLE III THE HOUSE OF YORK

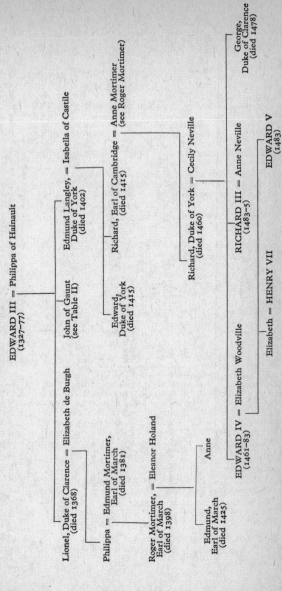

BOOKS FOR FURTHER READING

General

Some general introductions and textbooks:

D. M. Stenton, *English Society in the Early Middle Ages, 1066–1307* (Pelican
History of England, 1951).
A. R. Myers, *England in the Late Middle Ages, 1307–1536* (Pelican History of
England, 1952).
G. W. S Barrow, *Feudal Britain, 1066–1314* (1956).
V. H. H. Green, *The Later Plantagenets, 1307–1485* (1955).

A full account of the period is contained in three volumes of the Oxford History
of England:

F. M. Powicke, *The Thirteenth Century, 1216–1307* (1953).
M. McKisack, *The Fourteenth Century, 1307–99* (1959).
E. F. Jacob, *The Fifteenth Century, 1399–1485* (1961).

Many aspects of medieval life are described in:

A. L. Poole, ed., *Medieval England* (2 vols., 1958).

Introductions to the Continental background are contained in:

C. W. Previté-Orton, *History of Europe, 1198–1378* (3rd ed., 1951).
W. T. Waugh, *History of Europe, 1378–1494* (3rd ed., 1949).
E. Perroy, *The Hundred Years' War* (trans. W. S. Wells, 1951).
Cambridge Medieval History (vols. vi, vii, viii, 1929–36).

Sources

Most of the sources for the thirteenth and fourteenth centuries and many of
those for the fifteenth are in Latin or French. Here are a few which happen to be
in English or have been translated:

B. Wilkinson, *Constitutional History of Medieval England, 1216–1399* (3 vols.,
1948–58), includes many translated extracts.
Vita Edwardi Secundi (Life of Edward II) (ed. N. H. Denholm-Young, 1957).
The Brut (English Chronicle) (ed. F. Brie, Early English Text Society 1906–8).
Froissart, *Chronicles* (trans. Lord Berners or T. Johnes).
Sir Gawayne and the Grene Knight (ed. B. Stone, 1959).
William Langland, *Vision of Piers Plowman* (ed. J. F. Goodridge, 1959).
Wycliffe, *Select English Writings* (ed. H. E. Winn, 1929).
The Book of Margery Kempe (ed. W. Butler-Bowdon, 1954).
The Paston Letters (ed. J. Gairdner, 4 vols., 1910).
The Libelle of Englysshe Polycye (ed. G. Warner, 1926).
Sir John Fortescue, *The Governance of England* (ed. C. Plummer, 1885).

Lay Institutions

Two Victorian masterpieces from which much of the modern writing on medieval
institutions stems:

W. Stubbs, *Constitutional History of England* (3 vols., 5th ed., 1891–1903).
F. Pollock and F. W. Maitland, *History of English Law before the Time of
Edward I* (2 vols., 2nd ed., 1898).

Some modern theories about parliament:

M. V. Clarke, *Medieval Representation and Consent* (1936).

261

B. Wilkinson, *Studies in the Constitutional History of England in the Thirteenth and Fourteenth Centuries* (1937).

G. T. Lapsley, *Crown, Community and Parliament in the Later Middle Ages* (1951).

J. S. Roskell, *The Commons in the Parliament of 1422* (1954).

K. B. McFarlane, 'Parliament and Bastard Feudalism, T.R.H.S. (1944).

H. G. Richardson, 'The Commons and Medieval Politics', *T.R.H.S.* (1946).

(*Law and the Legal System*)

W. Holdsworth, *History of English Law* (vol. i, 1956; vols. ii and iii, 1922–3).

T. F. T. Plucknett, *The Legislation of Edward I* (1949).

H. M. Cam, *The Hundred and the Hundred Rolls* (1930).

H. M. Cam, *Liberties and Communities in Medieval England* (1944).

M. Hastings, *The Court of Common Pleas in the Fifteenth Century* (1947).

(*Royal Administration*)

J. F. Baldwin, *The King's Council* (1913).

S. B. Chrimes, *Introduction to the Administrative History of Medieval England* (1952).

T. F. Tout, *Chapters in Medieval Administrative History* (6 vols., 1920–35).

J. F. Willard and W. A. Morris, *The English Government at Work, 1326–37* (3 vols., 1940–50).

B. P. Wolffe, 'The Management of English Royal Estates under the Yorkist Kings', *E.H.R.* (1956).

(*Other Institutions of the Lay Nobility*)

K. B. McFarlane, 'Bastard Feudalism', *Bulletin of the Institute of Historical Research* (1945).

R. Somerville, *History of the Duchy of Lancaster* (vol. i, 1953).

W. H. Dunham, *Lord Hastings' Indentured Retainers, 1461–83* (1955).

A. R. Wagner, *Heralds and Heraldry in the Middle Ages* (2nd ed., 1956).

G. A. Holmes, *The Estates of the Higher Nobility in Fourteenth-century England* (1957).

(*On Warfare and Castles*)

Sir Charles Oman, *A History of the Art of War in the Middle Ages* (2 vols., 2nd ed., 1924).

R. Allen Brown, *English Medieval Castles* (1954).

A. E. Prince, 'The Indenture System in the Reign of Edward III', *Essays in Honour of James Tait* (ed. J. G. Edwards, V. H. Galbraith and E. F. Jacob, 1933).

K. B. McFarlane, 'The Investment of Sir John Fastolf's Profits of War', *T.R.H.S.* (1957).

Politics

Some notable examples of political history in detail:

F. M. Powicke, *King Henry III and the Lord Edward* (2 vols., 1947), includes a character study of Edward I.

J. E. Morris, *The Welsh Wars of Edward I* (1901).

T. F. Tout, *The Place of the Reign of Edward II in English History* (2nd ed., 1936).

J. C. Davies, *The Baronial Opposition to Edward II* (1919).

P. E. Russell, *The English Intervention in Spain and Portugal in the Time of Edward III and Richard II* (1955).

S. Armitage Smith, *John of Gaunt* (1904).

G. M. Trevelyan, *England in the Age of Wycliffe* (3rd ed., 1904).

A. Steel, *Richard II* (1941).

R. Bird, *The Turbulent London of Richard II* (1948).

Sir Charles Oman, *The Great Revolt of 1381* (1906).

J. E. Lloyd, *Owen Glendower* (1931).

R. A. Newhall, *The English Conquest of Normandy* (1924).

K. B. McFarlane, 'At the Deathbed of Cardinal Beaufort,' *Essays in Medieval History presented to F. M. Powicke* (ed. R. W. Hunt, W. A. Pantin and R. W. Southern, 1948).

Social and Economic History

The best general account is E. Lipson, *Economic History of England*, (vol. i, 11th ed., 1956).

For a wider background: *The Cambridge Economic History of Europe* (vols. i–iii, 1941–61).

Other useful general books:

H. C. Darby, *Historical Geography of England before 1800* (1936).

M. W Beresford and J. K. St. Joseph, *Medieval England: an Aerial Survey* (1958).

(On Agrarian Society)

G. C. Homans, *English Villagers of the Thirteenth Century* (1941).

R. A. L. Smith, *Canterbury Cathedral Priory* (1943).

A. E. Levett, *The Black Death on the Estates of the Bishopric of Winchester* (Oxford Studies in Social and Legal History, ed. P. Vinogradoff, vol. v, 1916).

F. G. Davenport, *The Economic Development of a Norfolk Manor* (1906).

R. H. Hilton, *The Economic Development of Some Leicestershire Estates* (1947).

M. W. Beresford, *The Lost Villages of England* (1954).

J. M. W. Bean, *The Estates of the Percy Family, 1416–1537* (1958).

W. Rees, *South Wales and the March, 1284–1415* (1924).

M. M. Postan, 'The Chronology of Labour Services', *T.R.H.S.* (1957).

M. M. Postan, 'Economic Evidence of Declining Population,' *Econ. H. R.* (1950).

(Trade and Industry)

E. Power, *The Wool Trade in English Medieval History* (1941).

E. M. Carus-Wilson, *Medieval Merchant Venturers* (1954).

E. Power and M. M. Postan, *Studies in English Trade in the Fifteenth Century* (1933).

L. F. Salzman, *English Trade in the Middle Ages* (1931).

A. A. Ruddock, *Alien Merchants and Shipping in Southampton, 1270–1600* (1951).

L. F. Salzman, *English Industries of the Middle Ages* (2nd ed., 1923).

L. F. Salzman, *Building in England down to 1540* (1952).

(Towns)

A. S. Green (Mrs J. R. Green), *Town Life in the Fifteenth Century* (2 vols., 1894).

S. L. Thrupp, *The Merchant Class of Medieval London* (1948).

J. W. F. Hill, *Medieval Lincoln* (1948).

M. Dormer Harris, *Life in an Old English Town: a History of Coventry* (1898).

The Church

Monks and friars are dealt with in the first two volumes of:

Dom David Knowles, *The Religious Orders in England* (1948–55).

(On the Rest of the Church)

J. R. H. Moorman, *Church Life in England in the Thirteenth Century* (1945).

A. Hamilton Thompson, *The English Clergy and their Organisation in the Later Middle Ages* (1947).

W. A. Pantin, *The English Church in the Fourteenth Century* (1955).

K. L. Wood-Legh, *Church Life in England under Edward III* (1934).

M. E. Aston, 'Lollardy and Sedition', *P. and P.* (1960).

(*Some Individual Churchmen*)

D. L. Douie, *Archbishop Pecham* (1952).
C. M. Fraser, *A History of Anthony Bek* (1957).
K. B. McFarlane, *John Wycliffe* (1952).

Literature, Thought, and Education

The Age of Chaucer (ed. B. Ford, Penguin Guide to English Literature, i, 1954).
C. S. Lewis, *The Allegory of Love* (2nd ed., 1938).
H. S. Bennett, *Chaucer and the Fifteenth Century* (1947).
E. K. Chambers, *English Literature at the Close of the Middle Ages* (1945).
G. Leff, *Medieval Thought from Saint Augustine to Ockham* (1958).
D. E. Sharp, *Franciscan Philosophy at Oxford in the Thirteenth Century* (1930).
J. A. Robson, *Wyclif and the Oxford Schools* (1961).
G. R. Owst, *Preaching in Medieval England* (1926).
H. Rashdall, *The Universities of Europe in the Middle Ages* (ed. F. M. Powicke and A. B. Emden, 3 vols., 1936)
A. F. Leach, *The Schools of Medieval England* (2nd ed., 1916).
R. Weiss, *Humanism in England during the Fifteenth Century* (2nd ed., 1957).
H. S. Bennett, *English Books and Readers, 1475–1557* (1952).

Architecture and Art

P. Brieger, *English Art, 1216–1307* (Oxford History of English Art, 1957).
J. Evans, *English Art, 1307–1461* (Oxford History of English Art, 1949).
J. Harvey, *Gothic England* (1947).
G. Webb, *Architecture in Britain: the Middle Ages* (Pelican History of Art, 1956).
M. Rickert, *Painting in Britain: the Middle Ages* (Pelican History of Art, 1954).
L. Stone, *Sculpture in Britain: the Middle Ages* (Pelican History of Art, 1955).

INDEX

269

All Sphere Books are available at your bookshop or newsagent: or can be ordered from the following address:

Sphere Books, Cash Sales Department,
P.O. Box 11, Falmouth, Cornwall.

Please send cheque or postal order. No currency, and allow 6d. per book to cover the cost of postage and packing in U.K., 9d. per copy overseas.